101 REASONS WHY PRAYER IS NOT FOR WIMPS

Lessons In Spiritual Warfare

JAMES TRANQUILLA

101 Reasons Why Prayer Is Not For Wimps
Copyright © 2022 by James Tranquilla

Scripture taken from the New King James Version.
Copyright 1979, 1980, 1982 by Thomas Nelson,
inc. Used by permission. All rights reserved.

All rights reserved. No part of this publication may be reproduced, distributed, or transmitted in any form or by any means, including photocopying, recording, or other electronic or mechanical methods, without the prior written permission of the author, except in the case of brief quotations embodied in critical reviews and certain other non-commercial uses permitted by copyright law.

ISBN
978-1-956529-46-3 (Paperback)
978-1-956529-45-6 (eBook)

MISSIONS in Spiritual Warfare
A Manual on Prayer for Prayer Warriors

Table of Contents

Introduction xi

Mission 1	Opportunity And Authority	1
Mission 2	Effective Strength	3
Mission 3	Too Late To Make A Difference	5
Mission 4	Failing To Secure The Spoils Of Victory	7
Mission 5	We Don't Know What To Pray	9
Mission 6	We Must Prepare To Go Back	12
Mission 7	Are We Praying Out Of A Surplus Or A Loss?	14
Mission 8	Praying For Effect	17
Mission 9	The Power Of Loudly Praying The Truth	19
Mission 10	Support As An Element Of Spiritual Warfare	22
Mission 11	Some Assembly Required	25
Mission 12	The Lord Will Provide	28
Mission 13	What Happened To The Others?	31
Mission 14	Don't Go Alone	34
Mission 15	Overtaken By Joy	37
Mission 16	What Are We Fighting For?	39
Mission 17	Prayer Warrior Yes; Superman No	41
Mission 18	Time To Clean House	43
Mission 19	What's The Big Deal About Prayer?	46
Mission 20	Sounds Like School!	50
Mission 21	The Power Of Prayer or The Prayer Of Power?	55

Mission 22	Thermometer Or Thermostat?	58
Mission 23	No Such Thing As Bad Publicity?	62
Mission 24	Seeking God's Face	66
Mission 25	The Super Weapon	70
Mission 26	Breaking Through	73
Mission 27	Valuing The High Ground	76
Mission 28	Are You Being Followed?	80
Mission 29	The Easy Way Out	82
Mission 30	Things Unseen – Part 1 Where Are We?	85
Mission 31	Things Unseen - Part 2 How Things Work	89
Mission 32	What Does God Sound Like?	93
Mission 33	Follow Orders	97
Mission 34	Soldier -	100
Mission 35	Fighting On Two Fronts	103
Mission 36	Need To See	107
Mission 37	What Does God Do With Our Prayers?	111
Mission 38	Prayer Warriors Are Nice People (Really!)	115
Mission 39	Mr. Predictable	118
Mission 40	Ultimate Power	121
Mission 41	Who Protects The Warrior?	125
Mission 42	What Do You See?	129
Mission 43	Never Quit!	132
Mission 44	Windshield Or Rear-View Mirror?	135
Mission 45	It's Not Time Yet!	138
Mission 46	Welcome Home	141
Mission 47	Waiting To Be Called	144
Mission 48	Primary Objective	148
Mission 49	Danger Ahead!	152

Mission 50	Sneak Preview	158
Mission 51	Denied Access	162
Mission 52	Move Out!	167
Mission 53	God Has Secrets	172
Mission 54	Step On It!	175
Mission 55	Kingdom Warfare	178
Mission 56	Spirit-Man, spirit-Man	182
Mission 57	What If Nobody Notices?	185
Mission 58	Surrender Theology	189
Mission 59	How Much Is "All"?	194
Mission 60	Burn The Boats	197
Mission 61	Face Value	201
Mission 62	Night Vision	207
Mission 63	Exam Time	211
Mission 64	Situational Awareness	214
Mission 65	Complacency	217
Mission 66	Take Cover!	222
Mission 67	Intense	226
Mission 68	Not Big Enough!	230
Mission 69	Defeating A Strong Man	234
Mission 70	Flying Blind	239
Mission 71	Remove Before Flight	244
Mission 72	Eagle's Wings	248
Mission 73	Warriors Through the Ages	251
Mission 74	Just Ask!	254
Mission 75	Warrior Watchman	257
Mission 76	Big, Expensive, Irrelevant	263
Mission 77	This Is Not Home	267

Mission 78	Wounded!	270
Mission 79	Communicating Clearly	277
Mission 80	Stolen Messages	283
Mission 81	Do Not Cross The Line	288
Mission 82	Restore the Glory	292
Mission 83	Closing Ranks	295
Mission 84	Open Immediately!	301
Mission 85	Crack of Light	309
Mission 86	Extraction!	313
Mission 87	Dinner Is Served!	318
Mission 88	Complaining!	322
Mission 89	The Enemy's Plan – Part 1	327
Mission 90	The Enemy's Plan – Part 2	332
Mission 91	The Enemy's Plan – Part 3	336
Mission 92	The Enemy's Plan – Part 4	339
Mission 93	The Enemy's Plan – Part 5	342
Mission 94	The Enemy's Plan - Part 6	346
Mission 95	The Enemy's Plan - Part 7	350
Mission 96	The Enemy's Plan – Part 8	354
Mission 97	The Enemy's Plan – Part 9	359
Mission 98	The Enemy's Plan – Part 10	364
Mission 99	The Enemy's Plan - Part 11	368
Mission 100	The Enemy's Plan – Part 12	373
Mission 101	The Enemy's Plan – Part 13	377

Final Mission Briefing	385
Index of Scripture References	389

Introduction

God has always been in the business of answering prayer, and His people have always known at least something of the importance of praying. Still, Satan, our enemy, continues to try to confuse and blind us to the truly incredible power of prayer, especially as we engage in this thing called "spiritual warfare". Here, we often must admit that our praying lacks direction and power, that our heart is sometimes not filled with fire and conviction, and that we somehow fall short of the mark in this department. We expect our "spiritual warfare" prayers to be effective because God provides the delivery system for them (Romans 8:26); we want them to always hit their target with supernatural effect. But do they? Why does the situation so often seem unchanged in spite of our prayers? Is there something wrong with us or our praying? And exactly what do we understand about spiritual warfare? It may be that we still have a lot to learn about this weapon called prayer, Spiritual Warfare prayer. That's what this Manual is about.

The simplest definition of spiritual warfare, as it affects us, may be this: the direct confrontation between Satanic forces and God's Kingdom, all of which is a consequence of Satan's original rebellion against God. Satan has established specific rulership and influence over geographical areas (from nations to neighborhoods), institutions (from governments to families), and people (groups to individuals). Spiritual warfare takes place when the gospel of God's Kingdom confronts Satan's claimed domain. Not every illness or infirmity that Jesus or the early Apostles encountered was of demonic origin, but many were. Not every unanswered prayer was the result of demonic interference, but some were. Not every region that was opposed to the gospel being preached by Jesus or the early church was a stronghold of Satan, but some were. It comes down to discerning the difference, seeing the spiritual reality and knowing what to do about it.

I believe that many of us have arrived at this time in our faith journey having been taught little about spiritual warfare or the kind of prayer that is expected of us as spiritual warriors or the means which God has provided for us to fight this war. Directly or indirectly, prepared or not, spiritual warfare has deeply touched the life of every person, believer or unbeliever, and continues to do so to this very day.

In this spiritual war, our enemy is none other than Satan and his host of demonic forces (Ephesians 6:12). Many Christians today simply dismiss this as being fantasy, but the Bible is unapologetic; Satan and spiritual warfare are both very real!

I believe that we are living in a time of approaching darkness, a time when the vision and skills of the practiced spiritual warrior will be absolutely essential for the advancement of God's kingdom and for the health of His church. Spiritual warfare is not, nor has it ever been, optional for the believer. Not for anyone! Every last person on the planet is affected by this war; most are victims, never suspecting what is really going on behind the scenes, driving the events that we see in this flesh-and-blood world. The war is spiritual, but the consequences are played out in the physical as well as the spiritual realms. Sadly, many believers today, at least in our part of the over-comforted, self-consumed church, are no more aware of or better prepared for this war than are the lost. The need for training in Biblical spiritual warfare is great, and I believe the situation is urgent.

Many believers may simply disregard this warning as they have many others, and nothing will change for them, but I believe the world will quickly change around all of us; Satan and his forces are seeing to that. But I also believe that God will show His great power even more clearly to those who have eyes to see, and He will exercise His grace and gifts to those who are ready to "know the season" as we move into this darkening time.

The first printing of this book was written in 2018, when many of the things we covered were only on the horizon. But since then, we have found ourselves thrown further into an age of insanity that defies imagination, with more and worse to come! Wrong is right, dark is light, truth is irrelevant, power is everything. Wicked people and wicked agendas are multiplying and apparently winning. A thick veil of deception has fallen everywhere, and too many self-proclaimed believers are completely comfortable with it, even swallowing it as "truth" and promoting it. It's hard to imagine that it can be allowed to go much further, but it will. And what are we to do in the middle of this end-time insanity? This book is a call to spiritual awakening. Spiritual warfare.

My conviction is that spiritual warfare is not a solo event; it is a team effort. There is no such thing as an army of one. If ever we needed to come to a fuller understanding of why God describes His church as a body, functioning powerfully through the coordinated work of every individual part, that time is now. Spiritual warfare demands that we get a vision of the whole body of Jesus, the church.

I want to pray differently, starting now. And I want to be part of God's army of Prayer Warriors before whom the powers of darkness will flee and through whom the Kingdom of God will be stretched.

> *These lessons on prayer are not for everyone; they are intended for those of us who are responding to God's call to engage in prayer as a weapon of spiritual warfare, and while the principles may apply to every kind of prayer (there are many), they are especially directed to our engagement as an army of God against the forces of our enemy Satan. These lessons, or Missions, become progressively more challenging as we grow in spiritual strength and awakening. They are filled with Scripture references; please read them all, for only what is based on God's Word will endure.*

Mission 1

Opportunity And Authority

When I started this book project we had witnessed amazing victories in our church fellowship in praying over our family members; I have been reminded that this is based on the Biblical principle of spiritual authority. One by one, we have witnessed the effectiveness of the prayers of husbands and wives, fathers and mothers; these are the ones who have been given the spiritual authority *by God* to pray over their household. That's an individual authority grounded in God's Word (Ephesians 5:23, 1 Peter 3:7), so it is recognized spiritually as being authoritative and powerful, supported by Divine authority, and it cannot be overcome by the enemy.

Not all of the spiritual battles involve only family members; sometimes there are many others involved. Friends, extended family, church family. Sometimes whole communities of people, sometimes organizations and institutions. It's complicated!

There are many prayer objectives that cannot be tackled by individual prayers, nor, I believe, has God equipped every individual believer and placed him/her in authority to single-handedly attack every target in a spiritual battle. In secular warfare, snipers have specific, important missions but they cannot destroy bridges or buildings, for example. Someone else has been given the ability to direct specific firepower against such targets. Enemy fortification simply cannot be destroyed until the appropriate force is employed and coordinated against them.

In spiritual warfare, we must begin to learn some of the same tactics that are used successfully in secular warfare. We need to know the appropriate lines of command (ours as well as the enemy's), and we need to know how to employ the full range of weapons that are available to us. Sometimes we must "spy out the enemy" before we can effectively engage him. Sometimes we need to disrupt his communication or control systems before the battle begins. Sometimes we need to disarm his defenses before the main attack can begin.

Our first concern should be to discover who has been called (given authority) to be the Prayer Warrior(s) who can break, confuse or disarm the enemy's weapons in each situation, opening the way for other warriors to close in on the objective. The one(s) in authority may not be obvious, and it is not always the same person in each case.

So, the first Mission is to determine exactly which weapons are needed in each case. Where is the line of spiritual authority in each case? Are we willing to admit that we may not be the one with the authority to lead the prayer battle in this instance? Can we see the urgent need for the prophetic voice, the word of wisdom that can only come from God? It's not a matter of everyone doing his "thing" and hoping for the best; no battle can be won that way. We must discover God's battle plan, his lines of authority, and it will take more than one Prayer Warrior.

Mission 2

Effective Strength

This is a humbling discovery for me. 2 Chronicles 7:14 is not about individual praying; it's about a lot of people praying together, unified to make the prayers effective.

If we are not willing to call others together with us or are too proud to allow ourselves to take our place among others (or even under their authority) for this prayer offensive, then the praying will be relatively ineffective.

When we come together in prayer against our spiritual enemies, we might well ask the question "What does the enemy spirit see when we attack him?" The quick, "easy" answer might be that the enemy sees Jesus in us. I do not think that answer is correct! Jesus said that He would build His church and that the gates of Hell would not prevail against *it* (Matthew 16:18). The enemy must see believers (the church) standing prepared and armed. That enemy should see a squad of Prayer Warriors, each with a raised shield of faith, standing behind the one in the lead. And in the hand of each of those warriors is a weapon designed to be completely effective, *when used together*, to defeat the enemy. I believe that each demonic spirit has the ability to immediately size up the force brought against him, and he is able to determine if it is God's force acting in God's authority. He cannot win so he must retreat. This is tactical prayer.

In Acts 19:15 we see an episode that clearly demonstrates this principle. The sons of Sceva, along with other exorcists, attacked a demon but were quickly overpowered when the demon recognized that they had absolutely no authority against him. The demon acknowledged Paul's legitimate power, as well as the authority of Jesus. The demon knew which battles he could win and which ones he could not win.

In Acts 12:5 we see Peter in prison and the whole church (together) moved to prayer for his release; the result was immediate and powerful.

The second Mission is that we must be willing and trained to pray *together* for very specific battles in this war.

Mission 3
Too Late To Make A Difference

During the Battle of Gettysburg, one of the contributing causes of the Confederate defeat is generally reported to be the failure of General Stuart to maintain contact with General Lee to report the location and size of Union forces leading up to the battle. The Confederate army was surprised by the Union location and strength, and General Stuart's powerful cavalry unit was late in arriving at the battle after the decisive opening fighting had begun. General Stuart arrived too late to swing the battle in favor of the Confederate Army, although he may have been able to do so had he arrived sooner.

There is something important here for us to learn. This is a tough lesson to take to heart. If we are not prepared to rise up immediately in prayer (and that includes being in the proper line of authority before God), the enemy will snatch the victory away from us without a contest. So, we forfeit the victory by simply not being able (or willing) to respond quickly enough.

When we attack the enemy, we choose the timing of the battle, and it is usually a time in our favor. The enemy does the same! So, he likes the dark hours, often when we are physically, emotionally or spiritually weary. He almost always comes at us when we are alone. He knows very well that if we can't even organize a Sunday morning meeting where everyone enthusiastically shows up together at a very convenient time, there is little chance that he will be confronted by a Rapid Response Team of well-armed and well-prepared Prayer Warriors called in the middle of the night or at short notice. Powerful, unified prayer on short notice! What a radical idea that would be! Not exactly the "Now I lay me down to sleep" kind of praying that many believers are willing to offer up to God.

Peter, throughout both of his epistles, repeatedly stresses the need to be alert and to have our minds attentive and disciplined (1 Peter 1:13, 4:7, 5:8, 2 Peter 3:1).

Timing is important!

The third Mission is to set up a workable communication system *between those who are of the same mind in this matter* so that we can enter the battle while it can still make a difference. Never mind a long list of "believers" who don't really care or who are not willing to endure the inconvenience; they're not in the battle and their efforts won't make any difference.

MISSION 4

Failing To Secure The Spoils Of Victory

This one is hard to admit; actually, it is most embarrassing. After having fought *and won* a spiritual battle, we often fail to secure the prize. We leave the trophy lying on the battlefield. So, what happens next? Jesus taught in His parable (Matthew 13:19) that the enemy (none other than the devil himself, the master scavenger) comes along and snatches the seed away from where it has been planted. Jesus warned of the danger of casting out an evil spirit, only to have it return later with more friends, in which case the latter situation is far worse than the former (Matthew 12:45). The enemy does not give up just because he has lost the battle. It's not about winning the battle, it's about winning the prize!

I believe that we must enter into a different phase of our spiritual warfare, one in which we bind and secure the prize.

We may pray that God would post His angels for the preservation of the prize, or it may require more than just praying about it. In any case, we must attend to the necessary work of bringing the harvest into the barns. Leaving it lying in the fields for the enemy to snatch away or spoil is a terrible mistake.

We must secure each other at the end of each battle. I think the enemy hates Sundays around our churches, but he often likes Mondays a whole lot. Why? Perhaps Pastor and some others have expended a lot of spiritual capital, perhaps tiredness at the end of a long day, perhaps an elation at the victories we have just seen on Sunday. If we leave each other in just whatever condition we are in on Sunday night, we probably will hear about it by Monday evening. We are vulnerable, not necessarily to any particular sin (although that is not an unusual consequence), but to failing to bind up and secure each other's spirits exposed to the enemy. In a sense, we are uncovered.

What if we concluded our Sundays (and any other days in which we are collectively engaged in ministry) by praying over each other for the securing and binding power of the Holy Spirit, adding to that the strengthening in our spirits that we need at the conclusion of these battles?

We must secure the ground that is still being fought over. The enemy returns when we go home. We often find the situation entirely different (and not in a good way) when we return to re-engage the enemy. God knows that we cannot sustain the level of activity 24/7 but I believe that He has made provision for us to place the battle into His hands so that we may continue another day. We bind the enemy and hold him powerless to steal back what has already been won. Again, how many of us should sense the great need for a word of wisdom, of prophecy, of encouragement as we disengage from battle for short periods of time? Do we imagine that Satan has given up so easily?

If we were to invest long, hard training in order to compete in a sport event and win a gold medal, it would be unimaginable to go home without the prize medal.

The fourth Mission is to keep our eye on the prize, not leaving it lying on the battlefield after the battle has been won. It's not about winning the battle; it's about bringing home the prize!

MISSION 5

We Don't Know What To Pray

This isn't the situation in which we "just run out of things to pray about". It's much more fundamental than that; after all, if we don't know *what* to pray about, then it hardly matters much *how* we pray.

It seems that we should all know what to pray about, and in a general sense, we probably all do know *many* things to pray about. But when confronted by a spiritual battle, a "general sense" is not good enough. Like a soldier on a battlefield, coming under fire from an enemy, it is critical that the soldier determines exactly where the enemy is located in order to return effective fire.

In Luke 11 Jesus responded to his disciples' request to teach them *how* to pray. He reinforced the lesson with a parable, out of which we have the unforgettable "Ask, seek and knock". The parable, as well as the examples, were all about asking for things that we need (such as food). Nobody could miss the great practical lesson: we are to ask God for all of the things that we need in daily living, even though it may seem that all (or many) of these things are well within our own ability to get them for ourselves. But it only takes one of life's upsets to remind us that we can suddenly find ourselves helpless and in need of even these simple things. Jesus' irrefutable argument in verses 11-12, again speaking of those same basic, practical needs (such as food), concluded by stating how much more our heavenly Father can be depended upon to satisfy those very needs for us. That's when Jesus throws in one of His curves; He says that, in response to our needs, our Father gives us the Holy Spirit. So, we're hungry, we ask Him for a fish, and He gives us the Holy Spirit! That just doesn't make any sense at all; we're missing something. And, by the way, this text (in context) has little to do with asking God for the Holy Spirit, or the Baptism of the Holy Spirit, even though we have all probably heard the text wrongly used for that purpose. We'll have to look elsewhere for teaching on that subject.

Paul fills in the missing part in Romans 8:26. The Holy Spirit shows us what we should be praying for (even in the middle of what might seem to be quite obvious); as Paul says, "We do not know what to ask", so the Holy Spirit comes to our rescue and directs our prayer, not only getting the correct target but also taking over the very expression of our needs directly to God's heart in such a way that no words could ever express.

So, Prayer Warriors, here we are confronted with the basic fact that we, in our own wisdom, do not know what to pray. That comes as a shock; after all, we are in a spiritual battle where we see the problem, we know where the answer comes from, so let's get to work on it. Ready, aim, pray! So why didn't that work?

Well, for one thing, the enemy is an expert at camouflage and deception, so much so that, according to the Holy Spirit speaking through Paul, we will often aim our prayers at the wrong target.

It is critical, therefore, that our first response to a prayer need must be to seek the wisdom of the Holy Spirit in showing us the real target, and all the more so when the "obvious" answer is staring us in the face. In the midst of a spiritual battle, it is crippling if God's army is so unfamiliar with seeking His wisdom that we have to call time out for a holy huddle just to cover the basics of knowing what to pray. The enemy knows that the battle will be over by the time we get our act together. Equally as bad, without the ready direction of the Holy Spirit, we could be shooting in all directions, hitting nothing and producing nothing but a lot of smoke and noise. We think that we have been fighting a spiritual battle, but we have not been anywhere close to the real target. More deception.

We must be trained in the use of all of our spiritual weapons and we must have the supernatural eyesight of the prophet through whom the Holy Spirit can direct our actions. It's too late to go looking for a prophet (or one operating in a prophetic gifting) after the battle has already started. *That critical piece must be practiced and in place before the battle starts.*

We also need the prophet's ability to see "over the horizon" to know what will be the next battle. Before the battle begins, we must scout out the ground, clear away the enemy strongholds, disrupt his communications, loose prisoners, build strong points, clear out anything in our own lives that will hamper our movements or give the enemy anything that he can use against us. Carrying dirty secrets into spiritual warfare is like pulling the pin out of a hand grenade and then stuffing the grenade into our pocket. Achan's secret (Joshua 7:4) cost the lives of 36 other men.

This Mission warns us of the sin of presumption (assuming that we already know the answer) and drives us to seek God's wisdom first.

Mission 6

We Must Prepare To Go Back

Our attitude in spiritual warfare may be that we are only passing this way once, no going back. So, our praying takes on that same hit-and-run mindset. We are mistaken!

We don't think of the Good Samaritan (Luke 10:25-37) as having much to teach us about praying, but let's give him another chance. After having done all that he could to aid the poor victim, including putting him up in a motel with a pre-paid expense card, he then told the manager that he was planning to return on a certain date and that he would check to see if there was anything else that was needed, and that he would attend to those matters as well. He knew that he was on a round trip.

Spiritual warfare is not hit-and-run fighting; it is taking and occupying enemy "territory" in order to release captives. Every good military commander knows the necessity of patrolling the borders of taken territory and posting sentries. Why? Because the enemy is waiting to see if we are going to come back or if our interests have taken us somewhere else. The enemy doesn't mind losing a battle to us as long as he can re-occupy the territory after we have moved away. We must patrol our borders and be prepared to fight as hard to keep them as we did to win them.

I recently saw the blessing of "binding up" (as in applying medical dressing to scrapes and wounds) my friend after a busy day of ministering, after which he was exhausted and felt "exposed" spiritually. The enemy had no way to attack him as long as he was covered, and he (the enemy) could not take away from the work that had been accomplished that day as long as it was "sealed" by the Spirit. Well done, but is that the end of it? Unless

I'm prepared to patrol that border regularly, how long will it be before the enemy attacks again to re-take the territory?

Somehow in our praying in spiritual warfare we need to leave the devil with the clear message that "I'll be back!"

Good for you, Good Samaritan.

Mission 7

Are We Praying Out Of A Surplus Or A Loss?

It comes as no surprise that everything that affects our life affects the way we pray. Or maybe you thought that you could pray in a vacuum? Sadly, a piece of forgotten "baggage" may be robbing us of power in prayer.

I've been reading the little book of Ruth again. We are familiar with the story line, how Naomi has lost her husband and two sons and is now returning to Judah with her daughter-in-law Ruth. She is quick to recite her misfortunes: "the Lord's hand has turned against me" (Ruth 1:13 NIV), and "I went away full, but the Lord has brought me back empty" (Ruth 1:20,21 NIV).

There's no denying her losses, or ours; we all have at least some. The question is "What are we doing with them?" Somewhere in the hurt of our losses we watch those precious things in our life pass into the realm of memories; they must. But for some of us, those memories harden into monuments, solid souvenirs. Memories pack easily and travel lightly; monuments do neither. They are hard and sharp-edged, denting and demanding accommodation from everything they touch. And they grow heavier with time. Naomi returned to Judah carrying monuments.

Boaz, on the other hand, is an inspiration. He was probably only a bit older than Naomi's sons, but he had obviously stayed in Judah when Naomi and her family fled to Moab to escape the famine. So, Boaz would have remembered those lean years of famine, too, but now we see him in the midst of a plentiful harvest. Even Naomi had heard that the Lord had come to the aid of His people and had broken the famine. Boaz welcomed these family/strangers with an unforgettable greeting: "May you be richly rewarded by the Lord, the god of Israel, under whose wings you have come to take refuge" (Ruth 2:12 NIV). To him, God's richness and bounty were more than sufficient to satisfy the needs of His people PLUS the needs of any others who would flee for refuge to those same protective wings.

Now to the part that may hurt.

> Have you suffered a great loss (loved one, family, friend, position, reputation, fortune, etc.) in your life?
>
> Have you measured your "success" at this point in your life and are now disappointed?
>
> Have you started to think that your current circumstance isn't where you expected to be by the time this year rolled around?
>
> Have you found yourself looking back to an earlier time in your life when you "had it all", only to have to admit that you have lost it and now you don't have time to get it all back again?

Our enemy loves to draw our attention to these things, because he knows that as long as we are dwelling on them, we are hardening them into monuments, reminders of how much God has taken from us, how poor He has left us and how hopeless our circumstance is. We count our walk with God as a cost, instead of a dividend. Naomi was counting the cost; Boaz was counting the dividend.

How can we pray with that spirit of blame hidden away in our heart? How can we hope to engage in spiritual warfare when there is a secret (or not secret) doubt in the integrity of our Commander-in-Chief or of His ability to do the best for us? We may not even be aware of that evil spirit hidden in the dark corner of our heart, but our enemy knows it's there and he'll pull it out when it suits his purposes. The only way to be sure that it's dealt with is to take the lead: ask the Holy Spirit to search our hearts, *especially if we already know that our life has suffered one or more losses that could become the source of this deadly blame game.* Name it before God and ask Him to seal it up against the enemy, then ask Him to sanctify it to His glory so that we may finally begin to see God's dividends.

Boaz was right and his prayer was prophetic. He and Ruth became the great-grandparents of King David and the ancestors of the Messiah. Naomi even got her baby boy (Ruth 4:17).

We must let God show us that we can only be effective Prayer Warriors when we see ourselves praying out of a surplus of a generous God.

Mission 8

Praying For Effect

Have you ever seen the effects of a prayer assault against the enemy? We usually do not; we are content to be on the "sending end" and we give no thought to what may (or may not) be happening at the "receiving end". Our prayer "bombardment" goes pretty much the way we assume it will go without any confirmation of the effects it has on the enemy. We may be fooling ourselves!

There are a couple important lessons that we can learn from observing military operations, particularly when it comes to artillery bombardment. First, the shells are BIG (up to 2700 lbs. apiece); second, they are fired a long way from the target (up to 38 km); third, there must be some feedback to the gun to allow for accurate aiming. The first rounds fired are usually just to produce smoke, so the spotter can see where the round is landing with respect to the target. After some aiming corrections, the command is then given to "Fire For Effect", meaning this is the real thing! I have seen as many as 6 artillery guns firing altogether at the same target from different positions, with up to a dozen rounds in the air at the same time. When they all start coming down together on the same spot, it gives a whole new meaning to the word "effect"!

What if we could pray like that? Take a look at Acts 4:24-31. Those few believers all set their sights on the same target and with great boldness and focus they sent a prayer barrage that shook the building and set off spiritual explosions all around their city. They had seen enough of the enemy's attempts to quash the Holy Spirit and to eliminate His servants. They had seen how powerfully God could move. They were justifiably "ticked off", to the point where they all marched into God's presence with one thing in mind: destroy the enemy's plan! If we had been there, we might have heard them shout "Pray For Effect!" I doubt that anyone dozed off during that prayer meeting, and I don't think that anyone was mumbling aimlessly that "God would bless all the missionaries everywhere and make everything work out OK Amen". On the contrary, I believe that those prayers were highly coordinated and loud and enthusiastic. And I think there were a lot of tears and "Amens".

What if WE were to come to this aspect of spiritual warfare with this same attitude, determined to Pray For Effect? Not all of our praying will necessarily take this form, and that does not mean that God does not answer those prayers, *but when it comes to prayer as a part of spiritual warfare, let's do nothing less than to Pray For Effect.*

Mission 9

The Power Of Loudly Praying The Truth

Many of us were probably taught somewhere along the way that prayer is a private (almost secret) conversation with God. While there certainly is a lot of truth to the fact that many of our conversations with God are deeply personal, so much so that it is not necessary for anyone else to be part of the conversation, nevertheless, when it comes to spiritual warfare, the opposite is more generally true. I believe that a necessary element of our warfare praying is the fact that we are <u>not</u> secretive about it. We need to learn the importance of not being silent.

My mother lived through the Nazi occupation of Belgium during WW2. Among the personal treasures that I have from her is a tiny diary that she kept with her during that time. In this diary are bits of handwritten information that she had learned either from listening to the BBC (on a hidden radio; like the note that she inscribed in January 1941 when the Allies succeeded in taking Tobruk, Libya) or from her own observations (like when she saw a formation of Allied bombers flying east en route to a target, especially after what we now call D-Day). This information was shared among friends; social networking isn't something new! The penalty for being caught with a diary like that was immediate execution.

There were two reasons why the enemy did all that it could to stop this sort of thing: it didn't want the occupied people to know that the Allies were making advances that would one day lead to Germany's defeat, and it didn't want its own troops to hear the news. For the occupied people, it was hugely encouraging and led them to become bolder in their resistance against the enemy. For the enemy troops, most of whom did not know the news either, it would be hugely discouraging, demoralizing, and might even lead to defection.

Have you ever thought of your prayer in spiritual warfare as being a critical piece of communication? The enemy wants to keep us silent for the same two reasons, so we are told to pray silently (if at all). No!! We loudly proclaim the Lord's victories among us to encourage one another and to announce to the devil's forces that they are in a losing battle. What we don't see is the bigger picture. That enemy engaged against our brother or sister in a seemingly unrelated battle of cancer is intended (by the devil) to come over to join the forces already fighting against us. Our situation is "supposed" to become a lot worse just as soon as that cancer battle is won by the enemy. But what happens when the Lord prevails against that cancer, bringing healing and salvation? Suddenly the enemy fighting against us learns that he isn't going to be getting help from his friends anytime soon. He is weakened by the power of the truth of God's victory and we are greatly emboldened. We are reminded that the walls of Jericho fell at the shout of God's people (Joshua 6:20)! I can already hear the sound of God's reinforcements!

I believe that we must develop a much better sense of the interconnection between the parts of the body of believers that are most directly connected with us in spiritual warfare. We all have our spiritual battles, but there is only one enemy with limited resources. We must be led to pray strategically for one another; what may seem to be unrelated to our personal struggle is likely to be connected to us in ways that we cannot see with human wisdom. A word of wisdom or prophecy from the Lord can reveal it to us and direct our prayers.

Openly declaring God's victory in someone else's battle announces to our own opponent that he has lost again, that he is not going to be strengthened against us, and that we are about to receive reinforcements from the Lord's army.

How many of those powerful prayers that we read in Acts start off with a declaration of God's mighty works against the devil's forces? We can be sure that the enemy cringes when God's people loudly declare the Lord's victories to one another, and he hates to think that his own forces are being reminded of their own certain defeat.

Our warfare praying ought to be anything but silent; it needs to be loud enough to encourage the fellow believer next to you and loud enough to remind the enemy that he cannot win.

> *Now thanks be to God who always leads us in triumph in Christ, and through us diffuses the fragrance of His knowledge in every place*
>
> 2 Corinthians 2:14 NKJV

Mission 10

Support As An Element Of Spiritual Warfare

When you picture yourself engaged in spiritual warfare, how do you see yourself? Do you see yourself as the General in the front line in combat with the enemy? That may be a problem if that's all you can see. We usually see ourselves as being the hero at the front of the parade!

Military commanders understand the importance of supporting roles in combat, and they understand that the ones most effective in front-line combat are also the ones who have the best appreciation of the supporting role, not just because they see the need for others to support them, but because they also realize the importance of switching positions and being the supporter. We don't appreciate the supporting role if we only view it as something that serves us; *we need to step into the shoes of the supporter in order to gain a proper appreciation for the next time we need support.*

Luke 22:31 presents us with a powerful example of the critical importance of the supporting role in spiritual warfare. Here we might expect that Peter would be assigned the supporting role, with Jesus in the lead, but this is not the case. Jesus, seeing Satan's designs on Peter, moved immediately into the supporting role. His prayer was immediate, powerful and to the point. And it brought Him into face-to-face combat with Satan himself. There can be no doubt that Jesus was engaged in spiritual warfare. His objective was to provide supporting cover for Peter. It was to the point: Satan wanted to shred Peter and Jesus jumped in front of him and smashed the devil's plan.

When was the last time that you jumped in front of the enemy when it was clear to you that he was about to attack a brother or sister? It's fair to say that you won't get much closer to the enemy than when you jump between him and his intended victim.

This may sound a bit "theoretical" and distant since none of us is likely to bump up against Peter in the scenario described in Luke 22. Not likely to happen to us, or so we think. As it turns out, this is one of the easiest ways to get involved in spiritual warfare, and, unlike many situations in which the players are either distant or "spiritual" (invisible), this one involves people whom you can see. It is also one of the few situations where you can actually see the results of your battle. It can be quite revealing; are we ready for an honest evaluation of how effective we are as a spiritual warrior?

Pick someone close to you, someone who is engaged in their own battles. Someone who is a spiritual warrior. Don't pick someone sitting in the bleachers; they're too busy with themselves to be of any interest to the devil. Get down with God and come to the side of that warrior as a supporter before the Lord. Pray that the Holy Spirit will allow your heart to feel what they feel. Loneliness, defeat, disappointment, despair, shame, fatigue, ... then beg God with great boldness to deliver and restore that one. Confront the enemy, stand by the side of the one under attack, deny the devil's wish, foil his plans, jump in front with your shield of faith and your weapons ready for use.

So, when do you want to start? If you're serious, you will start right now! Here's a suggestion: stand in the gap for Pastor and his wife. Do it even if you don't know the details; your effectiveness has nothing to do with how much you know, it has everything to do with your determination to make a difference where it counts. Then pick another one and so on. How about that brother in a wheelchair? Do you suppose that he ever gets discouraged? Just do one at a time; "multitasking" is a myth, so don't be fooled into thinking that you're any different!

Your next assignment is to pray for your wife or husband or son or daughter like that.

If a brother or sister close to you is being "sifted" (or shredded), maybe it's because you haven't offered yourself as the only available supporter willing to jump in front of the enemy.

Mission 11

Some Assembly Required

We all remember having bought something that came in a box with the simple warning printed "Some Assembly Required", and the tiny picture of a single screwdriver next to those words, as if to announce that anyone could put this thing together in no-time with nothing more than that little screwdriver. The fully assembled BBQ that we saw in the store didn't resemble this pile of pieces and bags of nuts and bolts!

Or what about that free software package? It does some of the things that we want, but we soon discover that if we want the full-featured version (with no pop-up advertisements) we must pay a subscription price, possibly every year!

Why do we think that our experience as a Prayer Warrior will be free and easy and full-featured right out of the box? Praying for miracles, looking for God's wondrous signs in healing, salvation, deliverance, miraculous provision, holy boldness, unexplainable openings for the gospel, …….. surely this shouldn't demand much from us, should it? After all, we are believers, and God is on our side, isn't He?

Well, believers yes, but full-fledged Prayer Warriors probably not. At least not yet. It doesn't come automatically with our salvation membership; it is optional, and it does cost. It costs more than some are willing to pay. There is a lot of assembly required, and it is not maintenance-free.

We must become teachable. Sounds simple and obvious but try telling that to someone who has been a believer for many years, done all the usual "church" stuff, maybe even held an office in the church. Maybe a Pastor or Elder. Become teachable? You must be kidding; that's for novices, not for me!

In Matthew 10 Jesus personally commissioned his disciples, called them his apostles and gave them explicit authority to perform miracles, and yet in Matthew 17:20 we see these same disciples powerless to drive out a demon from a boy. Jesus' explanation: they lacked faith and they were weak in prayer. Maybe they thought that it would be enough just to be deputized by Jesus, to be known as one of His disciples, to be repeating His words. They discovered that they were not ready for tough spiritual warfare as-is; there was some assembly required, and it was going to cost them. We may argue that they had not yet experienced Pentecost, that Jesus had not yet been crucified and risen ..... all true, but the basic truth is that they simply had not yet fully invested their lives into the Kingdom. Jesus didn't offer the Pentecost excuse; he simply told them that something vital was missing from their ministry. That "something" was a costly, tough, demanding, disciplined attitude toward their own faith walk, including a different kind of prayer. A casual approach wasn't good enough, and their experience up to that point (even having heard Jesus' teaching) wasn't sufficient either.

No believer engaged in spiritual warfare is strong enough to carry his pride; it's got to go before anything else can happen. Refusing to do so is a sure sign of an arrogant heart, an un-teachable spirit. God pushes the proud away (James 4:6). Really bad place to be as a spiritual warrior!

Then we come to the maintenance. Spiritual warfare quickly reveals that we are not maintenance-free! Secret sins, old favorites, have to go. New secret sins too! There seems to be an endless supply if we are willing to subscribe to them. But the truth is that they, new or old, will prevent God from hearing our prayers! (Psalm 66:18). Another bad place for a spiritual warrior to be!

Then we come to our personal relationships; a husband who is not holding his wife up in that place as an honored, cherished, sanctified vessel cannot be strong in spiritual warfare because his prayer life is hindered (strong interference, weakened, confused and unclear) (1 Peter 3:7). Don't be counting on him to be at your side when the battle is raging because the enemy already knows his weakness.

We must recognize that our faith walk as Prayer Warriors will cost us some sleepless hours, some inconvenience, some effort, some sacrifices, some real changes in the way we live every day.

Some assembly required!

Mission 12

The Lord Will Provide

My grandfather was a godly man, a Pentecostal man. He came to Canada as an immigrant railway worker, and somewhere between arriving here at age 18 and a few years later, when he married my grandmother, he came to a new faith in Jesus. I can imagine that it was not a quiet event! He was known as a man who dearly and unashamedly loved his faith, a man who had a gift of healing. He didn't talk a lot, as I recall, but he had a kind, strong voice with which I often heard him pray. He didn't argue with others about his faith; what he believed, as far as he was concerned, was just quite simply *true*.

He had a saying that I heard him repeat many times: "The Lord will provide". I heard him pray it many times and I heard him say it many times when he received exactly what he was asking for. Not just big things but more often ordinary things, like when he would return from hunting grouse with a bird in his hand. He didn't say it too loudly, just loud enough to be heard if you were paying attention, but it was as if he wasn't speaking to anyone present; he was saying it more like a "thank you" to God. The Lord will provide, and He did over and over again. I'm reminded lately of that truth as God sends little reminders that he is still the Provider.

That got me thinking about the fact that one of our greatest spiritual battles is against our enemy, the father of lies, as he continually whispers doubt into our ears and hearts. "Has God really said that?" First heard in the Garden of Eden, it has been repeated countless times. Maybe you've heard it in your heart lately. Did God really say that He could heal your loved one? Did He really mean that He would come through for you this time? Did He really mean that He would hear you every time you cried out to Him, even after you failed Him? So, I've been asking God to speak to me about how He does provide.

We must come to Abraham, the one to whom God first revealed Himself as the Provider (Genesis 22:14). We all know that God provided the ram caught in the thicket just as Abraham was about to offer his son Isaac. So, where was that ram all the time that Abraham was building the altar, arranging the wood, getting his son prepared? Did Abraham just not notice? How about this idea: the ram was NOT there all that time; God created it at the same moment that He withheld Abraham's hand from killing Isaac. Preposterous you say? Possibly God the Provider is none other than God the Creator.

Here's another one. Where were all those millions of quail the day before they flew through the wilderness Hebrew camp on that east wind? Not once but every day. They might have been flapping around out there over the Sinai, or they might have been created just as they were needed to serve the purposes of God the Provider and to bless His people.

So, what does this all matter and what does it have to do with spiritual battles over faith? Just this. Do we understand miracles to be arrangements of circumstances that lead, like joining the dots, to a miraculous conclusion? A parade of secondary causes? Perhaps. Or perhaps sometimes God is not just God the Arranger but God the Creator/Provider. When we pray for the miraculous, do we presume to know the sequence of events that must lead to the desired miraculous outcome? Are we praying for those precursor events, convinced that is surely the route God will use to arrive at the miraculous outcome? In a way, we'd like to think that we understand at least a bit of the "how" God does things. So maybe God really doesn't have to be the Creator, just the Arranger. Who knows, we might even be able to do part of the arranging for Him. So maybe we don't have to hang ALL our hopes on an all-or-nothing Creator God. Doesn't that sound like something that Satan would come up with just when we're fighting the spiritual battle against doubt?

Take a deep breath in your spirit. Our God, the God of the Bible and the God of our faith, is the Creator/Provider. I believe that ram may not have been there before Abraham got there. Those quail may not have been flapping around out there over the Sinai desert. That healing miracle you're praying for may not necessarily be coming as the result of a sequence of clinical events; I believe that it may be coming out of nothing, the same way that God created the universe, and when it arrives it will be instantly whole. Same thing about those other needful things for which you are waiting on God. If God the Provider is, in fact, the God of Creation, and if His work of providing for all of our needs is intimately connected with His power in creating all things, then there is no limit to what He can do or how He can do it.

Please don't misunderstand what I'm saying. Sometimes God does use a series of visible events to work to a miraculous conclusion. I'm thankful for the miraculous healing in my back and for the surgery that God chose to use to effect it. What I am saying is that God doesn't require *any* circumstances in order to bring a miraculous conclusion.

So, the next time you are fighting the spirit of doubt and he reminds you that the circumstances don't look very promising, just remind him that our God doesn't need circumstances. The circumstances at Lazarus' tomb weren't very promising! He creates miracles, and He still does it today.

The Lord will provide! Amen!! (I think that was a Pentecostal Amen!).

Mission 13

What Happened To The Others?

This Mission forces me to seriously evaluate my walk as a Prayer Warrior, as a disciple of Jesus, as one called and sent by Him.

Luke tells us (Luke 10:1-24) that at one time Jesus had 72 "sent ones" - disciples, apostles. This number may or may not have included the "twelve". In any case, there were many. These were men whose names were written in the Book of Life (v.20), called by Jesus, commissioned by Him, empowered by Him to perform miracles (v. 19), anointed by Him to speak in His Name. They went out as instructed and their experience was, to say the least, life-changing for them as well as for many others. Upon returning, their testimony included exercising power over demons (v.17). It would be hard to imagine how these men, having experienced what they did, could ever be the same again! I think that we all envy their experience, their victories against some of those same demons that we face in our own spiritual battles.

But wait! We never hear again about at least 60 of those men. What happened to them, that after only a short space of time there would remain only 12 to accompany Jesus at the Last Supper? It may be no coincidence that this account of the 72 follows immediately after Jesus' warnings about the real cost of following Him (Luke 9:57-62).

But that's enough speculation about those disciples; I'm more concerned about us. The hard truth is that even disciples who have experienced wondrous things in Jesus' service can lose their way, become less than they were, "fall" from those high places they once knew and become satisfied with much less. Still believers, but not demon-chasers. Not Prayer Warriors. No more miracles.

So now it's question time.

> Did you once know an intimacy and power in your praying that you no longer experience?
>
> Did you once know the familiar voice of the Spirit and move in obedience to Him but now find it hard to recognize His voice at all?
>
> Did your faith once know the all-powerful Jesus and His ability to do the impossible, but now finds it hard to summon any real confidence in His power or provision?
>
> Did your preaching once resonate with God and men but now you find that neither seem to be impressed?
>
> Was there a time when your spiritual weapons were sharp and familiar in your hand but, today they lie unworn in the corner of your memory?
>
> I could go on but by now you know what I mean.

If there was a time when you stood on higher ground than where you are standing today, then something very dangerous has happened.

I don't believe that any of those 60 men intentionally quit one day or ever thought that they would; they drifted away one step at a time until they lost the fire in their hearts and then they no longer felt the fire in God's heart. Like Jesus said, there is a high cost; the day that we are no longer willing to pay that cost is the day the fire begins to go out. Could never happen to you, you say? Paul disagrees (1 Corinthians 10:12) and the deceitfulness of our hearts was well known in the Old Testament (Jeremiah 17:9).

God's call came again to Jonah and it can come to you; there is no need to "forfeit the grace that could be yours" (Jonah 2:8). God IS calling you to renewed service.

In our walk as Prayer Warriors, we must remind ourselves that our own best intentions are not enough to keep us on the high ground; we need the humility to ask God daily to renew His fire within us.

Mission 14

Don't Go Alone

I learned to hunt and fish from my Dad, who knew how to do both well. The lessons started long before I was aware of it. First, he told me countless stories of his hunting and fishing trips, and each new experience was added to the story list. I heard them many (many) times, enough to make me want to know more. Then, when I was old enough to step over the windfalls or wade across the brook, he began to take me along with him. In fact, I really didn't do much hunting or fishing on those first trips; I was just following my Dad, keeping my eyes on him and listening to the short tutorials along the way about how to recognize that track or scuff mark or how to know just where a trout would lie next to the stream bank or under that log. Finally, the day came when he passed me the fishing rod and I first felt the tug of a trout on the line, or he passed me the shotgun after we had spotted the partridge. Finally, I began to hunt and fish.

One day Jesus took three of his disciples up into a mountain to pray, and during that time He was transfigured in their presence (Matthew 17, Mark 9, Luke 9). He met and conversed with Moses and Elijah; the conversation focused on Jesus' coming death and probably also his resurrection. I would love to have heard that conversation and to have seen Jesus, Moses and Elijah standing together in glory!

But why did Jesus take those three disciples along with him? The meeting with Moses and Elijah had nothing to do with Peter, James or John and they weren't even involved in the conversation. Luke records that the disciples were actually asleep during part of the meeting, and when Peter did blurt out something, it was only because he didn't know what to say so he said the first thing that came into his head; not at all inspirational, as usual! Jesus even cautioned them not to mention the incident until after His resurrection. The Transfiguration was an intensely personal experience for Jesus, intimately connected with his coming death. So why did He bring His disciples along?

Of course, we don't know all the answer to that question. Jesus had been telling them who He was and now He was showing them who He was in a very special way. But the day would come when each of these men would have to come to their own personal encounter with the power and presence of God and his Kingdom.

So, what about us? Do we enjoy mountain-top experiences with God? Do we engage in intense spiritual warfare? Is our prayer time deep and personal, life-changing for us? Do we want others to know that about us? Do we frequently tell them about our faith walk, our mountain-top encounters with a miracle-working God?

Or are we willing to bring them along with us and show them, with the expectation that they, too, will come to that place in their faith walk?

You see, if our goal is to convince others of the intensity and power of *our* experiences, then we are probably doing it for the wrong reasons, no matter how much we sprinkle God into our story telling. It becomes all about *us, our* experiences, the things that *we* have seen, *our* walk, how close *we* are to God and how much of His presence *we* are enjoying.

Our goal must be to bring others with us so that they will step into their own experiences with God, perhaps even more spectacular than our own. Prayer Warriors cannot raise up other Prayer Warriors by simply recounting their own "war stories"; they must provide the model that allows others to see spiritual warfare first-hand and then to finally engage for themselves. The others are not there to allow us to be the superstars.

We must be willing to pass the fishing rod or shotgun to someone else for the first time. Like my Dad did for me so that I, too, could become a fisherman and hunter.

Can you pray for healing, deliverance, salvation, provision? Then show someone else how to do it, too. Show them how to speak before God, how to claim the Lord's victories, how to hold up others before the throne of God, how to confront the enemy, how to skillfully use the full armor of God. Show someone how to hold up *his* shield of faith over *his* family and how to exercise spiritual authority against the enemy for the protection of *his* household.

Next time don't go up the mountain alone.

Mission 15

Overtaken By Joy

I've been walking in a wonderful time of joy in my life and it doesn't show any sign of letting up! You might say that I've been overtaken by joy!

Lisa, my wife, has been experiencing a life-changing renewal of the Holy Spirit over the past many months, now over two years and counting. That's what she calls it. You can see it in how (and how much) she talks, how much she smiles, how she started getting up at 5:30 am just to have a time of prayer and Bible reading before going to work. You can see her new boldness in her faith and how it is even affecting her co-workers; she prays for them and gladly gives God the glory for answered prayers in their lives. They even thank her! She talks to God while driving to work, then she does stuff that He tells her to do. I'm surrounded!

It's hard to defeat a child of God who has the joy of the Lord in their heart. Nehemiah, upon completion of the rebuilding of the wall of Jerusalem and the reading of the Law, declared that "the joy of the Lord is your strength" (Nehemiah 8:10).

Prayer Warriors need strength, but we often equate strength with fervency in prayer, power in preaching or some other outward act of ministry. But the real source of our strength ought to be the joy of the Lord. Jesus was filled with the joy of the Holy Spirit (Luke 10:21) when he saw the Kingdom being unfolded and revealed to his disciples.

Maybe that's where we should look to find our joy, and from that, our strength. Can you see the Kingdom being revealed? Can you hear the voices of the bound ones being set free? Can you sense the nearness of the coming King? In your spiritual battles, can you see that the sound of the Lord's victory has driven fear into the enemy?

We know the difference between joy and happiness. I have a dear friend who has been through many losses during the past few months, including the home-going of his wife, his mother, and a dear friend. But he has joy, even if you have to look through his tears to see it in his spirit.

You may be praying for strength; start praying for a renewed joy. Psalm 51:12 is a good place to start. Prayer Warriors, remind one another that the battle is the Lord's and that the victory is assured. Rejoice aloud that our Lord reigns! Let the joy of the Lord rise up among the redeemed of God. This is something that we must decide to do as an act of our will; it won't just "happen" to us. Our strength will rise with our joy!

Mission 16

What Are We Fighting For?

We are called into spiritual warfare (Ephesians 6:10-13), we are armed for spiritual battle (Ephesians 6:14-17), but exactly what are we fighting to achieve? We spend most of our time and effort concentrating on *how* to fight and we may not be spending enough time figuring out *why* we are doing it in the first place. That's why we often find ourselves unclear about our objectives and at odds with other spiritual warriors over what the end result should look like.

For starters, I don't believe that we are fighting to capture the world and to thus make it the Kingdom of God. I believe that Jesus is the one who will personally come to reclaim authority over the world, its kingdoms and its governments (Revelation 11:15) and He is the one before whom every knee shall bow (Romans 14:11). So, what is our job in the here-and-now before this comes to fulfilment?

First, we are to oppose every effort of the devil against the building of the Kingdom that is going on right now. Jesus made it clear that Kingdom construction has already begun (Mark 1:15) and it may be nearing completion. Satan wants to destroy that Kingdom, or to spoil as many parts of it as possible. It is our call to oppose the enemy, so we pray for healing and deliverance and salvation so that men may be loosed from the chains of darkness and brought into the light of God's salvation (1 Peter 2:9). We have been given the authority to directly fight against the devil's schemes to destroy or delay the Kingdom of God.

Secondly, we are to advance into the darkness of Satan's domain to push back that darkness so that men may hear and respond to the gospel. We come against rulers who have been given authority over cities, regions, countries, neighbourhoods, homes and families; we come against these evil authorities in order that prisoners will be loosed and set free from their captivity (Ephesians 6:12). We pray for God's own angels to hedge and protect the advance of the gospel in these places.

Thirdly, we stand in the face of the enemy to declare that God's Kingdom has already come to us; that we who were once lost have been given new life and a holy boldness so that we are living proof that God's work will be completed exactly as He said it would (Matthew 16:18). We remind Satan that he has already lost us, and he has lost the war against God's Kingdom.

Fourthly, we fight in order to present Jesus as Lord. We do not present healing; we present the Healer. We do not present deliverance; we present the great Deliverer. We do not present prosperity; we present the Provider. We do not present salvation; we present the Saviour. We confidently lift up the Healer, the Deliverer, the Provider, the Saviour and in His Name we declare that He does all things according to His grace and mercy. Jesus is Lord, and we are given the authority to speak His Lordship into sickness and circumstances so that Kingdom work will advance and will ultimately be completed.

So, how will we know when we can stop fighting in this spiritual war? I think that a safe answer would be when we see Him coming again.

Mission 17

Prayer Warrior Yes; Superman No

Gaining strength in prayer doesn't mean that we spend all of our time fighting demons; sometimes the struggles we find ourselves in can make us think that, but we have all experienced what it means to trip and fall down. Maybe a familiar sin, maybe someone or something that suddenly brought out a side of us that deeply disappointed us (and maybe others). At those times we don't feel very mighty. We are quickly reminded of the weight of guilt and shame and, hopefully, as quickly of the infinite forgiveness we have in Christ (1 John 1:9). But the disappointment doesn't pass away instantly; we expected more of ourselves, but hopefully it was a reminder that we are not supermen or superwomen. It should also be a reminder that God fully intends for us to be continually casting ourselves on His mercy, humbling ourselves under His mighty hand, casting our cares (including our disappointments) upon Him and experiencing His grace being revealed in us (1 Peter 5:6,7).

So, does that mean that we have failed as Prayer Warriors? Certainly not. Does it mean that God now expects less of us, or that we have been moved out of the front line and relegated to a back-row seat on the sidelines? Absolutely not. Of course, our enemy would want us to think all of those things; suddenly the spiritual battle has come to us. The father of lies himself whispers defeat and failure in our ears but the Holy Spirit has a very different message that He wants us to hear (Galatians 4:6, Romans 8:15). God picks us up right where we fell down, and then, instead of leaving us to dwell on our fall, He directs our eyes toward the goal and kindly reminds us of our original commission.

We can all use a reminder once in a while that God values humility, so much so that I think He sometimes lets us have our own way just long enough to get the lesson. Growing mighty in prayer, if it means anything, must mean that we also grow in the grace of humility. How else could we be willing to get down on our knees to help someone up from a dirty gutter, or embrace them when they don't smell or look very presentable?

It then becomes a very short step from spiritual might to servanthood. Isn't that exactly what Jesus modelled to us (Mark 10:45)? And isn't that what He told us to expect (Mark 10:44)?

So, if our spiritual exploits have taken us to high ground and we have become accustomed to the shouts of victory, we might become a bit careless and begin to forget that we are not superheroes; no surprise to God (Psalm 103:14). We only become strong when we first become weak (2 Corinthians 12:10), but we would rather not *remain weak*; unfortunately, that's our problem. Continued strength comes through continued weakness.

As we take our place again as Prayer Warriors, mighty in God, let's remember to ask God to keep us in a place of weakness so that the victory we seek will reveal His strength instead of ours.

MISSION 18

Time To Clean House

The New Year is a good time to make some resolutions that we know we can keep; better yet, it's a good time to make some that will make a difference in the way we live the coming year, and there's no better place to start as a Prayer Warrior. The fact is, there may be some stuff lying in the corners of your house that have been causing you trouble, stuff that has to go before you can move to a stronger place in prayer.

I think there are some of you who will think that what I'm about to say is off the wall; you've gone over the top, Jim! But read through and pray it through and you may change your mind.

If you saw the film "War Room", you will recall the scene where the retired Pastor, who is looking to buy the house, wanders into the now-empty prayer closet. His clear impression is that that closet was once filled with prayer. Of course, that scene was made for dramatic effect in the film, but there is a truth beyond the film. Places have "memory". On one level, all we have to do to know this is true is to think about our childhood home kitchen; can you smell the bread baking in the oven? Or our grandfather's workshop where we can still "smell" the wood. Or what about a special spot that has deep romantic connections?

If familiar places can trigger such strong, clear memories even after many decades have passed, then it is possible that some places can have spiritual connections. Beyond memories, these are places that I believe have strong spiritual attachments. The ones that we need to know about are the ones that have a "dark" connection with past sin (ours or someone else's), because these are the ones that our enemy will use to build his stronghold right under our nose, right in the midst of our home, right among our family. If we do not clean out these places, then the enemy and his evil spirits that once reigned in those places will continue their dark work of stealing, killing and destroying (John 10:10). Persistent, repeated temptations or failures. A recurring darkness that just refuses to go away. Repeated spiritual attacks against us or our family members that seem to come out of "nowhere". Sound familiar? Maybe these are the hallmarks of a room with an unwanted guest.

I'm not talking about haunted houses! I am talking about something in our (or someone else's) past, something that we may have confessed to God as a sin, something perhaps strongly associated with a place in our home. Something very familiar to us, not a stranger although it may be something that we wish we had never known. Something that speaks of a time in our life when we lived under the power of the one who is now our enemy. By our actions back then we may have given him authority to "occupy" that room, and he has never left.

"Familiar spirits" in the Bible are associated with places and people, mostly people, who are known and identifiable. God's strictest judgment was pronounced on anyone who consulted these "familiar spirits" for the purpose of receiving advice, telling the future or exercising power over others (Leviticus 19:31, 20:6, 20:27, Deuteronomy 18:11). Some of the most tragic episodes in the life of God's people came as a result of leaders who resorted to these "familiar spirits" (2 Kings 21:1-16, 23:24-26). Saul is the arch-example (1 Samuel 28:7, 8-14). Beyond the Biblical examples, I believe there are modern versions of these "familiar spirits", some too close for our comfort.

Enough of a history lesson. Now let's get to work cleaning house, and even if you don't have one of those rooms, this is something that we all should do anyway.

1. We clean house by proclaiming that Jesus is the Lord of our house and home, absolutely every part of it, and that no part of it will be knowingly given over to sin of any kind.

2. We confront any evil spirit that we know was once associated with sinful activities in any particular room(s) and we speak aloud that Jesus is now the Lord and that any other spirit must immediately leave (James 4:7).
3. We break the attachment that those dark spirits have on our mind and memory and claim the release of our spirits from the influence of those enemy spirits.
4. We may wish to bring another Prayer Warrior to accompany us on this cleaning mission, not just for moral support but as a witness against the enemy that he has lost the authority to occupy those rooms where he once held power.
5. We pray through each room in our house, consecrating it to God and dedicating it to His glory.
6. We consecrate ourselves to the ministry of being a Prayer Warrior, asking the Holy Spirit to remind us frequently of this commitment. Perhaps even those places that were once under "different management" may be used to proclaim that the old has gone and the new has come.
7. Tell your story to another Prayer Warrior and give him/her the authority to remind you in those times when the road becomes rough.

I think that we all know that we cannot be mighty for God in our churches if we are not also mighty for Him in our homes. So, can you think of a better way to start a new year as a Prayer Warrior than to make sure you have first cleaned house?

Mission 19

What's The Big Deal About Prayer?

So, what's the big deal about prayer? Why is it such a hot item with God and why does Satan expend so much of his energy to disrupt (or destroy) it?

Let's go back a bit, almost all the way back to when God created the universe but before He created Adam. The universe included every part of God's creation, not only the physical universe but also the spiritual universe; together they summed up God's magnificent creation, all of it, in all of its beauty and glory. And it was Lucifer's ministry to channel and communicate ALL of that beauty and to express it as glory and praise to the Creator Himself. His name means "shining one", "light bearer", "Day Star", "morning star" and "star of the morning". Ezekiel 28 describes him as intelligent ("full of wisdom" v.12), beautiful ("perfect in beauty" and "every precious stone was your covering" v. 12-13), musically talented ("your timbrels and pipes" v.13), having an elevated position ("the anointed cherib who covers", "you were on the holy mountain of God" and "you walked back and forth in the midst of the fiery stones" v.14), and filled with perfection (the seal of perfection" v.12 and "perfect in your ways" v.15). Lucifer was the trunk line, the direct communication channel between all that God had created and God Himself. He had the monopoly, on authority from God, to be the channel of communication between God and His creation. Our human minds cannot even begin to imagine what that was like, what that beauty was or how it expressed itself to the glory of the Creator.

Then I can imagine that one "day" there was a new chat around the coffee shops of Heaven (if they have such things!). The angels were buzzing about something that the Creator had just revealed, a piece of breaking news unlike anything they had ever heard before. It was about a new creature that God was going to create, but absolutely different from any other that had ever been created. This one, called Adam, was not going to be an angelic being; it was going to be below that status (Psalm 8:5, Hebrews 2:7). It was going to be a peculiar combination of physical and spiritual. Made of dirt (Genesis 2:7, 3:19), it was going to be invested with the very *image of God* (Genesis 1:27)! Not another God, but a creature in whom God would dwell and express Himself. And even beyond that, although this creature would fall in what would become called sin, God would redeem him through yet another new Adam (Romans 5:14-17, 1 Corinthians 15:22) and so complete His ultimate plan of creation and redemption.

That's a brief history of the past and future! Well, almost; there's a very important part left.

I imagine that this heavenly chatter about a creature to be called Adam, and even more so the mystery of yet another "new Adam" who would follow, didn't go over so well with Lucifer. Somewhere in his heart that had known nothing but the praise and glory of God, about the time of his decision to assume a role that went beyond his God-given authority and to aspire to become "like God" (Isaiah 14:12-14), he already hated this creature Adam. After all, Adam was going to have direct, personal communication with the Creator without any participation by Lucifer. And somehow, all this investment by God in this creature to actually call him his own son (Galatians 4:6, 1 John 3:1) and to ultimately reveal the complete glory of God in him (Ephesians 2:6-7) was nothing but bad news to Lucifer. For all the reasons that persuaded him to rebel against the Creator, one of them must have been hatred for this Adam and envy for the privileges that were going to be his. So he rebelled, and we see the history of Adam and his descendants told in the pages of the Bible. Part of Lucifer's promise to himself and threat against God was that he would destroy, or at least defile, this Adam and his descendants, and more certainly prevent this "new Adam" from ever entering the picture.

But before we leave Adam in the Garden of Eden, let's catch a glimpse of him at the evening of each day (Genesis 3:8). God manifested Himself and walked and chatted with Adam; it was unimaginably wonderful for them both, and I suppose that more than once the sun went down while these conversations were going on into the night. Every day! Have we missed the important point that God had made a fundamental change in the way He was now communicating with His creation? Having stripped Lucifer of his authority to carry out that mission, it appears that now God was placing that mantle upon his Adam; the authority to communicate intimately and directly with the Creator. What became revealed later was that God was going beyond even that authority to communicate with Him, and that he would ultimately be the very means through which God would reveal His total, infinite, eternal glory to the amazement of all creation (Ephesians 2:6-7).

This God-given authority to communicate directly with God is what we call prayer. First bestowed upon Lucifer for the purpose of glorifying the Creator as nothing else could, we have now inherited that mission through Adam, and more importantly through the "new Adam" who is none other than Jesus Christ.; *we* have been given that privilege and responsibility, and the fulfillment of that mission has yet to be revealed (Ephesians 2:6-7).

So why do you suppose that Satan wants to destroy our prayer life? Well, you see, it's personal to him, perhaps because it reminds him of what he has forever lost. So, how important is it to you? A big deal, or nothing to be excited about? I suppose that our enemy is quite pleased with his efforts when he sees how little importance we place on it, how we run through our "Mighty Moments" calling that a prayer life and offering that up to the Creator as an acceptable service (Romans 12:1-2). So how does God feel about that? Do you suppose that He misses those evening conversations in the Garden and is disappointed that there are so few new "Adams" with whom He can resume those lengthy and intimate times together?

Prayer Warriors, we have a daily appointment that we had better keep. Not five or ten minutes or next to nothing sandwiched between the pages of our over-busy lives, but as long as it takes and as many times as it takes. Our highest priority, as if our lives and the well-being of our families depended upon it. Rest assured, when Lucifer had the job, he did it full-time; now he spends most of his time trying to get us off the job.

It doesn't matter to me whether or not you agree with my suppositions of coffee shop chatter in Heaven eons ago, but it does matter a lot to me how seriously we all take this matter of prayer. Our lives depend on it!

Let's ask God for a reality check on our lives.

- What is our attitude toward prayer? Really honestly! Shouldn't we ask Him to change that for us?
- What is our awareness of the responsibility that has been given to us in praying? Shouldn't we plead to God to give us His understanding (1 Corinthians 2:10-11) of this responsibility for which we will one day give an accounting to Him?
- How teachable are we in the matter of praying? Perhaps we should start all our praying with a confession of too-often having a proud, stubborn heart (a condition that causes God to withdraw from us (James 4:6) and rendering our prayers as useless). Shouldn't we plead with God to give us a genuinely teachable, steadfast spirit in this matter (Psalm 51:10)?
- How sensitive are we to the fact that Satan is spending so much effort to weaken our prayer life? Shouldn't we make that a big part of our spiritual warfare (James 4:7) in order that we would become mighty in prayer?

MISSION 20

Sounds Like School!

Training. That's another word for "school"! Chances are that we didn't really like school when we were in it, or at least we were happy when that part of our life was over, so much so that the thought of going back to school doesn't really thrill us.

Several years ago, I had a friend who was a military helicopter pilot. He used to tell me stories of just how much training the Canadian helicopter pilots got compared to their US counterparts, especially in low-level night flying using night vision equipment. So much so that, during joint Canada / US exercises, the US troops would always try to get a Canadian pilot; they could fly lower, faster and quieter than anyone else, and that made all the difference to the troops whose job it was to sneak undetected into position. I saw it for myself. I was standing in a clearing looking directly at the treeline only a few yards ahead of me; that's the direction I expected to see the approaching helicopter. I couldn't hear it but I knew it was coming. Then, suddenly it settled to the ground right in front of me! It didn't come over the trees, it came *through* (actually between) them, so quickly and silently that it was there before I knew it.

How could that pilot do that? At night!

The answer: hundreds of hours of training, not on simulators, but in the air. It was boring, tiring and frustrating, but it was the *only* way to achieve those results.

So, how much prayer training have you had? Oh, you just picked it up by yourself and it has just come more-or-less naturally ever since, perhaps with the help of hearing some older believers praying in church or at those old-fashioned prayer meetings. Pretty normal. I think that most of us are in that boat. The truth is, we have probably had extremely little actual training in the kind of prayer that we are seeking, wanting to become good at. Prayer Warrior grade praying. Military grade!

If we want that kind of prayer experience to become our new normal, then we've got to do something about it because it's not going to happen the way we've been going about it. We need training, lots of it, and it may become tiring but there is no other way. School of Prayer. There's no App for that.

I suppose that this should have been Mission 1 instead of Mission 20, but I hope that by now you have been challenged enough by what you've read to whet your appetite for a new level in your prayer life. Perhaps you've already begun to ask God for that.

I hope that you have noticed that these Missions are intended to be a sort of curriculum in our School of Prayer, however simply reading the textbook or agreeing with it won't give you a passing grade. We've actually got to *do* what it says, and if you have read all of the Missions you know that it's going to take some time and effort to do all that, and some of it will get downright uncomfortable. And there are demands that will be expected of us, not because I say so, but because God has said so.

Before we get to the demands, let's make a note of some things that do not, all by themselves, count as the kind of prayer that we're talking about here.

1. Thinking spiritual thoughts as we read Scripture. That's good, but not strong enough to pass as a prayer life.
2. That weekly meeting with a special friend where we talk and pray (mostly talk) together for an hour or so about things that are on our hearts. That's also very good, and necessary, but that's not enough to be called a prayer life.
3. Reading the short prayer that's included with your daily devotional material. Thoughtful, maybe even inspiring, but far too little.

4. Thinking about God frequently during the day. That's also great, but that's not called prayer and it won't get the job done.
5. Reading books or listening to (or preaching) sermons on prayer. Great but not the same thing as actually doing it.

So now we come right down to the subject of prayer and it's time for a heads-up on what it's going to involve. Please don't get discouraged if you suddenly realize how much it will involve; the best and first thing that we can do is to ask God to give us the desire to do it and the grace to do the job well. After all, if it could be done with human strength, we would have done it already! God is the One who is encouraging us to do this, and He is the One who is prepared to give us the victory in it. I know that we have all had the experience of making a resolution and then failing along the way, so I'd like to suggest that if you are serious about this one, please tell another believer who also wants to make the same commitment and give that person the authority to keep you accountable.

Here is what you can expect.

>Prayer demands time, lots of it. You simply cannot fit it into your schedule; you must reorganize your schedule to intentionally make time for prayer. You may have to get up an hour early to make it happen. Do it. Jesus said that we should always pray and not give up (Luke 18) and Paul said the same thing (1 Thessalonians 5:17-18). I'll go so far as to say that you need a prayer list with at least 500 names on it or you're not trying hard enough! At Hope, our Family Prayer Book has over 600 names so far, and by taking one page per day (plus reading one together as part of our corporate prayer on Sunday) we could get through it every 7 days. Let's raise the bar, but it will require time.

>Prayer demands faith (Matthew 17:20) and commitment, and if our faith is weak, then we must strengthen that first before we can move on in prayer. Some things about our faith may have to change. This kind of faith is not simply believing that God *can* do what we ask; it goes way beyond that. It is a stubborn determination to keep on

asking because we are convinced beyond any doubt that God *will* give us what we are asking in His will. It's a refusal to give up simply because we have not seen the results yet. Isaac and his wife entreated God (Genesis 25:21) to have a son. That means that they begged and pleaded with Him over and over again (Rebekah was childless, i.e. they had tried many times but she could not become pregnant). The language actually conveys the meaning that God allowed Himself to be entreated; He was pleased with the repeated pleadings because it brought Isaac and his wife closer and closer to Him. Some Rabbis suggest that the language conveys the idea of Isaac "digging a tunnel" to God, so strenuous and exhausting were his prayers. There was no Plan B. That kind of faith allows no room for quitting. That kind of commitment means "whatever it takes, as long as it takes".

Prayer demands humility. In Mission 19 we saw that a proud heart causes God to turn away from us (James 4:6) and our praying is futile. It's when we approach God in prayer that He often reveals to us that there is something that we must first get right. He may also show us that we may not be the one who is being directed by the Holy Spirit to lead the spiritual battle in this particular case; perhaps it is someone else who has been gifted with the faith needed (1 Corinthians 12:9). It takes a humble spirit to acknowledge someone else's gifting where we may have thought it was our place to lead.

Prayer demands submission, not only to God, but to others. James 5:13-16 is hard to practice because it leaves no room for playing masquerade with each other, even to the point of being willing to confess our sins before one another in order that we might be healed. That "righteous person" in verse 16 is someone who was first willing to ask, to make himself vulnerable and even to confess to other believers. It's easier to submit if we start out on our knees.

Prayer demands frequent repentance. When Jesus wanted to teach a lesson on the sin of self-righteousness, he chose a parable on prayer (Luke 18:9-14). If our praying is done to show others our vocabulary or virtues, then God is not interested. But if our praying is intended to let God show us how we look through His eyes, then we come to repentance. Even the prophet Isaiah, when confronted by the holiness of God, could only confess his utter unworthiness (Isaiah 6:5).

<u>Prayer demands that we put ourselves at risk</u>. Declaring our trust in God puts us on the line! What if we give ourselves no way out? What will people say if God doesn't come through? May I suggest that, if these questions frighten you, you are not alone. But let me also suggest that now is the time to push your faith past that limit. Openly declare your faith in God's power to do whatever it is. Pray for the holy boldness to do it in spite of whatever happens, because God is always faithful (Psalm 25:3) and this isn't the first time that He has been on the line.

<u>Prayer demands discipline</u>. Getting up early just to make time to pray isn't going to be easy for anyone, but you have no choice. Discipline is like Buckley's cough syrup; it isn't supposed to taste good but it is supposed to work! Better than Buckley's (and more effective), prayer is a service that we offer out of obedience to God; it's supposed to cost us something. An offering that costs us nothing is offensive to God (2 Samuel 24:24). Soldiers don't train and march and fight under hard conditions because they like it, they do it because it is demanded and expected of them, and to do less will bring consequences. Tough prayer is like that.

<u>Prayer demands priority in all circumstances</u>. The Psalmist could say that he would cry out to God at any time of the day or night (Psalm 55:16-17) as the need arose for God's help and deliverance. David's 911 number was connected to God. That wasn't his last resort, it was his *first*! Sadly we often only turn to God as a last resort when everything else has failed.

Mission 21

The Power Of Prayer or The Prayer Of Power?

Well, do you believe in the power of prayer? Be careful; it's a loaded question! Of course, we all believe in the value of prayer, in its importance to the Prayer Warrior and in its significance to God. We wouldn't be in Mission 21 if we didn't agree on those things. Let me get back to the question in a minute.

I recently completed a small wiring job at my house, nothing complicated and something that I have done many times before. I was wiring in some new outlet boxes in a line connected to some outlets that had been put in place when the house was built. The wiring was already in place so the job was a no-brainer. Looked great, as it should, but there was one problem that didn't become obvious until I plugged something into the outlet: no power! In fact, as far as I can tell, that entire circuit had never been connected to the panel when the house was wired at construction. All the outlets were nicely placed and they all looked great but none of them was connected to a power source. Just one piece missing …… the power!

So, does prayer have power? No! Not in itself. The power comes from the One to whom we pray, and more particularly from the Name of the One by which we pray. Now I realize that we all know that, at least intellectually, but it is a very critical point that is easily lost as we become deeply involved in the details of our prayer life. Sometimes the prayers become what it's all about.

Our prayers are as useless and powerless as my outlets until they are connected to the power source, and that source of power is much more than simply ending our prayers with the "magical" phrase "in Jesus' Name". Witchcraft and sorcery place power in certain chants, phrases, curses and incantations but the Bible recognizes none of that. Words are powerful but don't mistake that for being the same thing at all. **We must be grounded in the absolute truth that our power, and the power for all our praying, comes from Jesus.** There is power, all power, in the Name of Jesus. Our praying should be filled with His Name being lifted up as the source of our authority and the object of our praise. The Holy Spirit, who must direct our praying (Romans 8:26-27), must also direct our attention to Jesus (John 15:26). Without that, our praying is nothing more than a "form" (imitation) of godliness having no power (2 Timothy 3:5).

It is in Jesus' Name that chains are broken, prisoners are set free and the powers of Hell are forced to flee (Romans 14:11, Philippians 2:10-11). That's the Name in which there is salvation for our lost loved ones (Acts 4:12). That's the Name in which addictions are broken and diseases are healed, and life is restored to the faint (Psalm 103:3-4). That is the Name in which the wanderer is brought home (Psalm 107:4-9). That is the Name by which those in bondage are set free (Psalm 107:10-16). That is the Name by which the rebel is rescued from a wasted life (Psalm 107:17:20). That is the Name in which the storms of life are calmed (Psalm 107:23-30). Get excited about it!

Our prayers should ring loudly with the Name of Jesus! There's nothing to be shy about!! The devil hates that Name, but the Holy Spirit continually reminds us of it and the Father loves it. Our spiritual warfare must resound with that Name in which we are assured the victory (John 16:33, 1 John 5:5).

So as we pray, here are a few reminders:

1. Start by asking the Holy Spirit to exalt the Name of Jesus in us, especially as we pray,
2. Commit yourself to this prayer time as an act of obedience and an offering to Jesus,

3. As we pray, be mindful of how our requests will glorify Jesus and how He will be magnified when the Father gives us what we ask,
4. In our warfare praying, ask the Holy Spirit to reveal to our eyes of faith our Commander in Chief right there in the battle with us,
5. In our spiritual battles, ask the Holy Spirit to reveal to us how we are to be part of a larger company of Prayer Warriors so that our combined prayers will be more effective than ours alone.
6. Lift up the names of loved ones and friends who are among the lost, the prisoners, the sick and speak the power of the Name of Jesus into those lives. Break the chains, loose the blessing in that all-powerful Name.

Now, if you want to spice up your prayer time, sit down, fasten your seatbelt, raise your chair and table into the upright, locked position and listen to this:

https://m.youtube.com/watch?v=TIuq3q_GcoU

So, back to the question, but I think we already know the full answer. Where is the power in prayer? Better yet, where is the power in *your* prayer?

Mission 22

Thermometer Or Thermostat?

We've all heard the challenge "You're either a thermometer or a thermostat". The meaning is clear: a thermometer reads the temperature of its surroundings; a thermostat *sets* the temperature of its surroundings. That principle applies as well to our praying!

A praying thermometer is all about what the situation is, and that is usually not very good and, as a result, that praying is often filled with a sense of hopelessness and resignation. It's often also very self-centered and negative. Not the kind of prayer that is likely to lift anyone up. Not that God doesn't care about the situation, but this prayer doesn't invite Him to intervene. Sadly, it may be filled with "reality" but it too-often is lacking in faith. Sometimes reality simply sucks.

A praying thermostat starts with the situation but quickly moves to higher ground, where a mighty God reaches His hand into our world and changes it, changing us in the process. Our eyes may be filled with tears and our hearts filled with disappointment but through the tears and hurt we declare that our God is bigger than all that, that He cares for us, that He can be trusted even when we cannot see the light at the end of the tunnel, and that He invites us to ask Him for miracles. Miracles are our names for those things that God does in spite of circumstances and reality. And our God delights in being the God of miracles.

Sadly, much of the "average" praying that we hear is thermometer praying, a detailed recitation of the problem. Maybe you've begun to slip into this kind of prayer life yourself.

The praying thermostat looks reality in the face and trusts God to work anyway.

Abraham was 99 years old and Sarah was right behind him; having a child was not a reality. But God made a promise and Abraham was blowing out 100 candles on his birthday cake with Isaac on his lap! (Genesis 17, 21).

A few years later, God tested Abraham's faith with another reality; God asked him to sacrifice Isaac. Seeing no other possible solution, Abraham was obedient on the certainty that God would certainly raise Isaac back from death in order to keep His covenant with him (Genesis 22, Hebrews 11:19).

Joshua and Caleb saw the same reality as did the other spies sent to check out the promised land, but their report was much different (Numbers 13:26-30, 14:6-7), as was their reward. The naysayers who stirred up the Israelites against God and against Moses were judged harshly (Numbers 14:36-38) while Joshua and Caleb entered into the promised land. Caleb could lead a prayer meeting with his courage and faith stronger than ever at age 86 when he claimed the rough hill country as his possession (Joshua 14:6-13). Reality, take a back seat when that kind of faith stands up!

Peter was thrown into prison with little question what the outcome would be, but the church didn't accept that reality and came to God asking for a new reality (Acts 12:5).

In Lystra Paul was stoned and dragged out of town for dead; the believers (including Barnabas) stood around him and I can imagine that they prayed although the text doesn't say as much. Paul got up and they went right back into town (Acts 14:19-20). Then a few days later they returned to that same town. Reality is a poor match for that kind of determined faith.

John reminds us that we are (and will be) called upon to defy (and even overcome) the reality of the spirit of this world with a faith that is greater than this world (1 John 4:4, 5:4).

John again sees the ultimate victory of this faith over Satan himself (Revelation 12:11,17).

OK we've read again these Scripture accounts and we certainly agree with them intellectually. Now we must take the next big step and begin to make that our faith statement in our praying in the midst of our reality. Our reality may include sickness, heartache, disappointment, unemployment, frustration, fear and loss; *we are called to trust God in our praying that He is greater than all of that reality, to declare that He is not limited by that reality and that we will not be bound by it either.* Chains must break, prisoners must go free and walls must come down at the Name of Jesus. *So here are some things that we, as Prayer Warriors, must begin to do to change the spiritual temperature around us:*

1. We start right where we are; we bring ourselves to God with no pretences. If our faith is weak, we say so and ask the Holy Spirit to strengthen us. Whether we are the one being tested in this trial or someone else, we must begin at this point.
2. We must declare to God that we are not satisfied with the present reality, that we ask for holy boldness to pray for change and that we are committed to persevere with Him until He answers us or directs us to stop praying for it.
3. Because we are often weak, we should ask another Prayer Warrior to join with us in our praying.
4. We ask God for the courage to confront the challenge directly by name and then we ask the Holy Spirit to reveal to us His desire in the matter; then we ask for the grace to accept His desire as our own and that becomes our prayer.
5. We refuse to magnify the enemy by spending our prayer time reciting the details of what we are facing. God knows that, and reciting the problem is thermometer praying; stop it!
6. Start reading the Psalms and underline every passage that describes how God rescues His children from distress (Psalm 4:1, 4:3, 4:8, 5:2-3, 5:11-12, 7:1, 7:10, 9:10, 16:1, 17:6, 18:1-6, 18:16-19, 18:27-28, 18:30-36, 22:11, 25:1-5, 27:1-14). Keep going. It is simply amazing what this exercise will do for your faith. Then start

reading these back to God in your praying. Now you're moving past your reality and into God's new reality. This is the beginning of thermostat praying!

7. We look for an opportunity to declare God's faithfulness before others.
8. Ask another believer if you can have the privilege of joining with them in their praying. Bring your faith into his/her life as an added strength, humbly realizing that next time the roles may be reversed.
9. Find a song that raises up Jesus, glorifies Him and testifies to His mighty power. Not many songs are truly anointed, but some are, so ask the Holy Spirit to direct you to one of them.
10. Start by changing the spiritual temperature in your home, then among your close circle of friends and then to others.

Mission 23

No Such Thing As Bad Publicity?

Several years ago, I was starting my first business venture and I had the good fortune of meeting a man who worked in the government; his job was to help promote new business in the Province and, as part of that job, he invited me to accompany him on a trip to Toronto to connect with a company that he thought would be helpful. The invitation was special because the trip was to be on the government aircraft; turns out that the aircraft was making the trip at the request of a Member of the Legislative Assembly and we were just tagging along. Sweet!

Our flight was to make one stop in the northern part of the Province to pick up the MLA. It was winter, snow everywhere when we landed and waited for the limo to pull up. First off, the sight of a stretched limo in this impoverished part of the province was making a statement all by itself! What happened next took me quite by surprise; the man who emerged from the limo was wearing the biggest beaver fur coat that I had ever seen, with all the jewellery and fixin's that could go with it. A short man wearing a two-sizes-too-big tooth-filled grin, the beaver-wrapped dignitary fell upon me as a combination of Liberace and a hairy mammoth. I didn't know who he was until I finally saw his face; one could not have mistaken this man because his picture had recently been splashed over the newspaper pages due to his indiscreet, repeated use of his provincial credit card at several strip joints and prostitution clubs in Boston over the past months. When he sat directly in front of me on the plane, smile and fur fully intact, I thought it only polite to attempt a conversation, but what to say when all I could think of was the litany of scandals that had been revealed? So, I offered something like "I suppose that these are difficult days for you, sir". His answer floored me even more than his fur. Not missing a beat, he proudly replied with that same grin "In my business there's no such thing as bad publicity". I had nothing more to offer. Here was a man who proudly and boastfully wore his moral depravity as some kind of badge, sensing no hint of shame whatsoever and looking forward to going on doing the same. It was a very long flight to Toronto!

No such thing as bad publicity! But, you know, that is the devil's credo, too. He craves attention and, for him, it all works to his benefit. Sometimes I think that he gets as much airtime from believers as he does from the rest of the world, and I imagine that he is especially proud of the fact that he has somehow subverted so many Christians into being his unwitting publicists. How's that possible?

For starters, we are drowning in a sea of bad news of every kind, so there's not much to draw our attention away from the Devil's handiwork whether it be in Afghanistan, Syria or a high-school near you. Added to that is the relentless assault of every kind of moral perversion on TV and in the movies. "Harmless" sitcoms are cesspools masquerading as normalcy. The problem is that it is too easy to simply drown in it all, letting it slowly but surely adjust our moral compass. When it starts to fill our thoughts and conversation, we have become publicists for the evil one because we are exalting his handiwork of destruction and perversion simply by giving it so much of our attention and conversation. The Devil doesn't care that we disagree with him, just so long as we are willing to speak of his work or tolerate others who see it as the new normal. Lot learned godliness from his uncle Abraham but, because he refused to separate himself from the moral filth of Sodom, he gradually came to accept much of that culture of sin "for that righteous man, living among them day after day, was tormented in his righteous soul by the lawless deeds he saw and heard" (2 Peter 2:8).

Our prayers can become spoiled by that same influence. After all, what fills our minds and attention fills our prayers. And it is precisely in our prayer life that we must start this great battle against the prince of darkness who would like to spread that mantle of darkness over us, our homes, our families and our churches. Our praying has to take on the challenge of denying airtime to the enemy.

We cannot deny the news that we hear every day, but we must devise a strategy to combat its influence on us and others. We start with ourselves before we can influence others. And it will be immensely valuable to take these steps in partnership with another Prayer Warrior with whom you can become mutually accountable.

1. Ask the Holy Spirit to make us increasingly sensitive to the things in our life that offend Him, and to give us the conviction to agree with Him,
2. Pray for the Holy Spirit to reveal just one thing in our thoughts or habits that agrees with the Devil's message. That thing is sin to us, and we must confess it and turn away from it before we can go any further. We are to capture every thought and bring it into submission to Christ (2 Corinthians 10:5), so for starters we must permanently put off-limits all those shows, games and internet sites that are designed to feed our fleshly appetites and lead us as slaves into habitual sin (Romans 1:18-32). Shut down the Devil's broadcast channel to your mind.
3. Start your prayer time with a simple confession that we need His cleansing daily, aware that the Devil constantly seeks to remind us of our past habits and sins for which we have been forgiven; now ask God to break the chains of habit and to set us free.
4. Pray for the Holy Spirit to bring to mind those things in your life that fit into the category listed in Philippians 4:8 and speak them to God with thanksgiving.
5. Spend more time simply reading God's Word; it has supernatural power to change our focus and to do exactly what needs to be done in our lives (Hebrews 4:12) and God guarantees the results.
6. Pray against the spirits of darkness that have captured the minds of our children and other loved ones; name them and oppose them in the Name of Jesus. Husbands and fathers, claim the authority given to you as the head of your household.
7. Deliberately include in your praying that God would drive away the darkness from the hearts and minds of our loved ones and those others for whom we pray, so that the light of God's gospel will shine in and bring life (Psalm 119:130).

8. Pray that God will show you ways in which you can advance His kingdom into this world of darkness.
9. Speak openly about God's wondrous works, His care for you and the miracles you have seen.

Shut down your part of the devil's publicity machine and become a broadcast centre for Jesus. Capture your home for the glory of God and make that a place where the kingdom of God is proclaimed and lived. Let the sounds of victory be heard in the houses of the redeemed (Jeremiah 33:11, Psalms 118:15)! Now *that's* bad publicity for the enemy!

Mission 24

Seeking God's Face

When Solomon had finished the temple of the Lord and the royal palace, and had succeeded in carrying out all he had in mind to do in the temple of the Lord and in his own palace, the Lord appeared to him at night and said: "I have heard your prayer and have chosen this place for myself as a temple for sacrifices. When I shut up the heavens so that there is no rain, or command locusts to devour the land or send a plague among my people, if my people, who are called by my name, will humble themselves and pray and seek my face and turn from their wicked ways, then I will hear from heaven, and I will forgive their sin and will heal their land. Now my eyes will be open and my ears attentive to the prayers offered in this place. I have chosen and consecrated this temple so that my Name may be there forever. My eyes and my heart will always be there."

2 Chronicles 7:11-16 NIV

Several years ago the National Gideon Convention was hosted in my home city where I was a member of the organization and a part of the organizing team. The theme was 2 Chronicles 7:14 and each devotional speaker was assigned a part of that verse. I was given the part about seeking God's face. I don't remember everything that I said then, but I do remember that the verse has been very important to me ever since.

I copied above the several verses that make up that conversation between God and Solomon, of which verse 14 is a part. Please take time to read it again.

Seeking God's face. It's a subject that's taken up at least 15 times in the first 5 books of the Bible:

Genesis 33:10
Exodus 33:11, 20, 23
Leviticus 17:10, 20:3, 5, 6, 26:17
Numbers 6:25, 26, 12:8
Deuteronomy 31:17, 18, 32:20

It's important, to say the least. We cannot fail to get the message that God's face brings His approval and blessing; turning His face away is very bad news indeed. Little surprise that God tells us to seek the former and to avoid the latter.

I know that you can search those verses as well as I can, and there are many good commentaries to help us understand them. I'd like us to examine how we can apply that to our prayer life because prayer was the context of the passage in Chronicles that we are focused on today.

First, if we are to seek God's face, this implies that we must become aware of where God is looking. *The prayer is to seek His face, not to get Him to seek ours.* So the big question is "do you sense that God's face is not directed toward you?" There are things that God simply refuses to look upon.

- If we are consumed by our work (as I was), allowing it to eat up all of our meaningful attention and time at the expense of everyone and everything else, there's a name for that: it's called idolatry, it's a sin and God hates it. He turns away from it and completely refuses to allow it in His sight.
- If we are harboring a known sin in our life, God refuses to turn toward us and He does not hear our prayers (Psalm 66:18).

- If we hold our family or loved one(s) as the dearest part of our life, even before God, there's a name for that too: it's called idolatry and, although it may seem godly and right to hold our children, spouse or parents in such a high place, God never intended for that to be so and He sees it as sin. He cannot look that way and He cannot bless it.
- If we hold our possessions or hobbies as the most valuable part of our life, we know what to call that. But sometimes we are not aware of just how those things have really crept in and usurped God's place in our life. We count them as proof of God's blessing, and so they may have been in the beginning, but, quite simply, when we sacrifice other things (like church attendance in the summer, prayer time or spending time with our spouse and children) in order to give our devotion to this "stuff", they have become idols and they have cut off God's face from us.

So the first key to seeking God's face is to take an honest look at which direction God is looking. If we're not looking in that same direction, then we're not seeing what He sees and we're not going to see His face because we're not in agreement with His priorities.

Second, if we are to honestly seek God's face, then at some point we must turn around. Even if we are looking in the same direction as God is looking (and we must pray to gain His view of everything), there comes a point when we must be willing to take our eyes off that thing and turn around; at that point, He must be all that we are looking at. It's an unfortunate truth that sometimes God's work can consume our vision. We are truly seeing with God's eyes, but when that becomes our only passion and priority, then we stop facing Him and a new idol has crept into our life.

Prayer Warrior, let's be sure to include these priorities in our praying:

1. Ask God to give us a clear understanding of the things that are precious to Him. Ask the Holy Spirit to direct our vision to the very things that God is looking at, and ask Him to give us the grace to willingly change our view from where it is right now.

2. Ask God to reveal to us those things that we have put into our lives that would cause God to turn away from us. Confess them and ask God for the strength to put things in their proper order in our hearts.
3. Ask the Holy Spirit to give us the courage and confidence to turn around and face Him.

Mission 25

The Super Weapon

In every age, military forces have sought a weapon that would automatically give them superiority over any enemy force. A super weapon. In recent history the tank was such a weapon, then the airplane, then the atomic bomb, and the list goes on.

There is a spiritual warfare super weapon; it's called PRAISE. It's like prayer on steroids!

So, what is so different about praise and what makes it so powerful?

First, in the context of our spiritual warfare, we know that the biggest difference between prayer and praise is that the former includes asking God for things; Jesus told us to ask the Father for many things (Matthew 7:7, Matthew 18:19, Matthew 21:22, John 14:13). And asking isn't something that just appeared in the New Testament; one of the best examples is Solomon's invitation to ask anything of God (1 Kings 3:5). So, asking God for things is an act of obedience so long as our heart is in the right place (James 4:3).

Praise has only one focus; it lifts up and magnifies God. Heaven is filled with it. It is not only a reflection of God's glory in His creation (as it was before man was created), but it is the deliberate act of ascribing glory to God as voiced by His created beings (angels and mankind). God loves praise, and He is completely worthy of it (Revelation 5:12). His throne is situated in praise (Psalm 22:3 NKJV); He literally inhabits praise!

As a weapon of warfare, God reveals some of His mightiest power in response to praise. In 2 Chronicles 20, Judah was in a desperate situation under attack by three enemy nations. Jehoshaphat and the people had prayed, God had promised the victory and now the army set out to meet the enemy. At the head of the army was the song and praise section, and as soon as they began to sing and praise, God confused the enemy to such an extent that they completely slaughtered each other.

Even the praise of children is a stronghold against the enemy (Psalm 8:2 NIV).

Paul and Silas had been badly beaten and chained in prison (Acts 16:24); now around midnight they were praying and praising God so loudly that the other prisoners were listening to them. That's when God sent an earthquake that shook the building, opening all the cell doors and breaking all the shackles (Acts 16:25,26).

Praise, the right kind of praise, really gets God's attention and draws Him right into our situations. So, what does this praise look like?

<u>Praise is not simply an add-on to our prayers</u>. It's not an appetizer or a dessert; it's the main course. It must be the desire of our hearts and the reason for coming to Him.

<u>Praise involves sacrifice and our voices</u>. It's sacrificial when we intentionally direct our voices away from other conversations and toward God in thanksgiving. Picture yourself holding up your words as a personal gift to God.

> *Therefore by Him let us continually offer the sacrifice of praise to God, that is, the fruit of our lips, giving thanks to His name. But do not forget to do good and to share, for with such sacrifices God is well pleased.*
> Hebrews 13:15-16 NKJV

That same passage in Hebrews reminds us that <u>service to others is a springboard for praise to God</u>.

<u>Praise may also be most sacrificial when it's the hardest thing to give</u>. Paul and Silas had many other things that could have occupied their thoughts and conversation. It takes a peculiar strength of faith and courage to turn our attention away from the crisis (and our ideas for fixing it) and to begin to praise God instead.

<u>The language of praise should fill our prayers</u>, and there is no reason why it should not <u>also spice our conversations</u> with each other (Ephesians 5:19, Colossians 3:16).

Praise to God is an out-loud <u>reminder to our enemy</u> that we refuse to be dominated by circumstances, trials or attacks of the evil one. Satan wants us to stare into our problems, but praise happens when we intentionally turn away from our problems to look into the face of God and to say "Thank you, Lord"

> *Praise the Lord,*
> *For His mercy endures forever.*
>   2 Chronicles 20:21 NKJV

We would be wise to strengthen our walk as Prayer Warriors by holding a praise gathering on a regular basis. We have the Super Weapon; let's use it!

Mission 26

Breaking Through

My father missed his intended wedding date in December 1944. He was in the Canadian Army that liberated Belgium (where he met his intended bride) but was suddenly (and without notice to anyone) sent to a Dutch hospital with a suspected case of diphtheria. That's where he was when he was supposed to be getting married; meanwhile, back in Belgium, the wedding was cancelled, literally at the last minute, when nobody knew where the groom was.

The diphtheria was a false alarm, and my father was proceeding to get back to Belgium by any means possible. He was in the Belgian Ardennes when he was caught in a German offensive that came to be known as the Battle of the Bulge, one of the major battles of WW2. German forces were attempting to break through the British – American lines in hopes of turning the tide of the war. My father spent the battle fighting alongside the American Army, cutoff and surrounded by German forces, until they were relieved by British and American units sent to break through to reinforce the cut-off troops. The battle lasted two months. My father made it to Belgium, my mother apparently believed his excuse for the earlier no-show, and the wedding took place in January 1945.

A breakthrough usually decides the outcome of a battle however breakthroughs are not limited to earthly battles. In Daniel 10:10-14 we have the account of God's messenger angel (probably Gabriel) coming to deliver the answer to Daniel's prayer of three weeks earlier. In fact, the messenger was on his way to Daniel when he was attacked by a satanic force called the prince of the kingdom of Persia. The battle lasted twenty-one days until Michael arrived to reinforce the messenger; that breakthrough allowed Daniel to receive God's message.

Some spiritual battles are not over quickly; the enemy's forces may be strongly fortified and under the command of high-ranking powers. They are not going to run away easily. In fact, they are not going to surrender until they are confronted by a superior force, and that force may have to include some reinforcements from God's angelic army.

The gospel gives us the account of a forty-day campaign between Jesus and Satan (Luke 4:1-13, Mark 1:13). Satan tried to break through Jesus' Kingdom agenda, but he failed and finally withdrew.

There is a powerful lesson here for Prayer Warriors, one that we must learn sooner or later. Spiritual warfare is serious business with real consequences. We have been given God's armor (Ephesians 6:10-18), however many times we fail to grasp the seriousness of what we are doing. This is not our armor, it is God's armor (v.11) and the forces arrayed against us are not cartoon boogymen; they are the very angels and administrators of the devil's kingdom. By engaging in spiritual warfare, we must be aware that we may easily "bite off more than we can chew" by ourselves, so we must be prepared. We are pressing a battle into the kingdom of darkness in order to establish God's kingdom in the lives of people; we're not seizing territory, we're after the prisoners, the sick, the broken …… the very ones that Satan has shackled as his prize. We're dismantling Satan's kingdom one person at a time and he doesn't like it!

So here are some things that we must do to prepare for our battle:

1. Get at least one (and preferably more) other Prayer Warrior(s) to join with you (Matthew 18:19-20), someone with whom you are "of one accord" in this battle,
2. Pray through Ephesians 6:10-18 together before the Lord, asking Him to cleanse you of any unconfessed sin, and asking for a humble heart (James 4:10) knowing that pride will always result in our downfall,

3. Ask the Holy Spirit to reveal what you are up against in the spirit world; what are the enemy strongholds that first must be demolished?
4. Ask the Holy Spirit to show you how you should position yourself to be in God's line of authority,
5. Search the Scriptures and ask the Holy Spirit to show you the Biblical basis for your engagement. Has God given a promise that you should claim or has He written a principle in His Word upon which you are taking your stand? Have God's Word open before you as you pray and read it aloud to Him and to the enemy.
6. Ask God to send His angels before you, to form a hedge around you and to do the same for the one(s) for whom you are praying (Job 1:10),
7. Start the battle with a season of praise to God,
8. Prepare for a long battle, so that means securing and sealing up each gain throughout the battle,
9. Expect that the enemy will usually attempt to distract you from the decisive battle by creating another threat nearby; don't take your eyes off the main battle,
10. Ask God for the breakthrough that you need in order to gain the victory and remember that the breakthrough will always be preceded by the fiercest resistance.

Mission 27

Valuing The High Ground

One of the key tenets of military strategy is to recognize the value of high ground. On any battlefield, the high ground is always the most valuable and the most hotly contested. The army that controls the high ground almost always wins the battle.

The Battle of Gettysburg was the pivotal battle of the American Civil War. It lasted 3 days, from 1-3 July 1863, during which over 53,000 men were killed. On the evening before the first day, a small Union cavalry force scouted the probable site of the upcoming battle; the commanding officer instantly recognized the value of the ridge overlooking a field that stretched almost a mile in front of him. He also saw a large approaching Confederate infantry force and he knew that they recognized the strategic value of that same ridge. During the opening battle, the small Union cavalry force was able to hold the ridge against overwhelming odds. The Union position was quickly reinforced with a much larger force and, on the third day of the battle, it withstood an attack by over 12,500 Confederate infantrymen supported by 175 Confederate cannons spread along a two-mile line. The disadvantage of being on the downhill side of the battle was that the Confederate troops had to march uphill nearly a mile in 87°F heat while being raked by cannon fire. The Confederate force lost more than half its men in the first few minutes; the outcome was almost inevitable. One day earlier, a single Maine regiment defended a hill against a force three times its size, using up all of its ammunition in a non-stop battle that went on for an hour and a half, finally ending in a downhill charge with empty guns, completely routing the Confederate force.

So, Prayer Warrior, what is your "high ground"? What is the most treasured part of your life, the piece on which you spend nearly all of your money, talent and time? Is it your job? ...your family? ... your toys?

Paul tells us that there are two types of believers; carnal and spiritual (1 Corinthians 3:1). The text makes it very clear what are the characteristics of each group. For the carnal man, the high ground is marked by comfort, pleasure and ego; these are the same marks pointed out by John (1 John 2:16) as the lust of the flesh, the lust of the eyes and the pride of life. John tells us that these things do not come from God and that they are, in fact, the enemy of God.

The high ground for the spiritual man is marked by righteousness, salvation and truth; these are, in fact, key parts of the armor of God (Ephesians 6:10-17). Righteousness is the presence of God's own character in us. Paul describes the "weapons of righteousness" in each of his hands (2 Corinthians 6:7). Salvation is the believer's unity with God in His Kingdom (which starts here). Truth is so close to God's nature that Jesus called Himself the Truth (John 14:6).

Prayer Warriors must settle the question of where is their high ground. Honestly. You see, if your high ground is somehow anchored in the things of this world, then all the enemy needs to do to defeat you is to shake the foundations of your world. Your world is in *his world*! Some day you will realize, too late, that life was given to you, not as a gift to spend on yourself, but as a trust out of which to build something to present to God. We will all present our "high ground" to God. The wealth, the medals, the promotions, the "stuff", the wood, the hay, the stubble .... (1 Corinthians 3:12-15). This is not the baggage of a Prayer Warrior!

Only the one who stands on God's high ground will win the battle, the war and the crown (1 Corinthians 9:25, James 1:12).

I do not think that any of us would claim to be standing completely on the highest ground yet, but we must be headed in that direction. As Prayer Warriors, we must make that our goal, and we must ask the Holy Spirit to show us the things that still need to be corrected on that journey. Without that, our praying, as well as our faith, will be weak at best. Our enemy knows exactly where is our high ground, even if we are unwilling to admit it to ourself; that is where he concentrates his attack because he knows that, when he defeats you there, he has won the battle. He also knows that if your high ground is anchored in his world, then he has already won the battle!

It's time to abandon the "lower ground" and to take our positions on God's high ground where our victory is already secured in Jesus. Let me suggest some practical ways to take that next step upward to the high ground:

1. If you find yourself in a dry time right now, with God seemingly silent in your life and your prayers sounding like echoes from the ceiling, then promise God that you will start to seek Him right now, that your only desire is to hear His voice and to feel His comfort, not asking anything else. Make that your heartfelt plea every day for a month, asking God to show you anything that may be in your life that may hinder your fellowship with Him.
2. When David found himself in a time when he could not seem to hear from God, his sleepless nights filled with groans and unanswered prayers, he resolved to break through by remembering the great things that God had done for him in the past (Psalm 77:10-12) and to recite them to God. *"The years of the right hand of the Most High"*. If you haven't done so already, or even if you have, go back to point #6 in Mission 22.
3. Give yourself to God with the simple prayer that He would use you to do just one thing for someone else that would bring God's blessing into their life. When God has identified that person to you, commit to pray for him/her, asking God to provide the same things that you would pray for yourself.
4. Ask God to begin to transform your prayer life into something that you could present to Him as your personal offering, your sacrifice of praise (Hebrews 13:15). Start your prayer time with this conscious offering.

5. Start to include a short portion of Scripture in your praying, speaking it to God as its Author, and offering it back to Him with your thanks.
6. Honestly tell God frequently that you want your feet to be planted on the high ground.

Mission 28

Are You Being Followed?

This is not what you are probably thinking. Normally we wouldn't like to think that we might be being stalked, spied on or crept up on by anyone, possibly even an enemy!

This will make you think differently; did you know that God has promised to follow you? Now I'm sure that you can immediately think of a few verses that support that idea, but you may not have thought of this one, but you all know the verse by memory. I laughed out loud when I read it again and it suddenly caught my attention. Psalm 23:6 says simply *"Surely goodness and mercy will follow me all the days of my life"*.

Whose goodness and whose mercy? Why, God's of course! SURELY (as if to emphasize who else's could it be?).

Prayer Warrior, maybe you find yourself at times wondering just where God is, how close is He to where you are at right now. Does He know the situations that you are facing at this moment? How do you recognize His presence, even when He stands right in front of you? How do you know that it is His hand that is holding yours? It may be that our constant reminder comes in the form of His goodness and His mercy stepping right into our tracks behind us.

His goodness? Exactly what is that? Well, I think that a child could give us the simplest definition that's hard to beat. Goodness is just the opposite of badness! Goodness means good stuff from God. The Psalms are especially full of the description of God's goodness. It is connected with His blessings (Psalm 21:3); we would lose heart and faint in discouragement without it

(Psalm 27:13); it was prepared for us beforehand (Psalm 31:19); it is the icing on the top of every other blessing that God pours on us (Psalm 65:11); it is the basis of our praise (Psalm 107:8). God's goodness is His grace to us; it's getting what we don't deserve. God's goodness is filling every second footprint behind you!

The other is being filled with His mercy. We know that mercy is not getting what we deserve. Forget what we think we deserve; if we think about it from God's perspective, we see a different picture. We don't deserve good stuff from God; quite the opposite! But God has shown us His mercy, not just once or twice, but in every step that we take!

Surely, we could not ask for more than that! Surely that should stir up praise from our lips! Surely, we must be moved to tears of thanksgiving at just the thought! SURELY, He will never cease to follow us with His goodness and mercy!!

So, Prayer Warrior, let us step aside and simply offer a prayer of thanksgiving, from our heart, to our Lord God who is so close. Let us be sure to ask Him to give us eyes to see and faith to believe these signs of His faithfulness to us. Counting our blessings may be as simple as counting our footprints!

It occurs to me that Prayer Warriors should be the most grateful people on earth, the most instant in praise to God and the most ceaseless in worship. We should lead the parade of the grateful redeemed. The enemy surely wants us to do otherwise, to be so taken by the battles before us, that we forget to look behind at the divine follower filling our steps, step after step, with His goodness and mercy.

Mission 29

The Easy Way Out

This Mission is dedicated to my friend Jeannie who, as I write this, is undergoing heart surgery after a serious heart attack this morning. Jeannie doesn't take the easy way out of situations. Right now, my praying for her is not looking for an easy way out.

Sometimes we take the easy way out, and so much the better if that easy way also comes with a religious coating that sounds so "right". Like using the phrase "Not my will, but thy will be done". We all know where that phrase comes from; let's get back to that in a minute, but first let's listen to one of the parables taught by the One who spoke that phrase.

In Matthew 25:14-30 and in Luke 19:11-26 we have probably two accounts of the same parable. We know the parable very well; it's about the servants who received money from their master and then had to give an accounting to him. I'm thinking about the servant who buried the money and then had to explain himself to his master. His excuse amounted to something like this: "I knew that you would do whatever you wanted to do anyway, so why should I get all bent and worked up about it. You're in charge, so do whatever you want to do with it".

That servant's example should teach us something about prayer, especially the praying of a Prayer Warrior, not the least being that we will have to give an accounting of our prayer investments to the Master when He returns.

Prayer is not meant to be easy. Searching out God's will is not meant to be easy or quick. Seeking God's presence is not meant to be free and easy. Labouring in prayer for as long as it takes is not meant to be easy. Presenting a sacrifice to God is not meant to be cheap. Giving up because we haven't found the answer (or one that we like) is not an acceptable excuse. Opting out with the excuse that "Well, God, I know that you're going to do whatever you want anyway so there's no need for me to work at this: Your will be done" is really just a cop-out, just like that unwise servant in the parable.

God tells us to seek His will, not just in a general way (2 Peter 3:9), but in detailed ways.

Jonah got the message twice (Jonah 3:1-3).

Abram needed to know how God would deal with his heirless (not hairless!) condition (Genesis 15:2).

Jacob was determined not to let go of God until He blessed him (Genesis 32:24-26) even though it came at a considerable cost.

Gideon needed to know if he was to lead Israel (Judges 6:36).

David needed to know whether or not to attack the Philistines (1 Chronicles 14:10).

Daniel needed to know the interpretation of a dream (Daniel 2:17-19).

Paul and his companions needed clear instructions about where to preach the gospel (Acts 16:6), and in the absence of clearer instructions, they simply started out in the best direction that they knew and allowed God to correct them. The old adage says that it's easier to steer a moving ship than one that is anchored.

We are told how to present ourselves to God in order that His will is evident in us (Romans 12:1-2).

Paul makes it clear to servants that they are to serve willingly and submissively (Ephesians 6:6) and to the Thessalonian believers he makes it clear that sexual purity is not negotiable (1 Thessalonians 4:3).

Paul himself is an excellent example of praying repeatedly for the removal of his infirmity, until finally God settled the issue (2 Corinthians 12:8-9).

Clearly these issues about knowing God's instructions, His will in a particular situation, were not simple, nor was the labour involved in finding the answers. Sometimes it took a long time to get the answer, and sometimes the answer was not what was expected. But God insisted that the work be done, that the prayers be continued, no matter how long it might take. There was no escape clause.

And now to the greatest example of all, and the source of the phrase that we started with. Jesus prayed in Gethsemane (Matthew 26:36-44) with great sorrow and anguish, to the point that his sweat was like drops of blood (Luke 22:44) and an angel came to comfort Him (Luke 22:43). He prayed until He knew the answer. He knew God's will in the matter, and it was only then that He said "Your will, not mine". It wasn't a way around prayer, it was the conclusion of prayer.

We are entitled to repeat that phrase only after we have been willing to put the time into finding the answer through laborious prayer. We don't say it instead of praying, we say it after praying.

Like that servant in the parable, we will all give an accounting to the Lord concerning our investments in prayer. *Really, it's not so much about God's will as it is about ours.* On that accounting day, He already knows what His will is; let's make sure that, when our will is revealed, it will be lined up with His.

Mission 30

Things Unseen - Part 1 Where Are We?

Imagine being able to hear only one sound frequency (note), or being able to see only one colour. How much would you be missing if you sat in front of an orchestra or looked at a sunset? Or what if you could see only objects within a short distance from the doorstep of your house? How distorted your perception of the universe would be! We realize, of course, that the frequencies within the range of human hearing are only a very small part of the entire acoustic spectrum, and that the range of frequencies to which the human eyes are sensitive is only a very, very small portion of the entire electromagnetic spectrum. And even today's most powerful telescopes can see only a small part of what we imagine to be the size of the physical universe.

We estimate that the edge of our *observable* physical universe is *at least* 500 thousand million million million kilometres from Earth (and is increasing all the time) and that it contains about 100 billion galaxies (like our Milky Way Galaxy), each containing about 100 billion stars.

The Bible complicates the problem even further by revealing that, in addition to the physical universe (of which we are a part), there is another universe, a spiritual one, probably larger than the physical one, which includes God's heaven and to which we have only limited access while we are alive in our bodies.

The significance of this spiritual universe is that it intimately affects what happens in the physical universe. Furthermore, although we have not yet received our spiritual bodies, we have been given citizenship in the spiritual realm (Philippians 3:20) and one day that will be our permanent residence (2 Corinthians 5:2-8).

First, let's consider some of the examples given in Scripture.

Elisha's servant had his eyes opened so he could see God's army of flaming chariots on the hills surrounding him (2 Kings 6:17).

The army of God was before David, attacking the Philistines, but neither David nor the Philistines could see them although they played the decisive role in David's victory (2 Samuel 5:24).

We are told that we are surrounded by a great cloud of witnesses in Heaven (Hebrews 12:1-3).

Paul describes the world in which we live as also being filled with spiritual beings called principalities, powers and rulers of darkness (Ephesians 6:12), all part of Satan's legion that was cast out of God's heaven. Daniel encountered one of these rulers, known as the prince of Persia, during his prayer (Daniel 10:13).

John tells us that the Holy Spirit is here but that the unbeliever can neither see Him nor receive His truth; the believer cannot see Him but can certainly receive His truth (John 14:17).

Both the Old and New Testaments describe incidents in which angels have become visible and have interacted with humans.

God assigns angels to guard our way (Psalms 91:11).

God Himself is present throughout His creation, however He has created humans such that we cannot survive looking at His face after being expelled from Eden (Exodus 33:20); we will, however, be able to look continually on His face when we receive our new bodies at the resurrection (1 John 3:2).

John's wonderful revelation of Jesus is filled with heavenly creatures (and Heaven itself), including instances of how these creatures will interact with this physical world (Revelation 6-10).

So, what are we missing by being able to perceive such a small part of all that God has created and why is this important to the Prayer Warrior? Simply because the Prayer Warrior is responsible to connect these two universes, to join a war in the spiritual domain with consequences in both the physical and spiritual worlds. All of the Prayer Warrior's resources are in the spiritual domain, and, although we cannot see the spiritual world with physical eyes, we must be able to both "see" and "hear" accurately what happens there (2 Corinthians 4:18), to draw on those resources from the spiritual world and to use our authority to command forces in the spiritual realm.

Here are some vital things for us, as Prayer Warriors, to keep in mind as we stand in awe of all that we can see and are puzzled and intrigued by whatever it is that we cannot see:

1. All of creation, both physical and spiritual, was brought into being by Jesus and for His purposes; He also personally sustains His creation by His power (Colossians 1:16-17);
2. God fills His creation, but He is not limited by it (Ephesians 1:20-23);
3. Although creation has been scarred by the presence of Satan's rebellion, so much so that it is "groaning" awaiting its redemption (Romans 8:22), it is all destined to be brought again under the lordship of Jesus (Ephesians 1:21-23);
4. We will be given active roles in the administration and stewardship of God's redeemed creation, and the degree of our glory in that role will be determined by our service and faithfulness here (1 Corinthians 15:35-49, 2 Corinthians 5:10);
5. Although we appear to be completely insignificant compared with all that God has created, nevertheless He has chosen to elevate us to a special place that even the Angels cannot attain (Psalm 8:5);

6. There are two means of communication between mankind and the spiritual universe: (1) witchcraft, demonism and satanic worship …… all of which are absolutely condemned by God, and (2) prayer and worship of the one, true God;
7. Prayer is the ONLY means of talking with God and, as Prayer Warriors, it is our lifeline. By it, we make requests and receive instructions. By it, we respond to the leadership of the Holy Spirit and exercise our authority against the devil and his forces.

So, to answer the question "Where are we?", we see that God has placed us in a unique position in both His physical and spiritual creation and, for reasons that we will be able to comprehend only when we have been united with Him in His Kingdom, He has reserved for us the centre stage of His eternal revelation (Ephesians 2:6-7) as joint-heirs with Christ (Romans 8:17).

Of course, Romans 8:17 reminds us that we are not there yet, and that while we are here, we have a duty to take our places in the building of the Kingdom of God.

> *Therefore, we do not lose heart. Even though our outward man is perishing, yet the inward man is being renewed day by day. For our light affliction, which is but for a moment, is working for us a far more exceeding and eternal weight of glory, while we do not look at the things which are seen, but at the things which are not seen. For the things which are seen are temporary, but the things which are not seen are eternal.*
> 2 Corinthians 4:16-18 NKJV

Mission 31

Things Unseen - Part 2 How Things Work

I have always been fascinated by those wonderfully illustrated books that describe complicated machines and how they work. It's the engineer in me, I guess, and for many years I taught young engineers the skills they would need to be able to understand complicated systems, like machines. I still love those wonderful, big books filled with detailed pictures and now I give them to my grandson, who seems to love them too.

In Part 1 of this Mission, we took a small peek at the enormous extent of God's creation and our place in it. In this Part 2, we're going to look at what makes things work in this creation of which we are a part, both the visible as well as the invisible.

In the physical world, we have come to understand some of the basic rules governing how things normally work. I use the word "normally" because there are some important exceptions to the "normal", but we'll get to that in a minute. God created the physical world to operate according to certain rules; as man has learned these rules, he has become able to use them to his advantage to do things that were impossible before. A match can start a fire because we understand something of the laws of chemistry. A machine weighing several tons can be made to fly through the air because we understand something of the laws of gravity and aerodynamics. Radio and television signals can be broadcast anywhere on the Earth or into space because we understand something of the laws of electromagnetics. And so on. Of course, our understanding of these laws, as marvellous as it is, is only in its infancy. Not surprisingly, many of these laws were discovered by men of faith in God. I believe that the full discovery of the laws governing the physical universe awaits the redemption that will come when

Jesus' lordship is fully restored over His creation. Mankind, redeemed and transformed from the penalty of sin, will resume the mission that God gave to Adam, but which Adam forfeited when he sinned and was cast out of Eden; along with that came something called death, which limited his time on this Earth and also greatly limited his ability to understand God's revelation in creation. The builders of Babel had to be stopped before their intelligence and creativity, now corrupted by sin, went too far (Genesis 11:1-9). Read verse 6 again to realize what they might have accomplished if God had not intervened by scattering their efforts and greatly shortening their lifespan.

The lesson is clear: understanding *how* things work enables us to control them, and ultimately to create outcomes that were impossible before.

So much for looking at the physical world. How do things work in the spiritual universe? What are the "laws" or rules that govern how things work there, and how can we control them? Quite simply, the Bible doesn't fill in the blanks for us to explain what are the spiritual equivalents of the laws of gravity, thermodynamics, electromagnetics, etc. The only glimpse that we are given allows us to understand that **the spiritual realm operates on the principle of *authority*.** All of the Angels and spiritual beings respond to authority. In fact, we are told that even the act of creation (of both the physical and spiritual universes) was accomplished solely on the authority of God's spoken word (Genesis 1:3,6,9,11,14,20,24,26,29, Hebrews 11:3). By that same authority, He created the "laws" that govern the physical world, but He is not limited by those laws and He reserves the right to act outside of those laws; we call them miracles. And so iron axe heads can float on water (2 Kings 6:6), donkeys can speak (Numbers 22:28), men can walk on water (Matthew 14:25,29) and even the dead can become alive (John 11:44).

In an even more practical way, we are taught that this authority, God's authority, can be brought to bear on the events of this world as well as in the spiritual world. Jesus was amazed when He saw how well the Centurion understood this principle (Matthew 8:5-10). Jesus did not need to travel to the soldier's house to heal his daughter; He need only speak the command based on His authority as the Son of God, and the daughter was instantly healed. Later, Jesus taught that, indeed, *all* authority in both heaven and on Earth had been given to Him (Matthew 28:18). That statement brought to full circle the chain of events that started in the Garden of Eden when God gave authority to Adam. Adam handed that authority over to Satan in his sin, Satan understood full well his power when he tempted Jesus (Luke 4:6), and Jesus regained that authority when he cancelled the curse of sin on His cross (Colossians 2:13-15). Satan's rebellion against God's authority didn't end when he was cast out of Heaven; that battle continues today on this Earth (1 Corinthians 15:24), but all authority has been taken back by Jesus (Matthew 28:18) and He has given it to us. Although rebellious, the forces of Satan *must* obey when confronted with the superior authority delivered to us in Jesus' Name (John 14:12-14).

It might seem, then, that it is a simple matter to exercise power over the enemy and to bring God's power into our situations. Not so! Just as we had to learn the basic rules of the physical world before we could reliably use them, so we must learn how to use the tools that God has given us. Faith, first exercised in bringing us into the Kingdom of God through the new birth, must grow into an ever-stronger faith (Hebrews 5:14). Spiritual armor, not natural to us, must become worn and exercised to become effective (Ephesians 6:10-18). Our praying must grow up from the cries of an infant into the powerful expression of a righteous man or woman (James 5:16), impervious to the devil's fiery darts (Ephesians 6:16) and proof of God's kingdom come here on earth. There is a cost for this kind of maturing process; it's called discipleship. It's not supposed to be easy or free. The kind of praying that moves mountains must be learned and earned through becoming true disciples of Jesus.

So, Prayer Warriors, let's pull this together in some helpful pointers:

1. The Bible teaches us that, ultimately, all of God's creation responds to His authority (Ephesians 1:11);
2. Jesus has reclaimed the authority over this world in His act of redeeming mankind through the cross, thereby cancelling the curse of sin;

3. Jesus has given us the authority to act in His Name. This includes asking God for things as well as using that authority in spiritual warfare;
4. Our strength in spiritual warfare increases with practice and understanding;
5. There is simply no substitute for true, costly discipleship to gain power with God, including power in prayer;
6. This world is coming to an end. The spiritual warfare will be finally finished. God's Kingdom will be complete. We have been re-created for eternity. God has equipped us to join with Him in using His authority against the forces of evil;
7. In addition to His authority, God has also given us His Word, which is our operating manual. In it, we learn how to use the tools that God has placed in our hands. In it, we also are taught the *way* in which God will operate victoriously through us and the *pattern* that we must follow in order to be used effectively by God. God's authority is released in us by placing ourselves obediently into God's pattern.

MISSION 32

What Does God Sound Like?

The Battle of Midway took place on 3-7 June 1942; it was the pivotal battle in the Pacific theatre of WW2. Only six months after the Japanese victory at Pearl Harbor, the Midway attack was intended by the Japanese to finally drive the Americans out of the war in the Pacific. There was one flaw in the plan; the Americans had broken the Japanese secret naval code and had learned the place and date of the attack. Now, in order to turn the tide by a surprise attack of their own, the Americans had to spot the Japanese fleet *before* they arrived at Midway. It was not enough to *know* about the Japanese plan, the Americans had to actually *see* that the plan was being executed before they could make their move.

Spiritual warfare often depends on the same principle. Knowing the plan is one thing but being able to detect that the plan is underway is quite another matter. So, Prayer Warriors, what does God sound like when He is starting to move in battle? This is an extremely important question because we are responsible to coordinate our spiritual battles with God's forces. Let me give you an example.

2 Samuel 5 gives the account of David capturing Jerusalem and establishing himself as the king of Israel. The Philistines answered that by attacking David's army. David prayed to God for instructions (v. 19) and was told to go out and attack the Philistines head-on; in the resulting battle, David saw the Philistine army shattered in front of him like a mighty wave breaking through a dam (v. 20). A short time later, the Philistines attacked again, and once more David prayed for instructions. This time, God told him to use a completely different strategy; they were to move around to the rear of the Philistines and to position themselves in front of a grove of low trees or

bushes (v.23). From a military perspective, that wasn't a good move since the trees would hamper the free movements of the army. However, God had a different plan to use those trees. David was to wait until he could *hear* God's army moving through those treetops so that he could know exactly when to *follow* in the attack (v. 24). Once again, David's army saw God's forces defeat the Philistines ahead of them.

The key in both of these battles was that David's army had to position itself *behind* God's forces. Getting ahead of God's army would be a mistake, as would finding themselves actually going in the opposite direction from God's army. Timing was everything, and for that it was necessary that they be able to not only know God's plan but to be able to know when He had started to move His forces.

In our spiritual struggles, has it sometimes seemed that, although we have the right plan, we somehow are out of step with God's timing? Maybe it's because we cannot see how God can possibly come through and so we take matters into our own hands, like Abraham (Genesis 16:2-4). Or could it be that we have put ourselves in a place where we simply cannot hear God's voice because of the noise and distractions around us. Lot knew what he was supposed to do, but he refused to remove himself and his family from the wicked noise of Sodom and finally had to be dragged out of town by two angels (Genesis 19:16, 2 Peter 2:7). Thistles and weeds in our life have the same effect (Matthew 13:22). Paul tells us that falling in love with the pursuits of this world will result in disaster (2 Timothy 2:4).

A wonderful example of doing it right is found in the book of Acts. God had revealed His plan in Acts 1:4; the outcome was to be the delivery of Jesus' (and the Father's) promise of the Holy Spirit. Knowing only that much, they were to wait in Jerusalem for a clear signal that the plan was being put into motion. The clear signal was the sound of a mighty wind (Acts 2:1-4). The invasion of planet Earth had begun, and the disciples moved into position with the proclamation of the Gospel. Before the day was out, over 3,000 people had come into the Kingdom of God, with thousands more to follow in the next days. Like the mighty wave that broke through ahead of David's army, this wave of the Holy Spirit was sweeping people into God's Kingdom and He is still doing it.

We cannot help but take note of one more signal from God. We have been told of Jesus' plan to return for His church, His bride, but we don't know the exact timing. How will we know that He has returned? We are told that there will be a clear signal (1 Corinthians 15:52, 1 Thessalonians 4:16). As wonderful as that day will be for many, there will be those who will have to be removed in much the same way as Lot (Jude 1:22, 1 Corinthians 3:15).

In this time we have before that trumpet call, we must learn how to hear when God begins a work. We must be able to hear the wind in the treetops, telling us that it is time to fall into place behind God's army. Rather than waiting for something to happen and then discussing and sermonizing it to pieces, the Prayer Warrior's responsibility is to hear the stirring of the Holy Spirit and to be ready to move into position. God has equipped His army with gifts ("gifted ones" Ephesians 4:11, 1 Corinthians 12:28) to hear, understand and declare God's voice and to respond to the moving of the Holy Spirit. Without the smooth operation of all these parts, the working of the Holy Spirit will, sadly, be missed or only seen from a distance as others are willing to respond. Perhaps that is why God's wondrous works, that are so plentiful in other places in the world, are so scarce here. The church that we are familiar with may have blinded and deafened itself by discarding the very gifts that are needed to both see and hear in this spiritual battle.

Here are some things that we must do:

1. We must pray that God will give us the spiritual sensitivity to become more aware of the moving of His Spirit;
2. We must place ourselves obediently in the correct order in the body of believers so that we can function together with them as God intends;
3. We must discipline ourselves to be prepared to respond quickly to God's call, meaning that we must be equipped with our spiritual

armor and be disentangled from the things that would prevent us from being of service;

4. We must become better in the use and understanding of God's Word, realizing that the Bible neither limits nor replaces the work of the Holy Spirit; both are needed together. We must seek the liberty and power of the Spirit in our praying, our worship and our living.

I'm excited that God has started to move among us; I can hear the wind blowing in the treetops. It is time to pray expectantly and boldly. Ask for much. Take big steps. Chains will fall, blessings will be released, and God's glory will be among us.

MISSION 33

Follow Orders

If there is one thing that every army drills into every soldier, it is the need to follow orders. To refuse to do so brings the harshest penalty. I think that we can all see the sense in that principle.

That principle holds true for Prayer Warriors, too. After all, if we are in the Lord's army, then we must expect to receive orders and, having received them, we are expected to follow them through. But sometimes orders can seem confusing; what are we supposed to do when they don't even seem to make sense?

2 Chronicles 20 gives the account of a most unusual battle. Jehoshaphat heard that three enemy forces were coming against him and he was vastly outnumbered. He immediately enquired of God and then he and all of the people stood waiting before God (V.13). We don't know how long they stood there, but that's what they did until the message was given that Judah's army was not going to have to fight in this battle; this battle was the Lord's (v.17). Then we see something strange. Having just been told that they were not going to have to fight, they were then told to march out in order the next day and to face the enemy from their positions (v.16, 17). This means they were to arrange themselves in military order just as they would do in a normal battle. Fully dressed, armed and in military order.

But why did they have to do all that if they were not expected to fight? Something didn't make sense, or so it seems. It is even stranger when we read that the fighting was over by the time the army of Judah arrived on the scene (v.24). The enemy never even saw the army of Judah, so why was it so important that they go to all this effort to get equipped and march out and take up their positions?

The answer is simply "Obedience".

I had a Jewish friend in Graduate School. Zev was a religious Jew and we had many great conversations together. One, I remember in particular, had to do with the question of why God gave the dietary laws to the Israelites in the desert; what was the purpose of those laws? His answer was simple: "God just said do it". No explanations, just a clear, unambiguous order to do it. That's it, of course! God does not need to explain Himself. And it is sheer arrogance for us to withhold obedience until we get the explanations we demand.

Jehoshaphat and the army of Judah followed God's order even when it didn't seem to make sense. Hopefully, when they saw the size of the army now lying dead before them, they realized that their fighting would have had little effect. Without God's intervention, they would have been destroyed and all Jerusalem (including their families) with them.

It was a lesson that had been taught when Moses brought the Israelites to the edge of the promised land (Numbers 14), only to have the people rebel against God and His leaders. Having refused to go according to God's orders and having suffered the consequences of their disobedience (v. 36-37), they now changed their mind and decided that they would go into the promised land after all. Too late! Moses told them that God was no longer before them (v.25), but they disobeyed again and were defeated by the inhabitants of the land (v. 40-44).

Saul should have learned that lesson (1 Samuel 15). Samuel summed it up by telling him that God values obedience above sacrifice (v.22). The arrogance of disobedience is the same as idolatry in God's eyes.

God still values obedience above sacrifice, repentance, or anything else that we are prepared to offer up when we simply do not follow orders. Whether we are called to fight a spiritual battle or to watch as God fights on our behalf, we are expected to follow orders without demanding explanations from Him. Sometimes we may rob ourselves of the victory simply by not following God's orders.

So now the tricky part. How do we hear God's orders? Let's go back to Jehoshaphat; he was the king of Judah, so he had the authority to appeal to God on behalf of his people, but God answered through a Levite standing in the crowd (2 Chronicles 20:14), respecting the authority that it was the Levites' place to be the spokesmen of God. God has His order, His pattern of doing things; Jehoshaphat understood that and respected it accordingly.

Here are a few questions to consider:

1. Are we willing to submit to God's pattern in order to receive His instructions?
2. Are we willing to recognize the necessity of the proper functioning of all of the parts and gifts of the body of Jesus, His church?
3. Do we think that God must explain Himself to us before we are willing to follow orders?
4. Do we presume upon God's mercy by knowingly refusing to obey His order, counting on being able to repent later and then to follow through?
5. Do we stop to consider that our unwillingness to follow God's orders will bring consequences upon others, even our own families?

Mission 34

Soldier - ....

We live in a hyphenated society. Double-surnames, double-nationalities. I recently heard of a Christian speaker who labelled himself as a Reformed-Charismatic; I believe that means Reformed as in the doctrinal sense, not that he was having second thoughts about the Charismatic part! I actually like that label, as you can see, since it stuck with me!

That got me thinking about our label as Prayer Warriors. It's a strong name, one with a great connection to Biblical men and metaphors (Ephesians 6:11,13-17, 2 Timothy 2:3-4). The question is ..... What do Prayer Warriors do when we are not fighting spiritual battles? Now I know that it seems rare that we are not engaged in some kind of spiritual battle, but the question remains. You see, we are used to a society in which we have armies of professional soldiers; that's what they do for a job every day. We may have automatically somehow hung onto that model in our thinking of ourselves as being Prayer Warriors, prayer soldiers, but we all realize that we are all something else, too. None of us is a "professional" Prayer Warrior in the sense that it's what we do all day every day, like a full-time job. Let me show you a couple examples of what I mean, and then we'll come back to our labels.

Nehemiah was a Soldier-Builder. Born a Jew in Babylon in the 5th Century BC, Nehemiah was a high-ranking official in the court of Artaxerxes of Persia. He was an administrator, not a soldier by training. He became moved by the tragic state of the city of Jerusalem after its destruction over 140 years earlier by the Babylonians in 586 BC, so much so that he made it a matter of fasting and prayer to know what he could do about it (Nehemiah 1:5-11). His answer was simple: rebuild the walls of Jerusalem and restore the worship of Jehovah! Now Nehemiah takes on the mantle of a Prayer Warrior, asking for boldness and favour with the King (1:11). He asked for permission to go to this task (2:5), added to that a request for letters of authority to act as the Governor of Judah and a special authorization for timber and other materials. The King gave him everything he requested plus a squad of royal cavalry to back him up (2:8). Not bad for a cup-bearer-come-Prayer Warrior! When he arrives in Jerusalem, he immediately takes command of the situation. He assesses the condition of the walls (2:11-15), he takes the lead in starting the rebuilding of the walls (2:57), he prays against the enemies of the project (4:4) and for God to strengthen his hands (6:9), he organizes the people so that each man worked in front of his family with another standing behind him holding a spear (4:13), he and his other leaders sleep in their clothes so as to remain ready (4:23) and every man wears his sword even while he was working (4:18). He withstood threats and attempted blackmail (6:5-7) but he completed the wall in 52 days (6:15).

Paul was a Soldier-Messenger. Well on his way to becoming a leading Pharisee prosecutor, we know of his conversion and call to become the Apostle to the Gentiles. His story fills most of the New Testament with his epistles to the churches that he founded and nurtured. The cost to him was extreme (2 Corinthians 6:4-5, 11:24-27) but he was driven by one single mission (1 Corinthians 9:22). He gave us the armor of God (Ephesians 6:10-18) and modelled its use for our example. He taught us the gifts and ministries of the Holy Spirit (1 Corinthians 12, Ephesians 4:11-13) and demonstrated them in practice. He longed to be with the Jesus whom he had come to love (2 Corinthians 5:1-10) and he died in prison for the gospel. He showed us what the return of Jesus would be like (1 Thessalonians 4:14-18) and the next time we see him it will be in the clouds!

Aquilla and Priscilla were Soldier-Artisans.

Timothy was a Soldier-Pastor.

The list could go on; these were all men and women of prayer, real Prayer Warriors, and they were all hyphenated; their life as a Prayer Warrior was completely interwoven with their life work. Not one of them was a professional Prayer Warrior; they were all full-time men and women of God who were moved to pray and live powerfully.

So what can we take from this? Perhaps just this: prayer, as important as it is, is not the end; it is a means to the end. We must become stronger and deeper in our praying, but never forget that the purpose of it all is to glorify Jesus and to build His Kingdom.

MISSION 35

Fighting On Two Fronts

The idea of fighting a war on two fronts can be good or bad, depending on whether one is on the offensive or the defensive. In both cases the campaign requires extra planning and deep resources.

During the opening years of WW2, Germany opened its campaign first against its European neighbours (notably Czechoslovakia, Hungary, Poland, France, Belgium, Holland and England) in 1940 and then turned against Russia in a new offensive on its eastern front in June 1941. Germany hoped that, by opening this second front, it could gain a quick victory and bring the war to a successful end without having to invade England, something that it had failed to do in the previous year. The two-front tactic was intended to take advantage of Germany's strength and high morale both on the battlefield as well as among the general population. With the exception of the failed attempt to subdue England during the Battle of Britain, Germany's army did appear to be invincible.

The tables were turned in September 1943 with the Allied invasion of Italy, followed in June 1944 with the invasion of Normandy; now Germany was fighting not only an eastern campaign (against Russia), but a two-front war in the west in France and Italy. Being on the defensive on two or three fronts was a formula for disaster for Germany; for the Allies, the two-front campaign in the west was the route to victory.

The strategy boils down to this: an army adopts a two-front campaign only when it believes that it has superior force and advantage and can secure a quick victory.

Paul tells us that our enemy, the devil, has launched a two-front campaign against us (Ephesians 6:12); he believes that he has superior force and advantage, enough to win the war.

First there is the war taking place here on the earth

> *For our struggle is not against flesh and blood, but against the rulers, against the authorities, against the powers of this dark world*
>
> Ephesians 6:12a NIV

These rulers, powers and authorities are present and operating in this physical world in which we live. They are spiritual entities, but they have real effects in the political, economic and social world in which we live. These powerful forces operate through human agents and governments. It is important to realize that they didn't get here by invasion, but by invitation. In his first act of sin in Eden, Adam handed over to Satan his God-given authority to subdue and rule the world (Genesis 1:28). Satan has taken advantage of that authority by planting and reinforcing his agents in strong positions throughout the world. These agents of darkness are here to hold the world in the grip of the prince of darkness and to strongly resist any attempt to break free.

The second front takes place in the heavenly realms

> *the spiritual forces of evil in the heavenly realms*
>
> Ephesians 6:12b NIV

This is certainly not meant to imply God's Heaven, from which Satan and his rebellious Angels were cast out (Luke 10:18). It refers to the spiritual realm in which the highest authorities of evil have their headquarters and about which they move freely. Unable to be seen by human eyes, these forces of evil orchestrate the devil's attacks against the Kingdom of God and His people here on the earth, not the least being their efforts to interfere with our prayer life and "one-mindedness" with other strong believers.

Little wonder that the Devil thinks he can win the war with such a terrible advantage against God's church, especially if we limit ourselves to only what we can see, hear and understand with human eyes, ears and wisdom. And so it would be, except for three game-changing factors:

1. Jesus defeated the Devil in His death on the cross and His resurrection, and took back the authority (but not the territory) that Satan had enjoyed (Matthew 28:18),
2. God has equipped His believers with the armor and weapons capable of withstanding the Devil's attacks and of defeating him in combat (Ephesians 6:10-18), and
3. God has given us the authority in Jesus' Name to attack and defeat the Devil in his strongholds and fortifications that he has built up in this world as well as those that he has established in the spiritual realm (2 Corinthians 10:4-5).

God has turned Satan's two-front strategy against him by giving us the power and authority to defeat him on both fronts.

But, in order to use this advantage, the Prayer Warrior must intentionally and effectively fight the battle on both fronts; we must confront the forces of the enemy in the circumstances and events they are attempting to control in this world, and we must attack the enemy in his headquarters in the spiritual realm from which he orchestrates and coordinates his demonic forces.

So, how do we go about this two-pronged attack?

- We ask the Holy Spirit to give us the vision and wisdom to see those real-world events and situations that are being orchestrated by the enemy against God's Kingdom,
- We ask the Holy Spirit to reveal to us how these earthly effects are connected to the enemy's forces in the "heavenly realms",
- We ask God to reveal to us the lines of authority that affect the people or groups being attacked. We may not be directly in that

line of authority, so we must ask the person(s) for permission to take that place,
- We praise God for bringing this situation to us at this time, we praise Him for calling us into battle against the enemies of His Kingdom, and we praise Him for our victorious position in Jesus (2 Corinthians 2:14, Colossians 2:15),
- We launch our earthly campaign by praying directly against those outcomes that the enemy clearly wants to achieve (a broken relationship, sickness, brokenness in the home or family, hatred or bitterness, materialism, etc); we forbid those outcomes in Jesus' Name; we take up intercessory support positions between the enemy and his intended victim (Mission 10), we petition God the Provider (Mission 12) to give the opposite of what the Devil wants.
- We launch our "heavenly" campaign by praying against the enemy himself, against the very tools that he is using to communicate with and control his forces, against his spiritual kingdom. We attack him in his very headquarters, disrupting his activities and hindering his movements. We call upon God to send His angels to stand around us, to hedge us in, to protect us and to fight alongside us against the forces of evil.
- We pray those Scriptures which tell us that, although Satan still occupies places of power in this world, he has lost the authority to do so since that authority now belongs to Jesus (Matthew 28:18), and the day is coming when He will regain possession of all that Satan now holds (Revelation 11:15),
- We must coordinate our own praying along with other Prayer Warriors; this kind of spiritual warfare is not something to do solo. God has not given all of the spiritual gifts and tools to us individually; we must come together to pool those resources that God has distributed among believers.

MISSION 36

Need To See

An army that is blind is always at a great disadvantage; the need to "see" is always the first requirement of any battle plan.

Before entering Canaan, the Israelites were commanded to send out spies to explore the territory ahead of them (Numbers 13). Their objective was to check out the strength of the armies that they would have to fight, to see if there were any fortifications, and to check out the suitability of the land as a place to settle and live. The twelve spies brought back accurate information, however we know the story of how the people rebelled against God's instructions and so were forced to spend the next 40 years (one year for each day that the spies spent in checking out the land, v.34) in the desert before they could enter the land and claim God's promise. When it came time to cross the Jericho River, again Joshua sent spies to check out the fortified city of Jericho (Joshua 2:2).

In 2 Kings 6 we are told of an episode during the time when the Arameans were at war against Israel. Several times the Arameans attempted to trap the Israelites, but each time the prophet Elisha warned the king by revealing the trap (v. 9-10). The king of Aram, being told that it was the prophet of God who was able to "see" and "hear" everything that was being planned against Israel, then attempted to capture Elisha; that plan failed miserably when his army found itself blinded and surrounded by the army of God (v. 15-23).

One of the big contributing factors behind the Confederate loss at Gettysburg was the fact that the cavalry, who were the eyes and ears of General Lee's army, failed to report on the strength and location of the

Union forces and, as a result, General Lee found himself confronted by an army of unknown size and location at the most critical point just before the battle. As it turned out, the Union force numbered 94,000 men against the Confederate 71,000, a fact that would have been most important in Lee's planning.

The reason for the importance of being able to "see" is quite clear: without sight, the army is vulnerable to surprise attacks, constantly forced onto the defensive and never able to plan ahead. Blind armies are usually defeated.

The same thing is true in spiritual warfare. Our enemy, the Devil, is always on the move (Job 1:7, 1 Peter 5:8), and we are the target of his attention. He is constantly devising snares and traps, creating situations intended to confuse and weaken believers. His attacks are relentless and powerful, and he makes full use of his demonic forces. Thus we are warned that the enemy we face is deeply entrenched in this world and has a variety of forces at his command (Ephesians 6:12). We are constantly confronted with situations, trials, tests, interferences, even tragedies …. all intended to weaken, confuse, demoralize and defeat us. Sudden sickness, loss of employment, financial collapse, family emergencies, failed plans ….. the list goes on. Sometimes the surprise is enough to knock us down and we find ourselves on the defensive. Often we don't even connect the dots to realize that this is the handiwork of our enemy and that we are on a spiritual battlefield, so we try to get through on our own strength. We know how well that works.

God has intentionally kept tomorrow a veiled secret, telling us instead to trust our Father to provide all that we need and to not worry about tomorrow (Matthew 6:34). But I also believe that God has equipped us to be able to "see" deeper into situations, to have a better understanding of the spiritual battles we face, and to move from the defensive to the offensive in our prayer as part of our spiritual warfare.

Our first course of action must be to ask the Holy Spirit to direct us to pray for the correct thing (Romans 8:26-27). Then we must exercise the gifts that God has distributed to various parts of His body, the church. That message of wisdom and understanding (1 Corinthians 12:8), that word of faith (1 Corinthians 12:9), the word of prophecy and the discerning of spirits (1 Corinthians 12:10) are intended to be our headlights in the darkness of the spiritual battle. We are able to discern that things are not as they appear on the surface, that God's wisdom gives us a deeper understanding, allowing us to "see" into the situation. The declaration of faith is what turns our fear into confidence that God has taken control of the situation; hearing that gifted one pray through the crisis and finish by victoriously declaring that "all is well!". Hallelujah right in the face of the Devil, and again Hallelujah!! Jesus is Lord! We have moved from the defensive to the offensive, giving God the praise for going ahead of us. What the Devil meant for our destruction has been turned to our blessing and God's glory.

If you are not used to this kind of praying, now is the time to get down and get deep with God. Maybe you're uncomfortable with the operation of the gifts of the Holy Spirit that I mentioned above; may I suggest that you just ask the Holy Spirit to be your teacher. He loves to be asked to teach, since that's one of His primary missions (John 14:26, 16:13). This kind of praying is what spiritual warfare is about, but it will take practice, so now is the time to start. It also requires that we pray in the company of other spiritual warriors who have the giftings that we may lack. The enemy wants to keep us blind but God wants to shed His light on our path.

Let's start:

1. Give the situation, with all of its confusion and disappointments, into God's hands. Lord, we don't know what to do.
2. Ask the Holy Spirit to be our guide and teacher, moving through the gifts that He has placed in the body, the church. Holy Spirit, give us wisdom, understanding and faith in this situation.
3. Praise God for this opportunity to see Him glorified in the very situations that the Devil intends for our destruction. Lord, be glorified in us as we wait on You and in the way that You will use this time for our blessing.

4. Lord, we tell You that we are aware of Your great love for us, even through our hard times. We can confidently declare that we have never been out of Your care; we know that You will not abandon us now.
5. Now, Holy Spirit, move in us and in this situation that confronts us. We speak the Name of Jesus into the situation, we come against all the forces of the evil one, we raise our shields of faith over each other, we claim our authority by the Word of God and we use it now to command the enemy to retreat.
6. Lord, we refuse to give up now; we've come too far to quit and we can already hear the sound of the wind in the trees! Hallelujah! Jesus is Lord!

Mission 37

What Does God Do With Our Prayers?

I know several people who have kept every special-occasion card they have ever received. Same thing with those romantic love letters they wrote before they married their spouse. Special souvenirs that remind them of a time that they don't want to forget. Somehow, having those very words still visible on paper makes them seem more "real" than just recalling them in our memory, and we all know that memory doesn't make the most accurate recording device!

Well, if our words to each other are so very important that we want to somehow accurately preserve them into the future, what about our words to God? Our prayers. And on the receiving end, what happens to those words after we speak them? Surely God has a perfect memory, so he has no need to "write them down" lest He forget. Where do our prayers go after we have spoken the words and God has heard them?

First, I think that we must understand what the Bible means when it speaks of our prayers. At its core, a prayer is a conversation between a believer and God. Notice that I said "believer". Although God certainly hears every word ever spoken by anyone, the Bible does not give any assurance that a non-believer can speak anything that qualifies as a prayer to God, *with the single exception of the prayer of repentance, which is a product of the exclusive work of the Holy Spirit*. In fact, with that only exception, the Bible makes it very clear that God's attitude toward the "prayer" of the non-believer is unfavourable, to say the least. Words like "detestable" (Proverbs 15:8, 28:9), "far from me" (Proverbs 15:29). He says that He hides His eyes and is not listening (Isaiah 1:15). Jesus told the proud Pharisees who prayed for public applause that they already had all the reward they would get (Matthew 6:5-6).

Now we know that the Bible is filled with assurances that God not only is attentive to the prayers of His children (Nehemiah 1:11, Psalm 34:15, 1 Peter 3:12), but that we have every reason to believe that we will receive what we ask in His will in Jesus' Name (Matthew 7:7,8,11, 21:22, John 14:13-14).

But the question remains: Do the prayers of believers simply "disappear" after we have spoken them, knowing, of course, that God is fully able to remember every word? After all, prayer is extremely important to God and there is hardly anything that He takes more seriously, as far as the believer is concerned. So, does God do anything with our prayers after He has heard them?

If we turn to Revelation 4, we see the Throne Room of God, a scene so magnificent and glorious that no language can do it justice. In the centre is the very Throne of God, with the Creator Himself seated on it. Around Him are four creatures and around them are twenty-four elders, each seated on a throne. We see and hear the ceaseless praise offered to God by these beings (4:8) and, in particular, the casting of crowns by the elders before God accompanied by the declaration of the absolute worthiness of the Creator to receive all praise and glory (4:11). It's as if we have just stepped into the most magnificent theatre imaginable and the performance is just about to begin with this opening chorus of praise. Breathtaking wouldn't even begin to describe it!

But then the best part begins, as if it could be more glorious than what we have already heard. The Lamb of God, the Messiah, Jesus, steps forward and takes the scroll from God's hand. This is it, the moment of the unfolding of time and eternity, and as soon as He takes the scroll into His hand the creatures instantly fall down in worship with the elders (Revelation 5:8) and we see something that we have not seen before: each elder is holding a bowl *filled with the prayers of every believer, and these prayers are released before the Lamb as a wonderful perfume, or incense.* Now listen to what happens next. Instantly, upon the release of this incense, the creatures and elders begin to sing a new song; this is the song of redemption that has never before been sung or even heard in Heaven (Revelation 5:9-10), at which the countless multitudes of angels join in the chorus "Worthy is the Lamb" (Revelation 5:10-12), after which every living creature in all of creation joins in the song (Revelation 5:13). Who can imagine what it must sound like to hear millions of millions of angels, together with every living creature, singing in a single chorus of praise?

Better yet, what would it be like to actually be *in* that mighty chorus, singing that redemption song that had never been heard before? Well, dear believer, look at those prayers that were released as an incense at the start of the chorus and that continued to rise before God throughout it; there was more than music rising to God, there were those prayers like a powerful perfume that pleased Him! Our prayers, together with the prayers of every believer who has ever lived! Think of it; God had saved up every prayer uttered by every believer for this occasion. This wasn't so He could grant all those prayer requests (He had long since done that); no, this was the perfume of praise (Psalm 141:2), an offering to God so special that even the Angels knew nothing of it. It was the praise of the redeemed of God. Every one of those prayers glorified Jesus. Every one of those prayers exalted the Name of Jesus. Every one of those prayers was used to bring forth the song of the Angels glorifying the Lamb of God.

The thought of "being" in that mighty chorus of praise and exaltation to Jesus makes me stop and think about some of my prayers, the ones where I'm asking for "stuff". Asking for the right "stuff" glorifies God (Matthew 6:25-33) because we are relying on Him as our Provider, but too often we go well beyond that. And, while we're at it, maybe we should add a lot more praise in our praying, since we know that the next time those prayers are revealed there is going to be a lot of praise going on. I wonder how our prayers might change if we kept that in mind.

There is one more glimpse of those prayers. Turn to Revelation 8:3-4. Now the singing is over and the horrific judgment of God is about to fall on the inhabitants of the earth. Just before the trumpets of judgment sound, a mighty angel comes before the alter of God and holds up another container with the prayers of all believers, and this incense rises up to God from the angel's hand. It's as if these prayers had somehow held back the terrible judgment that will now fall. I wonder how many of those prayers were for lost loved ones who were saved at the last minute. I wonder how many loved ones were lost because they were not prayed for.

When those golden bowls are opened and poured out before the Throne of God in the presence of all the Angels, how fragrant will our prayers be? And as Prayer Warriors, called to use our weapon of prayer, what will be our part in that perfume that rises before the Throne of God?

MISSION 38

Prayer Warriors Are Nice People (Really!)

Many of history's most famous soldiers were not nice people! They were good at their business of fighting, but that didn't necessarily include developing all of the positive character and personality traits that go into being a nice person to be with. I doubt that Mr. Goliath was selected for service in the Philistine army based on his good table manners and kindness toward pets. General Patton was not Mr. Nice Guy. Our movie version of what it takes to be a tough, strong soldier may be tilted more toward Rambo than toward Billy Graham. Unfortunately, we may bring along some of our movie misconceptions into the matter of being a Prayer Warrior. So let's ask this question: What kind of person should a Prayer Warrior be (or becoming)?

I think that we have a great example in the letters that Paul wrote to Timothy. We might say that Paul wrote the manual on what it means to be a spiritual warrior, how to be equipped, and how to use the weapons of spiritual warfare. So he should know a Prayer Warrior when he saw one. Clearly, Paul considered Timothy to be up to that calling.

In 1 Timothy 1:18,19 Paul links "fighting the good fight" with "holding onto faith and a good conscience". In 1 Timothy 6:11,12 he connects "righteousness, godliness, faith, joy, endurance and gentleness" in the same way. Then in 2 Timothy 2:3,4 he includes enduring hardship as one of the earmarks of a good soldier. It's hard to not see the direct similarity to the fruit of the Spirit listed in Galatians 5:22,23. The lesson is clear: becoming a great Prayer Warrior is not primarily about driving out demons and diseases (although both are expected!) as much as it is about developing godly character based on the transforming work of the Holy Spirit. That godly presence in us gives us the power to deal with demons, among other things. God doesn't want a cadre of spiritual "tough guys" (and ladies) who can knock heads in the spirit world; he wants men and women who reveal the character of Jesus shining through their armor. Paul describes his own stand in the face of opposition and suffering as holding the weapons of righteousness in the right hand and the left (2 Corinthians 6:7).

Paul's letters to Timothy also give him an opportunity to highlight some of the situations against which a great spiritual warrior must fight; little wonder that these enemies are the very things that war against godliness in our character. Things like falling into love with wealth (1 Timothy 6:9,10). Things like the terrible list in 2 Timothy 3:1-9 which will mark many professing believers in the last times who "have a form of godliness but deny its power", as well as those who fill pews and pulpits with useless myths instead of the truth (2 Timothy 2:3,4). Godly character: NOT! Among the responsibilities of the great Prayer Warrior is the protection of the integrity of the ministry of the gospel.

Then there is the foundational work of God's calling on our lives, including the call to become Prayer Warriors. God's appointment of Paul (1 Timothy 1:12) was also his command (1 Timothy 1:1). The same rule applied to Timothy's call (1 Timothy 6:12). It's the same for us.

Finally, Paul reminds Timothy of his commissioning through the laying on of hands (2 Timothy 1:6) in keeping with the prophetic word that had been delivered concerning him (1 Timothy 1:18, 4:14). This brings up something that has (sadly) become unfamiliar in many parts of the body of Christ. The gifts given to the church by Jesus Himself (Ephesians 4:11) include the prophetic voice, and the exercising of these gifts through the church leads to recognizing and raising up men and women who, like Timothy, will be great spiritual warriors, mighty in prayer and filled with the character of Jesus. It's not too late to start! Now is a good time.

Here are some things to do in our private devotions:

1. Read again those lists of things that war against godly character in us, and pray for the Holy Spirit to reveal where we may need to do some house cleaning. Do it!
2. Ask the Holy Spirit to grow the fruit of the Spirit in us, that our lives will flourish with this evidence of His presence in us.

Here are some things to do collectively:

1. Ask others to pray over you to receive affirmation of your calling;
2. Ask if any of the believers have a prophetic word concerning you, bearing in mind that this should be confirmed by at least two people;
3. Seek wisdom and godly counsel to determine if your call should be recognized and affirmed by the laying on of hands.

Mission 39

Mr. Predictable

I have a friend who retired as a commercial airline Captain. After a lifelong flying career, he had logged over 15,000 hours in several different aircraft types, from bush planes to Jumbo jets, with no accidents. That was no accident! He did everything by the book. Every procedure, every action, was done precisely the same way every time, and in the same order - no exceptions. He had been trained to understand that "freewheeling it" was a shortcut to forgetfulness, oversight, neglect and (too often) disaster. He believed in the adage "There are no old, careless pilots; there are old pilots and there are careless pilots, but there are no old, careless pilots". Even when we were flying small airplanes together, he was still the same Mr. Predictable. He applied that same routine to every part of his life; you could set your watch by his predictable visits to coffee shops and restaurants! Fortunately for everyone, he has always been a bachelor.

Although there can be some annoying things about being around someone who is so routine-driven, still there is a very important lesson here for the Prayer Warrior. Things like getting the job done right, counting results, being dependable, building skills, improving along the way, getting better not just older, avoiding disaster, building discipline into our lives.

Spiritual maturity requires discipline. Becoming stronger as a Prayer Warrior requires the same thing, and for the same reasons. Discipline involves forcing ourself into a pattern of behaviour that will produce the required results, even (and especially) when it becomes uncomfortable and inconvenient. Like physical exercise, there is a very good reason why we need it; without it we become lazy, overweight and unproductive. We also become generally discouraged and unhealthy.

Paul points out that physical exercise and spiritual exercise have something in common; both are designed to produce results (1 Timothy 4:8). If we want results, we must endure the exercise! The formula is simple: no exercise = no results. So, Prayer Warrior, what does your exercise routine look like?

PRAYER TIME

Seems like the obvious place to start (Duhhh!). This must be a time that we set apart from distractions and other activities. More than a couple minutes here-and-there. We need time to speak, time to listen, time to meditate before God. Leave some time to shed a few tears; prayer time with dry eyes is somewhat unconvincing, even to God. Every hero (men and women) in both the Old and New Testaments prayed. Jesus prayed. He taught His disciples how to pray (Luke 11:2-4) and He sent the Holy Spirit to show us what to pray for (Romans 8:26,27), even to express our prayers to God in ways that human language could not convey.

If you start missing prayer time, your spiritual health will immediately begin to suffer. We MUST pray every day, or else!

BIBLE READING AND STUDY

Every day, like taking Vitamins. And let's make it an adult portion, none of this daily crumb stuff. By all means make use of prepared daily devotional materials, but don't let that replace actually reading whole sections of Scripture, not just selected verses here-and-there. Make notes, underline, highlight, draw lines to connect thoughts, memorize it; do whatever it takes to get it from the page and into your head and heart. Think about it, speak it, pray it.

MEET REGULARLY WITH OTHER BELIEVERS

Forget the Lone Ranger myth; it doesn't work for Christians. Believers MUST come together frequently, not just because we are commanded by God to do so (Hebrews 10:25), but because that is how we are encouraged, strengthened and taught. It is also how we discover and learn to use our own spiritual gift(s). The Christian faith was never packaged as a self-taught course. Perhaps the clearest illustration of the extreme importance of this point is the great description of the body of Christ given in 1 Corinthians 12. Please read it again right now. And if you are asking God about your spiritual gift, it is highly unlikely that you will ever discover it by yourself.

ACCOUNTABILITY
We are too easy on ourselves! We were too busy to pray today? …. That's OK, we can make it up tomorrow! Same thing about reading the Bible? …. Well, nobody's perfect but we'll get back on track just as soon as things slow down a bit. That's just us lying to ourselves, and the Devil loves to hear it. We need to have another believer with whom we meet regularly (at least weekly) to talk about our faith and to pray together. It's not a confessional but confessing our failures to each other is taught (James 5:16) as part of receiving healing. It's one way to keep honest before God.

So, can we learn something from my friend Mr. Predictable? Please do have a life (!) but do remember the truth that he demonstrated to me, and it is as applicable to our spiritual walk as it was to his flying: "freewheeling it" is a shortcut to forgetfulness, oversight, neglect and (too often) disaster. If you find yourself drifting in that direction today, then now is the time to turn back and rediscover the joy of His salvation (Psalm 51:12).

Let's grow strong; let's grow up! Let's be found still standing (Ephesians 6:13) when our Lord returns. (Can anyone say "Hallelujah!"? I mean OUT LOUD)

MISSION 40

Ultimate Power

I'm sure that we are all aware that the most powerful force yet conceived by man is summed up in what we call the atomic bomb. To be more accurate, it is the thermonuclear bomb; that's the "holy grail" of bombs that uses a "regular" atomic (fission) explosion to detonate an even larger (fusion) explosion, followed by a second fission explosion. Today the world's arsenals contain enough of this power to destroy the Earth's population about 300 times over. Well done!!

The horrible irony in all of this human achievement is that all of that power is incapable of breathing life back into a single one of its victims. As great as is all that power of death, it is still infinitely less than the power of life.

We are about to celebrate the Resurrection of Jesus, the single most powerful event in the history of the Universe. Tortured, crucified to death, speared, embalmed and sealed in a tomb ….. Jesus rose from death, as He predicted, on that third day. No fireballs, no collateral damage, no collapsed buildings, no radiation or fallout …. just the miraculously resurrected Jesus and (this is the part that should really get us excited) the promise that we have that same power working in us!

> *… His incomparably great power for us who believe. That power the same as the mighty strength He exerted when He raised Christ from the dead and seated Him at His right hand in the heavenly realms.*
> Ephesians 1:19-20 NIV

Prayer Warrior, we have the ultimate power! So, what about those principalities, powers and rulers of the darkness of this world? Our Jesus is seated "far above all rule and authority, power and dominion, and every title that can be given" (Ephesians 1:21). FAR ABOVE! FAR ABOVE!! Hallelujah! God has released to us this same power, which Paul calls "His mighty strength" (Ephesians 1:19).

It is inconceivable that we who receive this power could live defeated, powerless lives, slaves to the flesh and the Devil; just as inconceivable as if death had been able to prevent the resurrection of Jesus.

There is one disturbing possible (and obvious) answer to the question of a lack of resurrection power that we must address up front. Could it be that the power is missing because you have never really accepted the resurrected Jesus into your life? You have read all about the Beatitude Jesus, the miracle-working Jesus, the Parable Jesus but you have never been at His cross where He took your sin in exchange for His righteousness. No cross, no resurrection, no power! Many have spent a lifetime with every form of liturgy known to man but have yet to encounter the real Jesus and to experience the power of His resurrection in salvation. Do not find yourself among those who will discover that terrible truth too late (Matthew 7:21-23).

So here we are in a world that has witnessed the resurrection of Jesus but is still the battleground between the forces of God and the army of Satan. We're in the middle, so to speak. We understand that the victorious resurrection of Jesus has not (yet) eliminated the very real power of Satan in the world. In fact, Satan is doubling his efforts as we approach the end of the age when Jesus will surely return. What is he doing, and how is that affecting our lives? In particular, how is that affecting our experience of that resurrection power?

First, we must understand that Satan cannot force his power onto our lives; we must allow him to do that. Most often that is accomplished a little bit at a time, step by step, and even though we may not be aware of the consequences, we will, by the same measure, have relinquished the power of God in our lives. In fact, I believe it's much worse than that. You see, whereas Satan is satisfied to have partial control of our thoughts and actions, God is not. When we yield a *bit* of the territory of our lives to Satan's influence, we give up *all* of the Lordship of Jesus and the power that goes with it (2 Corinthians 6:14,15). Lordship is an all-or-nothing proposition as far as God is concerned. Power flows from the Lordship of Jesus.

When Satan tempted Jesus in the wilderness (Luke 4), he wasn't after everything all at once; he would have been satisfied to share Jesus' position. Even in his rebellion against God, his desire was not to depose God but to be equal with Him (Isaiah 1:13,14). Satan wants us to believe in half measures, shared allegiances, part-time service, Dr. Jekyll and Mr. Hyde living. We believe him when we think that we can divide our loyalty and service and love. Jesus taught the opposite; there can be only one master at a time (Matthew 6:24), and divided loyalty is a complete lie. Paul agrees (Romans 6:16). Our lack (or loss) of that resurrection power must be connected to our failure to come under the lordship of Jesus, or our failure to understand that lordship is not an on-again-off-again proposition.

God made it very clear in the first Commandment (Exodus 20:3) that He would tolerate no other gods before His face. He has not changed His mind on that.

Secondly, coming under the lordship of Jesus does not happen by holy osmosis; it doesn't seep into our lives by simply being around others who are in that place. It does not automatically come after singing so many songs (old or new!) or attending so many conferences or revival meetings. It only comes when we finally become broken enough before God that He is all we want. Not Him plus happiness, not Him plus success, not Him plus family, not Him plus our dreams ...... just Him. All those "pluses" are other gods before His face; He is not interested. It's not that God does not see the importance of the many legitimate things that fill up our lives, but that He insists that we trust Him to provide them (Matthew 6:33). It's a matter of faith, of course, but it's also a matter of who we are willing to place in control (Matthew 16:25). If we want to have control (lordship), we will lose. I think this explains a lot of lost power. We must make the conscious choice to know His lordship, and having come to that place, we must understand that it's not something that we can turn on and off at our convenience.

Thirdly, let's not forget that God's resurrection power in us is not some inanimate "thing"; this power is the direct, exclusive product of the Holy Spirit (Acts 1:8). The lordship of Jesus and the activity of the Holy Spirit in us are inseparable and we can never have the one without the other.

Happy Resurrection Day! Be powerful!

MISSION 41

Who Protects The Warrior?

Armies have been known to advance too quickly or too far ahead of their supply lines. In June 1812 Napoleon invaded Russia with as many as 650,000 men against 200,000 Russian soldiers. The Russians kept retreating, mostly without a fight, until the French reached Moscow. In that battle, which lasted a full day, it is said that three cannon rounds and 7 musket shots were fired each *second*; 10,000 men were killed, and Napoleon entered Moscow only to find it in flames, set alight by the retreating Russians. Now it was September, an early winter was at hand, and the French army had far exceeded its supply line; with no food or proper clothing, they had no choice but to retreat, by now with as few as 100,000 men and no supplies. By December, only a small remnant of the army got home and the invasion had failed miserably.

In June 1941 Germany invaded Russia with about 3.8 million men against about 2.9 million Russian personnel. By December of that year, German forces, after having made it all the way to the gates of Moscow, were forced to retreat due to lack of supplies, harsh winter weather and Russian attacks. They lost 800,000 men. Russia lost nearly 4 million men, but they won the battle. Almost exactly as was the case with the French invasion 129 years earlier, the battle was over in six months with the defeat of the invading army.

History teaches some important lessons about how armies must operate if they are to be effective. At the top of the list is the need to keep the army from being exposed to loss of supplies and lack of protection. Even gigantic armies have been wiped out from loss of supplies and lack of protection.

So, spiritual warrior, who is looking after you and where is your supply line?

We can start by taking note of some very important Biblical events where God intervened miraculously in times of war:

- In 2 Chronicles 20, Judah was being attacked by three enemy armies; Judah's army did not need to fight, for the Lord had annihilated the invaders;
- In 2 Samuel 5, David twice defeated the Philistine army as God's army swept the enemy away ahead of him;
- In Exodus 17, the Israelite army was victorious over the Amalekites as long as Moses held his arms up.

There are many other examples, but we get the point. None of these battles came as the result of foolhardy, selfish actions on the part of God's people. Battles started out of prideful, foolish actions usually do not get God's rescue package. A quick look at "church" history shows that it is not lacking in examples of pride or foolishness, and too many of those examples stretch all the way into today's church. I guess that the first lesson we should learn is to clearly (and correctly) understand which battles the Lord wants us to fight. God is fully able (and willing) to provide supernatural power when we are joined with Him in *His* battles.

The second easy lesson we should pick up on is that armies never consist of just one person. That is *especially* true of God's army, where He has crafted the many parts together to create a body that is far greater than any individual (1 Corinthians 12). Prayer Warriors must (and do) pray individually, but spiritual warfare calls for much more than individual action; it demands the coordinated work of all of Jesus' giftings to the church (Ephesians 4:7-16).

That's the big picture; now, what about the small picture? Who is looking after the Prayer Warrior, even when he/she is standing alongside others? Who watches over you when you close your eyes at night?

David, a soldier's soldier, could say that "the angel of the Lord encamps all around those who fear Him, and protects them" (Psalm 34:7).

Peter tells us that we are "kept by the power of God through faith" (1 Peter 1:5). Here the word "kept" is a military term, meaning that a guard is posted to ensure the safety and security of the one being "kept". God has posted a guard over us to keep us. And the verse is more correctly translated "kept *in* the power of God". God's power is our fortress.

Paul tells us that "the peace of God, which surpasses all understanding, will guard our hearts and minds in Christ Jesus" (Philippians 4:7). That's the same word: "guard". God's peace guards us.

Peter reminds us that, even when our own thoughts tell us to be fearful, we are to "cast all our care upon Him, for He cares for us (1 Peter 5:7). That "care" that we are told to release to God consists of the distractions and confusion that often fill our mind, especially when we are in the midst of a pressing battle.

Then there is the irreplaceable encouragement of close friends, fellow warriors, through whom God can send comfort, strength and renewed hope. Paul, now after many tears of labor, appreciated Luke's companionship and longed for Timothy to come to him with Mark (2 Timothy 4:9-11). He asked Titus to join him at Nicopolis (Titus 3:12). He recounted the names of those beloved friends – Tychicus, Onesimus, Aristarchus, Mark, Justus, Epaphrus and Luke -- who proved their friendship by coming to his side, even in prison (Colossians 4:7-14). Jesus taught that His great commendation will be upon those who "visited Him in prison" (Matthew 25:34-36).

God has been careful not to leave us without supplies or protection, even when we are deep in enemy territory. It may even be that *we* are the supply line for another Prayer Warrior who needs to know that right now.

What are we to do when we feel that our strength and supplies are running thin? Allow me to suggest some things that we can all do:

1. Worship God by praising Him from your immediate circumstances; this will remind you of His mighty strength (Psalm 29:2, 100:2);
2. Call upon fellow warriors to help strengthen and support you;
3. Ask the Holy Spirit to remind you of His work of comforting and protecting you;
4. Renew your resolve to not let this time of testing lead you to unholy living or habits (1 Peter 1:13-15). That old phrase "gird up the loins of your mind" is something like "pull up your pants and tighten your belt; quit drifting and get ready for action"!

Mission 42

What Do You See?

I had the great blessing of having parents who inspired me; they painted a picture for me of a life that could be anything I imagined and was willing to work hard to achieve. They set very high goals and never doubted that I could reach them. They helped me to "see" what would be the reward of investing many years of work and commitment. There were times when I couldn't see much else, but I never lost that vision. I still have it, even after all these years.

Humanly speaking, it is wonderful to have had those who gave us youthful visions that could motivate us for a lifetime, giving us a life compass that could keep us on course toward some worthy goal. Even after stumbling along the way, that vision was strong enough to enable us to pick up and keep going.

But what about vision in our spiritual life? Have you caught sight of something that is just beyond reach, something real but as yet not attained? Do you have an understanding of something that cannot be humanly explained? Do you have a vision from God? Does your heart yearn for such a message from God? Do you even believe that such things are possible today?

Sadly, for many believers, the answer to those questions is simply "No". Their spiritual walk is really nothing more than following the herd, going through the usual routines, neither seeing nor expecting much to change from the ordinary. Lukewarm by all standards. If that's where you are, then now is the perfect time to make a drastic change, and it's not a minute too soon! Let's start by looking at a great example.

Moses was given a vision of the Promised Land (Deuteronomy 34:1-4). Because of his disobedience in the wilderness, neither he nor Aaron, his brother, were allowed to enter Canaan, but God wanted to let him see it, so He took him up to the peak of Mount Nebo on the east side of the Jordan River directly across from Jericho (27 km away). From there he could have seen Bethlehem 50 km away and Jerusalem 46 km in the distance. At that elevation, about 1000 m above sea level, he could have seen as far as about 100 km. Even at that, he could not have physically seen the full extent of the territory that God was giving to the Israelites, so his vision must have included not only the physical eyesight but also a spiritual vision. Although he did not enter the Promised Land with Joshua and the Israelites at that time, he did appear there 1400 years later at Jesus' transfiguration (Matthew 17:1-2). Moses was probably the first prophet to foretell the coming of the Messiah (Deuteronomy 18:15). Moses was also the only man to whom Jesus compared Himself (John 5:46-47).

Now back down closer to sea level. Without the benefit of height, the farthest one could see was a few hundred meters. From the base of Mount Nebo one couldn't even see the Jordan River, let alone the Promised Land beyond.

Things that limit or hinder our vision prevent us from knowing what lies beyond; they also keep us from knowing what direction to travel, resulting in aimless wandering, lost time and wasted lives (Proverbs 29:18). Do you believe that God will hold us accountable for all that aimless, wasted wandering? Doubly so if we are leading others along that path.

Things that hinder our vision also hinder our ability to expect great things. Moses didn't just see the Promised Land; he knew that God was delivering it into the hands of His people. The vision was going to be possessed. The time of talking about the promise was past; now it was time to take possession!

I believe that God has started something unusual, something wonderfully greater than we have seen so far. What started out as a distant hope has become much nearer to us; the Holy Spirit is fulfilling exactly what Paul spoke in Romans 15:13

> *May the God of hope fill you with all joy and peace as you trust in Him, so that you may overflow with hope by the power of the Holy Spirit (NIV)*

It is this unexplainable overflowing that is the earmark of the work of the Holy Spirit in those to whom He has given vision, and in whom He continues to do so. It's what Peter described as "joy inexpressible and full of glory" (1 Peter 1:8). It's the work of the Holy Spirit that directed the steps of Ananias (Acts 9:10), Peter (Acts 11:5) and Paul (Acts 16:9). It is the prophetic gift that was promised through the ministry of the Holy Spirit (1 Corinthians 12:8-11) and which I believe is operating today. The Word of God has not been replaced, but the Holy Spirit who breathed it is giving it new power in the lives of believers who want to go beyond the ordinary and experience "life extraordinary".

So, what do you see?

I am praying for vision and wisdom, not the human variety, but the Spirit variety. I'm asking that they be present and effective in me and in my church. I'm expecting the extraordinary to come along at any minute!

I'm challenging others to do the same.

Mission 43

Never Quit!

"Never give in, never give in, never, never, never, never—in nothing, great or small, large or petty—never give in except to convictions of honour and good sense."
Winston Churchill 1941

Sir Winston Churchill delivered that famous address to his boyhood school in October 1941, after England and the British Commonwealth nations had been engaged alone in nearly a year of war against Germany. Having narrowly survived the Battle of Britain the previous summer, Britain was pressed to its limit of resolve and stubborn commitment. Churchill's remarks have been quoted countless times since then to encourage people to keep going even (and especially) when the going is the hardest and the temptation to quit is the greatest.

Thomas Edison, himself familiar with frequent setbacks, said "Many of life's failures are people who did not realize how close they were to success when they gave up".

Prayer Warrior, you may be going through a time when you feel that the battle is too great and your strength has never been smaller; maybe you know someone who is in that place right now. The temptation to quit is never too far from any of us. Of course, we all know that our enemy, Satan, loves to use this tactic on us; we also know that God will be the ultimate Victor in this spiritual war that we are in, but sometimes it's hard to see how we can make it through.

That's where we must turn to God's Word, because it alone has the supernatural power to speak to our spirit in ways that no other person or no other thing can do. It's not inspiration that's needed at times like this, it's a transformation, an infusion of the Holy Spirit's strength; something that only God can do in us. Paul knew that:

> *That is why we never give up. Our physical body is becoming older and weaker, but our spirit inside us is made new every day. We have small troubles for a while now, but these troubles are helping us gain an eternal glory. That eternal glory is much greater than our troubles. So we think about what we cannot see, not what we see. What we see lasts only a short time, and what we cannot see will last forever.*
> 2 Corinthians 4:16-18 ERV

Reckoning what lies in store for us changes our perspective, and that's the first transformation that is needed. Our enemy constantly tries to get us fixated on the present trouble; our Father wants to gently remind us that the finish line lies ahead, not beneath or behind us. And the *finish* line is really mis-named; it should be called the *starting* line, because that's where we will truly begin to live into the fullness of what we have been called to.

There is also something more waiting for us; there are treasures that Jesus told us to put there (Matthew 6:19-21), and there are crowns that Paul knew awaited his arrival there (2 Timothy 4:8). There is also a prize at stake:

> *Brothers and sisters, I know that I still have a long way to go. But there is one thing I do: I forget what is in the past and try as hard as I can to reach the goal before me. I keep running hard toward the finish line to get the prize that is mine because God has called me through Christ Jesus to life up there in heaven.*
> Philippians 3:13-14 ERV

There is a lot at stake, and it is all ahead of us. I love that. And so much of it depends on how we conduct ourselves "down" here. Jesus told us to send treasures ahead for safe keeping. Paul's crown of righteousness might be called a crown of "right living before God". He ran hard toward the goal and stretched out to reach ahead for the prize. The message is quite clear that these treasures won't just "happen" without some strenuous input on our part. Paul declared that he had fought the fight and run the race, therefore ……. Without the contending and running and stretching there would be no reason to expect a crown or a prize.

God knows better than anyone how hard the battle can or might become. For that reason He gave us His very best, His most powerful asset. Stronger and greater in every way than an angel, He gave us Himself in the person of the Holy Spirit. Our Father did not entrust our victory to anyone else but Himself.

So let's do this when we are nearing our limit, or when we see another Prayer Warrior who is being pressed to quit:

1. Let's be quick to come before God to admit our own weakness. Admitting weakness is not the same as admitting defeat (2 Corinthians 12:10);
2. Ask the Holy Spirit to bring the Word of God alive in our spirit. Read it aloud before Him. Ask the Holy Spirit to cause strength to arise in our heart;
3. Keep going. Again, from Sir Winston "When life seems like you're going through hell, keep going". Really, this would be a very bad place to stop!
4. Ask for a spirit of praise, because nothing attracts God's close attention like praise;
5. Never give in to the enemy's demand that you should be alone at a time like this, and that you just need "some time to yourself". Run to the refuge of another Prayer Warrior and press into the company of other like-minded believers.
6. Refuse to quit and say so out loud so the enemy can hear it.

Now thanks be to God who always leads us in triumph in Christ

2 Corinthians 2:14 NKJV

MISSION 44

Windshield Or Rear-View Mirror?

Ahhhhhh!! Didn't see that coming! I guess this was a bad time to be looking behind me.

I know we would all agree with that thought; this would definitely be one time when we had better be looking straight ahead, and especially looking for whatever we have been warned about.

So, Prayer Warrior, as you barrel along in your Spiritual-Giant Mobile, in which direction are you looking? In particular, where are you looking for those miracles and great works of God that you say you believe in? Things like healings, salvations, deliverances, mighty provisions. Things like abundant living, Spirit-overflowing living, joy-unspeakable-and-full-of-glory living.

Sadly, for too many believers and too many churches, the only place they look to see these things is back in the book of the Acts of the Apostles, or maybe during the days when Jesus walked on earth. Way back in the rear-view mirror. Too many believe and teach that such things just cannot (or do not) happen today; that was for first-century Christians, not twenty-first century believers. Miracles simply are not for us today, or maybe just for those exceptional cases when God does something unexpected. Miracles and miracle-working power are only in the rear-view mirror; nothing like that up ahead!

Too true for most, but I am not willing to accept that! I'm going to use the prophet Elijah for my example. As we read 1 Kings, we start with the end of David's reign and the beginning of the time of Solomon. These were the greatest times in the history of God's people. Israel was established and safe, the Temple had been built and God's blessings were evident upon His people, so much so that foreign dignitaries came just to see if what they heard was true. The Queen of Sheba, after seeing for herself, exclaimed that even those things she was told did not come close to the full story (1 Kings 10:6,7). But with the passing of Solomon's reign, Israel came under poorer and poorer leadership. Those golden years were over. Elijah didn't have an easy job and he wasn't living in inspiring times. Then there was King Ahab! A wicked weakling with a witch for a wife! Jezebel ..... what a lovely name!! So what did Elijah have to look forward to for sermon material? In 1 Kings 17:1 he prophesied a drought! No doubt he thought that there were no more glory days ahead for him!

So Elijah was led by God out into a wilderness area east of the Jordan (remember that place? That's where the Israelites came *from* to get to the Promised Land!). But it was *the* place of miraculous provision for Elijah, as the Lord provided him with food and water (1 Kings 17:6). But then the brook dried up and, once again, it looked like the miracle days were in the past. Then the Lord led him to a particular house in Zarephath where he (and the widow and her son) was miraculously fed every day for up to three years. And during this time, he performed the miracle of raising a young boy to life from death. Didn't see that miracle ahead! OK, but the famine worsened (remember, he prophesied it to King Ahab). No miracles out there now, for sure, and to make things worse the Lord told him to go pay a visit to Ahab. Ouch! Queen Jezebel had been busy killing off all the prophets of the Lord that she could catch (1 Kings 18:4), so this meeting was already looking bad. But God had other plans, and the showdown on Mount Carmel (1 Kings 18:22-40) was probably the greatest miracle that Elijah had ever performed!

So here's the point I want to make. Elijah's miracles were always *ahead* of him, and they went from great to greater. All he had to do was to obey the word of the Lord and walk into them.

So where are your miracles? In the rear-view mirror or up ahead? If you've found yourself surrounded by those who deny the power of God to perform miracles today, then my advice is simple: move out. If you have believed that God has not anointed those in His church today to perform great works in the power of the Holy Spirit, then perhaps you should change company. Surround yourself with faith-builders. Turn around and look out the windshield; God is waiting to surprise you!

I just saw a sign that said "Miracles Ahead".

MISSION 45

It's Not Time Yet!

It's probably impossible to imagine how time must slow down for someone who is enduring an enemy bombardment or siege; it must seem as though it will never end. The longest battle in history was fought between 21 February – 20 December 1916; that was the Battle of Verdun, fought in Verdun, France during the First World War. France fielded 1,140,000 troops against Germany's 1,250,000 and during the battle there were an estimated 714,000 casualties, nearly 70,000 per month (more than 2,000 per day!). And that battle didn't end the war; it went on for another two years.

Some spiritual battles seem to last forever. The suffering of a loved one, an un-returned Prodigal son or daughter, a broken relationship. Sometimes it seems that our praying is not having an immediate effect; other times it is quite different. Still, we are instructed not to give up. I'm sure that we all understand that part of the mystery in such situations is that we are convinced what God *can* do, but we are not as certain of what He *will* do.

> "*whether or not God chooses to do something is a question of His sovereignty not His ability. Whether or not He will do it is His business but believing that He can - that's our business. His ability is not what's in question. It never has been. It never will be. You must be willing to settle this truth in your heart once and for all.*"
> Priscilla Shirer in God is Able[1]

---

[1] God Is Able, Priscilla Shirer, B&H Publishing Group, Nashville, TN USA, 2013, p 62

Peter wrote two letters to encourage believers who were enduring trials, and in the midst of those trials there were false preachers who told them that either God wasn't paying attention to the situation or that He simply was powerless to do anything about it. They taunted the believers with the fact that this Jesus, in whom they believed, had not returned as He said He would (2 Peter 3:4). They went on from there to ridicule the whole message of accountability to God in judgment.

Peter headed off that argument by making two landmark points: (1) God will judge the wicked, and (2) He will rescue His own. He knows how to do both, and He has proven it, enough for us to be assured that the scoffers are absolutely wrong. Here is his case:

1. God did not spare His own angels who rebelled against Him, but resigned them to Hell awaiting judgment (1 Peter 2:4),
2. God did not spare the world of Noah's day (1 Peter 2:5),
3. God did not spare the cities of Sodom and Gomorrah (1 Peter 2:6),
4. God did spare Noah and his family, and
5. God did spare Lot and his family.

His conclusion is that "the Lord knows how to rescue godly men from trials, and to hold the unrighteous for the day of judgment" (1 Peter 2:9). He then gets to the part that tells us that we and God operate on different time scales (2 Peter 3:8). This is where we find difficulty. God dwells in eternity (Isaiah 57:15) and, although we were created for eternity (Ecclesiastes 3:11), we are still creatures "imprisoned" in finite time and a mortal body. Little wonder that Paul longed for that immortal body that would no longer be subject to time or mortality (2 Corinthians 5:2).

In the meantime, we are reminded that God's seeming "slowness" is evidence of His great patience in allowing as much time as possible for men to come to salvation. Noah preached for 120 years as he built the ark, but the day came when it was time for God to shut the door. Those who are ultimately lost will never be able to accuse God of closing the door too soon. As Prayer Warriors, that means that God will keep us on duty until the last minute. One of us may be the one to lead the *last* person to Jesus!

That may be one of our own loved ones or friends. How grateful we will be then for that last five minutes!

Prayer Warrior, if it seems that the battle you are fighting is lasting too long, let's do some things that will make a difference:

1. Let's admit our tiredness to God (Psalm 103:14). It's not admitting defeat, nor is it a lack of faith.
2. Let's reaffirm our faith in God's wisdom and sovereignty; there is power and comfort in admitting that we are weak but He, the One who holds us and our circumstance in His hand, is mighty.
3. Let's ask the Holy Spirit for the comfort and peace for which He was sent to us.
4. Let's read aloud in our praying these Scripture passages which speak of God's provision of comfort to us through His Word, His people, and the promise of His return (Romans 15:4-5, 2 Corinthians 1:3-4, 7:6, Philippians 2:1, 1 Thessalonians 4:18).
5. Remember Peter's encouragement to those tried and tired believers; God is on time, never too early and never late. He will never forget us or our circumstance. If He has not ended our battle yet, it's because it's not time yet.
6. Let's do all of these things together, because, finally, there is <u>great</u> comfort and power in the unity of the body of Jesus.

MISSION 46

Welcome Home

I have to rely on the accounts of others who have served in war away from home, whether that time was months or years. From those accounts, it seems that the greatest heart-longing was to finally go home. After the adventure, the horror and the fun, it was the thought of being back where they "belonged" with friends and loved ones where life could go on. I imagine that a great many of those soldiers dreamed of the day when they would arrive back home, to see again those familiar faces and to be welcomed back into loving arms and lives.

We also know that many of those homecoming dreams did not come true. Loved ones were gone. Love was gone. Time was gone. And the returning soldier was not the same one who left those months or years ago. Amid the joy and laughter there were tears and heartache.

Prayer Warrior, when was the last time you thought of *your* homecoming?

Peter describes something wonderful, called a "rich welcome" (2 Peter 1:11). Rich. I guess that implies there could be different kinds of welcome, but he is talking about the *rich* welcome.

I think the Prodigal son got a rich welcome from his father (Luke 15:20-22). It started with the long, longing wait of the father whose heart was filled with compassion and his eyes with tears for his lost son. It sparked into life on the day he saw him in the distance, returning on the same road that had earlier taken him away. It overflowed as he ran to that son and threw his arms around him, not even waiting for or listening to the words of confession and apology. Mercy and grace. Rich, not because of the party that followed, but because there was a loving father looking and waiting for him. Rich.

I think that Paul was asking for a rich welcome for Onesimus (Philemon 10-16). He wanted Philemon to be looking down the road for Onesimus, longing for his return and looking forward to a new relationship with a friend and brother. Something new that would be rich for both of them.

Peter cautions his readers that they must do something to ensure that they will receive a "rich welcome into the eternal kingdom". But, you say, "I thought that every believer will be richly welcomed into God's heaven". Apparently not. Peter says that we must first "make our calling and election sure" (2 Peter 1:10) and he gives a roadmap how to get there (2 Peter 1:5-8). It's presented like an arithmetic formula

$$(F+V+K+SC+P+G+BK+L)^n = RW$$

It all starts with Faith (F).

The terms in this formula are not interchangeable; the order is critical. Faith first, for without that saving faith it is impossible to please God (Hebrews 11:6), let alone get anywhere near His kingdom. We cannot cut into the line further down.

Add Virtue (V). Some translations use the word "goodness", but I believe that "virtue" is the word. Some commentators even go so far as to suggest that, during Biblical times, that word was commonly used to reflect the particular evidence of the outward work and evidence of the Holy Spirit in the lives of believers.

Add Knowledge (K). Sounds like school. Things that must be learned, especially the knowledge of Scripture, and not just memorizing John 3:16. Get past the daily crumb and move to the tough stuff (1 Corinthians 3:2, Hebrews 5:12-13).

Add Self Control (SC). No mystery here; this covers everything from gluttony to sex (1 Peter 2:1). Whatever you give in to has become your master (2 Peter 2:19).

Add Perseverance (P). We really do know what this means. No way out. No Plan B. It's not what we start, but what we finish, that counts.

Add Godliness (G). I wonder if God looks like the person I see in the mirror. OK; I see what needs to change.

Add Brotherly Kindness (BK). By now, I believe that we should have come a long way toward recognizing that our brother, with all of his weaknesses and shortcomings, is not much different from us. No room for judgment or comparisons.

Add Love (L). Does it seem strange that this does not come first in the formula? Maybe that's because this kind of love is not the cheap, easy variety. This kind of love comes at a cost and it is very precious.

Well, so far, this is a tough list to fill, but now it's going to get tougher! Peter says that, not only must *all* of these qualities be present, but that they must *all continually increase* (1:8)! Like to the nth power, for you mathematicians. How would you like to go to the store with that shopping list?

The greatest news of all, of course, is that God has given us everything we need (1:3). That means that He has made everything available for us to fill the list and meet the conditions that will assure us of a Rich Welcome (RW). It does not mean that He will do the work for us; if we are not willing to invest our lives with work and determination to make these provisions our own, then we will miss out on the *rich* welcome.

Being a Prayer Warrior does not exempt us from any of these conditions; in fact, I think we can see that they are the very qualities that we must possess to really be effective as Prayer Warriors. Let's give ourselves with determination and Godly stubbornness to gain that *"rich welcome into the eternal kingdom of our Lord and Saviour Jesus Christ"* (2 Peter 1:11 NIV).

MISSION 47

Waiting To Be Called

Months of training and sacrifice, at your peak and ready to go! And then you wait …. and wait. Whether you are an athlete or a soldier, this can be the hardest part. When will the order come to call you into action?

We understand very well that, no matter how ready we may feel, we cannot simply decide for ourselves when to jump out onto the field (or floor or ice) to show everyone how good we are! We'd be off the team in a flash, or at least relegated to the bench for a very long time! And soldiers are given severe penalties for disobeying (or making up their own) orders.

Same rule applies in Kingdom service, but it seems that it is not taken as seriously. Sadly, we see too many men and women, committed believers, who have put themselves into ministry, usually with tragic (or at least unfruitful) consequences to themselves, their families and their churches.

We have a great example in the early church in Antioch. This church had been born as the result of the gospel message through men from Cyprus and Cyrene (Acts 11:20) after Stephen's murder in Jerusalem. The Antioch church grew quickly under the Lord's hand (Acts 11:21). News of this church soon reached Jerusalem, so Barnabas was sent up to Antioch to see what was happening. He immediately became powerfully involved in that work, leading many more to faith (Acts 11:24). He was the one who realized that someone else was needed on the team, so he was sent to Tarsus to bring back someone he knew ….. Saul, whom we know as none other than Paul. So Barnabas brought Paul back to Antioch, where they worked together for a year as that church continued to grow. The believers first took the name "Christian" at Antioch (Acts 11:26). When a famine was prophesied in the Antioch church, they decided to send a relief gift to the Jerusalem church; they sent Barnabas and Paul to deliver it.

Of course, Barnabas was no stranger in Jerusalem; he was in the first wave of believers there, and it was he who sold some property and gave the money to the Apostles (Acts 4:36). It was Barnabas who was called by the Holy Spirit to trust and then to introduce Paul to the Jerusalem church (Acts 9:27). Barnabas also had a sister (Colossians 4:10 KJV), Mary, living in Jerusalem, and it was in her home that many of the believers met regularly. Paul and Barnabas may have stayed (or at least visited) there while on their relief mission. During that time, King Herod decided to attack the church, killing James and arresting many others, including Peter (Acts 12:1-4). It was in Mary's house that the believers met and prayed for Peter's release, and it was there that Peter went after his miraculous escape (Acts 12:12).

All this to introduce someone whom we have not yet met, Mary's son, John Mark.

This young man had witnessed most of the events of the early Jerusalem church, including meeting and listening to many of those believers, among them being at least some of the Apostles, in his own home. He might have been at Pentecost, but at least he met many who were. He was probably brought to faith by Peter, who referred to him as "his son" (1 Peter 5:13) in much the same was that Paul referred to Timothy (1 Timothy 1:2). His mother was an activist in that church. On top of that, he was closely related to Barnabas, one of the leaders in both the Jerusalem and Antioch churches and now he was rubbing shoulders with none other than Paul. I would love to have listened to just one of those evening conversations to hear Paul tell his story of coming to faith and then having Jesus revealed to him. When Paul and Barnabas returned to Antioch, they took Mark with them (Acts 12:25). We are not told what led to Mark's decision to go, but we can imagine that he was an excited, young man who already saw himself following in the steps of men like Peter, Barnabas and Paul. Then he was introduced to the Antioch church, filled with Spirit-gifted men and women of God. He was there when the Holy Spirit set apart Barnabas and Paul for their first mission journey (Acts 13:2) and he was there when the church commissioned them, and the Holy Spirit sent them out (Acts 13:3-4). Mark went with them (Acts 13:5).

There is no doubt that Mark wanted to go with them (who wouldn't?), and probably Barnabas and Paul were happy to have him along. Who could be better prepared to be introduced to mission work, and who could ask for better mentors? Who could have asked for a more wonderful set of divinely appointed circumstances and events leading up to this? But the mission had no sooner begun than Mark left them and returned to Jerusalem (Acts 13:13). Later, when Paul and Barnabas were about to go out on their second mission, Barnabas once again wanted to bring Mark along but this time Paul disagreed and this division broke up the Paul – Barnabas team (Acts 15:37-39).

What happened to Mark? We know that, some years later, Paul came to regard Mark as a true partner in the faith and ministry (Colossians 4:10); he even asked specifically for him (2 Timothy 4:11). Mark was with Peter in Babylon (1 Peter 5:13). And Mark wrote the gospel record that bears his name. Mark turned out to be a treasured, gifted and called worker for the Kingdom. But what happened to him back there with Paul and Barnabas on that first mission, and what happened to turn him into such a powerful servant of the gospel?

Back in Antioch, Mark was committed and prepared, but he was not yet called into a ministry by the Holy Spirit. Being with men who were called was not enough. Hearing the Holy Spirit speak to someone else was not the same as hearing Him speak to him.

I believe that Peter became Mark's mentor, and who else could be better qualified to get him past his recent disappointment (and failure) and ready to hear God's call. Peter had his own story to tell. His denial of Jesus at the crucifixion (Mark 14:66-72) was not the end of his faith (Luke 22:31), but it was a bitter memory and an unforgettable lesson; back there Jesus had made Peter one of His disciples, but Peter had not yet "graduated" into his calling. That took place a few days later at Pentecost, and *then*

Peter was anointed for ministry. Peter had not failed his calling at the crucifixion; he had simply not yet been called. Peter was usually a few steps ahead of himself, and this time he got the message. God's timing and God's anointing are absolutely essential. Enthusiasm, commitment, even education, are not enough. Mark had not failed his calling back there with Paul and Barnabas; he had not yet been called. Now Mark was ready.

Prayer Warrior, are you waiting to be called? Who could be more committed or better prepared than a real Prayer Warrior?

Whatever God's plan is for us in the service of His Kingdom, we must accept the first and most important rule: the decision of what and when are entirely God's decision, not ours. And we must understand that, for the same reasons that He invests His gifts for the building up of the whole body (1 Corinthians 12:7,18), so He calls people into specific ministries. We must also accept that He does this through the working of the Holy Spirit in both the calling of the individual and the affirmation of the church through its leaders, themselves put in place by the direction and gifting of the Holy Spirit.

And God does not waste lives or time, nor does He keep players on the bench or His Warriors off the battlefield.

Mission 48

Primary Objective

Every battle plan has one clearly stated primary objective; there may be subordinate objectives, but these must all be directly linked to achieving the primary objective. The primary objective is what it's all about.

So, Prayer Warrior, what is your primary objective? This is a bit of a misleading way to pose the question, since it might imply that individual Prayer Warriors could have different primary objectives. In fact, this *is* very often the case, however it highlights a fundamental problem and overlooks a basic premise of battle planning. You see, there can be only *one* primary objective, and that objective must be established by the Commanding Officer. Individual soldiers cannot set their own objectives, no matter how much they might agree or disagree with the Commander's orders.

So, Prayer Warrior, what is *our* primary objective?

Jesus declared that *His* primary objective was to build His church (Matthew 16:18), and since He is the Commander-in-Chief, then we can take that as *our* primary objective. It is clear from the conversation with His disciples that was Jesus' meaning.

So, what is the basic element in the building of Jesus' church? Is it church planting? Is it discipleship training? How about leadership training? Is it the miraculous signs and wonders of the Holy Spirit? Church growth? Worship? Bible study? Home cell groups? Well, the list could go on, but the answer is "None of the above".

I'm sure that we can all agree that the basic element is salvation. *Salvation is the primary objective.* If we do not achieve that, no matter what else we may accomplish, it means absolutely nothing. As in all battles and wars, there is no second prize, just winners and losers. If we do not accomplish salvation, then we lose. It's that simple!

The irony, of course, is that we cannot save anyone, not even ourselves! But let's come back to that in a minute.

Our enemy, Satan, also has one primary objective: prevent salvation at any cost, and the only way he can do that is to prevent the entrance of the light of the gospel (Psalm 119:130). Tragically, he already "owns" the lost since we were all born with a sin nature that branded us as fallen and lost (Romans 3:23); barring a supernatural intervention (called salvation by grace), we would all remain in that lost state. Satan doesn't have to persuade us to become lost; we all started out that way. Satan's objective is to *keep* us lost by preventing that supernatural intervention. All of his schemes and activities are directed toward that objective. And he knows that this is a win-or-lose situation.

Sometimes it is necessary for us to re-evaluate our battle strategy. We may become so consumed in our particular battles that we temporarily lose sight of the big plan. For example, if we could heal every disease, but see no one brought into the Kingdom of God through salvation, then we would lose and Satan would win. If we could possess and perfect every gift of the Holy Spirit, but see no one brought into the Kingdom, then, again, we would lose and Satan would win. We could pray powerfully and preach mightily, but without salvation, all to no avail and Satan wins again. It's easy to see where Satan concentrates his efforts. If he can convince us that we are winning the war by doing all of these other things, then he achieves his objective, and we may not even know it. While we are celebrating our "spiritual powers", we are losing the war and God knows it. To make matters even worse (and more confusing), Paul warns us of a day when Satan, himself, will use "all kinds of counterfeit miracles, signs and wonders" (2 Thessalonians 2:9) to draw attention away from the true gospel. Miracles are no substitute for truth, but they will appear that way, and without the truth of God's gospel the lost cannot be saved. Satan wins again.

So, where do the miraculous works of the Holy Spirit fit into the picture? Well, they fit into our picture the same way they fit into Jesus' picture, and the same way they fit into the life of the early church described in Scripture; they draw attention to the One who is seeking the lost (Luke 19:10) and they are used to support the authenticity of the gospel message (1 Corinthians 2:4). They are never the ends in themselves, but they are a means to achieving the primary objective. And since our spiritual warfare is directly involved with opposing Satan and his forces (Ephesians 6:12), we know that we cannot do that without the power of the Holy Spirit. So there is no substitute for the anointing of the Holy Spirit in our battle. Even Jesus received that anointing before beginning His ministry (Luke 3:22, 4:1, 4:14, 4:18). Paul tells us that it is precisely the effective working of the Holy Spirit that is holding back the plans of Satan (2 Thessalonians 2:6), and we can understand that this work of the Holy Spirit is not being done in a vacuum; it is being done through anointed believers, like Prayer Warriors, who are equipped to do spiritual battle. That battle is to hold back the forces of evil *so that the message of the gospel can penetrate the darkness and bring salvation to the lost.*

If only we could battle the lost into the Kingdom! If we thought that spiritual warfare was a test of our faith, that's only the beginning! The real test of our faith comes when we see the gospel brought to the ears of the lost, and then we entrust to God the entire matter of taking that gospel of life into the heart and bringing about the new birth ..... without any interference from us! Salvation is of the Lord (Jonah 2:9). Either we believe that's how it must happen, and cannot happen any other way, or we have wasted our time.

If we think that we can achieve our main objective without the genuine, empowering anointing and gifting of the Holy Spirit, then we are telling God that we don't need Him to do the job. If we think that we can do it all by ourself without the other parts of the body of Christ, then we are telling God that He wasted His time in placing us into His church. If we think that it's all about seeing how many spiritual tricks we can master, then our church is nothing more than a circus act for the amusement of the deceived. Either way, Satan wins, the lost are condemned and we are accountable to God. Matthew 7:21-23 will be a terrible place to find oneself!

I do not want that to happen to me, or you. I plead for the work of the Holy Spirit to be effective in me. I ask for His giftings and I pray for His anointing, but I will not be satisfied until I see that it all results in someone yielding to the light of the gospel and coming into God's Kingdom. It's OK if someone else runs the ball across the goal line, but I want to be part of the winning team because I know that it takes a whole team to make it possible for one person to score a touchdown.

To get back to our battle plan analogy, every soldier who fights in the battle will share in the victory of achieving the primary objective. Then we all win!

Mission 49

Danger Ahead!

WARNING: Lisa tells me this is not a pick-me-up Mission. It's like cough syrup; good medicine but doesn't taste good! Maybe more like high-fibre cereal; good for you but takes a lot of chewing!!

During the First Gulf War, Iraqi forces laid over 9 million landmines in Kuwait, many of them in and around the oil fields. As the Iraqis were retreating out of Kuwait, they set fire to the oil fields and flooded them with over 60 million barrels of crude oil. The oil filled everything, including the oilfields, underground ammunition bunkers and trenches, and it also flooded the minefields. When the fires were extinguished and much of the oil had been recovered, what remained was about 4 million pieces of unexploded munitions, including land mines, and about 2 million barrels of oil that had seeped into the desert sand.

The most common anti-personnel mine was called the Valmera 69, with five spikes on its head. It contained 420 gm of high explosive; it was buried just below the surface of the sand and, when it was tripped (usually by stepping on it), it sprang about 18 inches into the air and then exploded, shooting out 1200 pieces of shaped metal fragments. It was lethal within 25 meters and caused injury out to 150 meters.

Now, the important thing to realize is that mines are not placed randomly all over the place; they are put intentionally in the places where they will inflict the greatest damage. They are placed around valuable assets and in the likely path of an attacking enemy. And they are never placed alone; they are placed in patterns that are deigned to multiply the injury or death.

As the oil workers moved back into the oil fields, the casualty rate was about 12 men per day due to encountering these unexploded mines buried everywhere. I was invited there to propose a method for recovering the oil and I had an opportunity to see the mess firsthand, including the mines. To say that it was a dangerous place would be an understatement! Nobody in his right mind would wander around in a place like that!

Land mines have killed or maimed more people than nuclear, biological and chemical weapons combined! Today there is one active, buried land mine for every 50 people on earth.

It's easy to see the common sense of avoiding a place as dangerous as a minefield, but Scripture describes situations that could be called spiritual minefields, where the damage and injury are even more serious than in earthly war zones. Prayer Warriors, like military soldiers, must be prepared to do battle even in places where the enemy has planted minefields set for our destruction. Actually, just as with physical mines, the enemy *intentionally* plants these mines in the places where he knows we will move. And make no mistake, these things really do work as intended!

Paul warned Timothy about the danger of making a "shipwreck" out of his faith in the course of spiritual warfare (1 Timothy 1:18-19); we can insert the picture of stepping into a minefield. Paul's advice to Timothy came in two parts: (1) maintain a solid grip on the foundation of his faith in Christ, and (2) do not abuse his Spirit-enlightened conscience. This last piece carries the meaning of willfully pushing oneself away from the clear voice of conscience; it is a deliberate choice of bad over good.

So, Prayer Warrior, what should we be looking for? What are some of these land mines that have already been set in our path, bearing in mind that, in our rush to engage the enemy, he has surrounded himself with these traps for the express purpose of stopping us before we can get to him? Look out for these.

1. *Wrong doctrine concerning the foundations of the faith.* Our enemy knows that wrong belief leads to wrong conduct. Paul described

the entanglement and slavery that results from wrong doctrine (Galatians 5:1), especially concerning the person of Jesus, His death, His resurrection, the exclusive sufficiency of His redemptive work, and His promised return. Proverbs 23:7 tells us that our thoughts (beliefs) direct our living. Unfortunately, wrong doctrine can be found everywhere from New Age celebrity gurus to mainline churches and even standing on your doorstep. This off-ramp leads to spiritual destruction. The differences between truth and error may appear to be very small in the beginning, and detecting these errors requires a deep understanding of God's Word and a keen sensitivity to the leading of the Holy Spirit.

2. *Materialism*. Plainly stated, this means love of wealth. It's another word for idolatry. This consuming addiction leads to ruin and destruction (1 Timothy 6:9-10). It sidelines important relationships, marginalizes faith, destroys commitment and cheapens everything it touches. It removes the guard rails that God has put around our lives and takes away our dependence upon Him as our Provider. It makes an enemy of God (James 4:4) and sets our "stuff" in God's place.

3. *Lust of the flesh*. This has got to be the devil's favourite trap, and probably his most effective one in terms of body count. David and Solomon both fell here. This weapon is designed to destroy the soul (1 Peter 2:11) and is effective regardless of age or gender. The tip of this iceberg today is Internet-based pornography, where addiction among boys has been documented at age 9 years. This week, the Governor of Utah has signed a Bill declaring pornography to be a "public health crisis". The explosive power of this weapon is demonstrated by its endless string of victims including families, marriages, ministries and reputations. It's the weapon that just keeps on killing. This weapon uses the God-created human physiology to actually enslave the individual and virtually remove the ability to resist. Believers are certainly no exception. It is impossible to be effective for God or to be empowered by the Holy Spirit with this baggage on board. Virtually every man that you know below the age of 60 has been directly touched by this, and more than 75% of those men are (or have been) addicted to

it. Today it would be exceptionally rare to find a teenage boy or girl who is not personally, regularly affected by pornography, most commonly by means of the Internet and YouTube videos.

4. *Idle spiritual curiosity*, including the many forms of mysticism and New Age spiritualism. These may appear to be very attractive, posing as open doors to "truth" and often embracing the language of Scripture, including recognition of Jesus. Individuals may seem unusually open to the message of the gospel. They are like the Athenians (Acts 17:22-23), filled with intellectual curiosity but no genuine spiritual appetite for truth. Paul warned Timothy of the danger of these "truth seekers" (2 Timothy 3:7). This is not the gospel by another name; it is *another gospel* (Galatians 1:7-9) and something to be immediately rejected. Prayer Warrior, we simply cannot dabble in these seemingly "harmless" curiosities; whether we're talking about Ouija boards, Mystics, white witchcraft, seances, pagan spirituality, Tarot card readers ……. you name it. They are NOT games and they are NOT harmless. They are traps and they will explode in your hands. God forbids it (Deuteronomy 12:29-30, Exodus 23:33).

5. *Schemes of the enemy*. These are deliberate traps set by Satan to cause us to fall. They may be very elaborate setups involving other people (knowingly or otherwise) with a complicated set of expected moves that will lead to our downfall. Saul's plot against David (1 Samuel 18:20-29) is a good example. This was not a spur-of-the-moment plan. It was carefully thought out and calculated (Psalm 38:12, 119:110). These plots are buried, unseen, so that we will not detect them until it is too late. We need words of wisdom and knowledge from God (1 Corinthians 12:8) in order to avoid these land mines.

6. *Pride*. Hardly seems necessary to say much about this one, except that it is so sly and crafty; it is an expert at camouflage. Ironically, it makes us expert observers of others but blind to ourselves (Matthew 7:3). It is one of the earmarks of a degenerate mind (Romans 1:30) and an enemy of the gospel (1 John 2:16, 1 Timothy 6:4). It always goes ahead of a fall (1 Corinthians 10:12, Proverbs 16:18, Proverbs 29:23) and shame (Proverbs 11:2). A spirit

of humility is the product of the Holy Spirit's presence in our life, and we must constantly ask God to refresh it within us.

7. *Uncontrolled tongue.* Solomon recognized this as a snare to the soul (Proverbs 18:7) and James has a lot to tell us about the power of the tongue (James 3:1-12), most of it not good. Our tongue can undo our ministry and bring the fire of Hell right into our homes and churches. Perhaps the best thing we can do here is to pray often that God would keep us silent.

8. *Submission to a spirit of fear.* Our enemy loves to use the weapon of fear against us, a fear that ensnares us and binds us (Proverbs 29:25). Of course, our enemy is also the father of lies, so it should come as no surprise that his campaign of fear is, itself, based on lies and false guilt. Fear paralyses us, keeps us from action and puts us into an endless cycle of doubt and second-guessing. Without that fear, he knows that we would be bold to move at the Spirit's urging, quick to grasp the word of faith and powerful in spiritual warfare. God's Word comes directly against this demonic spirit by declaring that "we have not been given the spirit of fear, but of power and of love and of a sound mind" (2 Timothy 1:7). God does not call us to be reckless, but He does call us to throw down the spirit of fear and to become filled with faith.

9. *A wicked reputation.* This is another way of describing a careless, loose, unrepentant lifestyle. Living a life that includes gluttony, drunkenness, loose sexual conduct, dishonest dealings with others, and hypocrisy is a hard secret to keep. If you think that this list could apply only to unbelievers, then think again; we're talking about people who claim to be believers, maybe even Prayer Warriors, but they are "hiding" a terrible secret that is all-too open to see. A wicked reputation robs us of our spiritual authority and that's why the enemy likes to use it.

Now, let's understand the difference between our *past* and our *reputation*. For the believer, the past has been forgiven and forever removed from us (Psalm 103:12). Paul understood perfectly that every believer, including himself, has a past (1 Corinthians 6:9-11), but that we have been separated from it by the cross of Jesus. Our enemy continually tries to project our past onto our path, making us re-live the guilt, and making us believe that our past is who we are today. That is a lie; we are new creatures in Christ (2 Corinthians 5:17).

Our reputation is based on what we are doing today. A wicked sinner who has been forgiven is a trophy of God's grace. A professing believer who lives wickedly is a hypocrite.

10. *An unteachable spirit.* Stubborn. Quarrelsome. Argumentative. Proud. Arrogant. Insistent on being right all the time. False humility. Strong on the letter of the Law but a stranger to the grace of God. Unwilling to submit to authority. If you admire any of these character traits, then you have something to pray about! I'm sure that we all agree that these cannot characterize any true disciple of Jesus, and they certainly cannot be included in the baggage of any Prayer Warrior. They are all the handiwork of the enemy and are designed to destroy us.

Our natural tendency is to consider these points as being theoretical, something that we can agree with intellectually, but we don't see how we are personally involved. The truth is, these are not just "things" out there somewhere; they are weapons in the hands of Satan, and they are being directed personally at us. He intends that we will be destroyed or injured by them. He wants to undo or hinder the building of God's kingdom, and he sees us as standing in his path to that end. Make no mistake; he knows who we are, where we live, our families, our churches. So, it's not hard to understand where he will plant these land mines, and what they are intended to do to us. We need to begin to operate as the whole body of Jesus, with all of the Spirit gifts given to us.

Now here is an even bigger challenge. We understand that, as Prayer Warriors, we are not supposed to live on the defensive; an important part of our warfare strategy has to be to actually, intentionally search out the land mines and to clear them out of the way. Dangerous work? Certainly, but we must know that God has enabled us to not just survive but to prevail. Necessary? Absolutely, because without it the Kingdom expansion will be hindered and many others will be wounded.

Mission 50

Sneak Preview

It seems that the first church had a short agenda; they expected Jesus to be right back, so they lived in excited anticipation of His return. What a perfect bookend to the Resurrection ... the risen Jesus had moved among them for 40 days and then He was taken up to Heaven with the angelic announcement that "this same Jesus ... will so come in like manner as you saw Him go into Heaven" (Acts 1:11 NKJV). And so they reasonably expected that He would be right back! I would have.

But then He didn't come right back, and then one by one those same believers died and their remaining loved ones and friends began to wonder what would happen to those who died before Jesus' return. Jesus had told them that He was going to prepare a wonderful place for them in Heaven (John 14:2), and that their resurrection had something to do with His return.

That was Satan's cue; his messengers of confusion began to preach that the resurrection of the dead had already occurred, while others said that there was no such thing as a resurrection from the dead. Still others preached that Jesus' promised return was a hoax. Still, even amid the confusion, the church clung to the promised return of Jesus as their "blessed hope". That brings us up to today; we are still waiting! And while we are waiting, we are also called to be Prayer Warriors.

Waiting and praying can become tiring; it's tough work, for sure, and all the while the enemy is playing his discouraging tune to anyone who will listen. Maybe you are tired and sometimes it's hard not to listen, even if you know that the tune is a lie. We could be one of those Corinthian believers, or maybe a Thessalonian Christian.

Enter Paul with a glorious reminder of the truth. Like the wall-builders of Nehemiah's day (Nehemiah 4:15-17), we should be holding this truth in one hand as we hold the weapons of the Prayer Warrior in the other. Here's the preview of the greatest show that this world will ever see.

To the Corinthian believers, Paul points to the glorious resurrection of Jesus as the ultimate proof that resurrection is real (1 Corinthians 15:12-16). It's even the cornerstone of the gospel and the bedrock of the faith (1 Corinthians 15:17). And Jesus' resurrection is just the *first* part of the resurrection anthem (1 Corinthians 15:20)! *Ours is next*!! But it gets better ….. the Holy Spirit propels Paul on to describe our resurrection body, how it will be **eternal** (no breakdowns), **glorious** (filled with the very character of God), **powerful** (same power that raised Jesus from the grave), **spiritual** (like God, finally able to see Him as He really is, 1 John 3:2).

Like the Corinthian believers, I want to shout "Hallelujah! How soon can this all happen, Paul?", to which he answers that there will be a generation of believers (perhaps us!!!) that will not see death (1 Corinthians 15:51). But whether we are that generation or not, **WE SHALL ALL BE GLORIOUSLY CHANGED**. And not over a long period of time, but instantly, in a flash, in the blink of an eye (1 Corinthians 15:51-52)!

To the Thessalonians believers (1 Thessalonians 4:13-17) who were worried about their loved ones, also believers, who had already died, Paul adds the wonderful assurance that Jesus will bring them with Him when He returns;

- *   then the archangel will shout the command,
- *   the trumpet of God will sound,
- *   the resurrection bodies of the dead in Christ will come out of their graves,
- *   followed by the instant transformation of those believers still living into their resurrection bodies,

- * together we will be raised to meet Jesus in the clouds
- * and from there we will be taken to our Heavenly home to be with Jesus forever.

What a day that will be!!! That is the vision before us as we endure trials and spiritual battles. Like those in Nehemiah's day, with the sword in one hand and a trowel in the other, we should be found standing in battle with our spiritual weapons in hand and our eyes fixed on the sky from where our Lord will appear.

And we can allow our minds to be at ease concerning those dear believers who have gone ahead, knowing that Jesus has already placed them at the front of the parade! Just in case we may have lost sight of the purpose for our spiritual warfare, this is the best reminder that the purpose is to see those loved ones come into the faith and be ready to take their place in that great resurrection day parade. Peter tells us (2 Peter 3:9) that this is the very reason why Jesus has prolonged His return, in order that the last one may be saved.

Now, this would be the ideal place to end this Mission, so we'll stop the bus and let all those who are not Prayer Warriors step off; Prayer Warriors, stay where you are because we're not there yet!

You see, we can all say Amen to the glorious expectation of the return of Jesus and to our own resurrection. *But what about those loved ones who are not ready?* What about those who are bound by the enemy, prisoners waiting to be set free? Why are we Prayer Warriors if it isn't to step into the battle for the stretching of God's Kingdom? If Jesus' return finds us simply standing and waiting, then what difference will it make that we are Prayer Warriors or just bystanders?

To start with, prayer has to mean something completely different than it once did. Our praying must show the strength, passion and boldness that we have learned. If you know some of those for whom the Lord is waiting before He returns, then claim them now by name and refuse to allow the enemy to keep his hold on them. Wrestle in prayer for them, plead for them, stand between them and the enemy, ask others to join with you in praying for them, and refuse to quit. Pray for them as if it meant the difference between life and death for them, because that is exactly what it means! Plead with the Holy Spirit to place a burden on your heart for their salvation, restoration, or whatever else is needed in order for them to be whole before God.

So, when we consider the soon return of Jesus, ask the Holy Spirit to not let us forget about our lost ones; our longing for Jesus' return ought to be tempered with our tears for them. Ask God for the boldness to run into the darkness of their lives and bring the liberating light of the gospel. It's not the nameless masses of the lost that I'm talking about; *run to the ones you know*. Some of them, like the Prodigal son, may already be running home and just need to know that someone has been looking for them, waiting and hoping (Luke 15:20).

OK, Prayer Warriors. We can get off the bus now. We've arrived in the enemy's neighbourhood, so let's get to work. And don't leave any of your spiritual weapons on the bus; you'll need all of them!

Somewhere out there is the last one who will be rescued before Jesus returns.

MISSION 51

Denied Access

One very important principle of warfare is to deny the enemy access to critical resources, strategic places or important communication and transportation routes. Makes sense; do everything possible to weaken and hinder the enemy. The formal name for this is Anti Access/Area Denial (A^2/AD). It's not a new idea. In the time of the Roman Empire, rows of sharpened stakes driven into the ground (pointy end up!) were used to prevent cavalry movements in certain areas. Through the ages, all kinds of booby traps and the like have been used to disrupt the movements of an enemy. During the German invasion of Russia in WW2, the retreating Russians adopted a scorched earth policy, essentially burning everything behind them, thus denying the German army any advantage of food or shelter. During recent conflicts in Iraq and Syria, air power was used to deny the enemy the use of airspace, thus protecting friendly forces from air attack.

So, how does this principle work in spiritual warfare? Whether we know it or not, Satan has been using it against us for a long time. We can look at it from two points of view.

<u>From the enemy's perspective</u>, he wants to prevent us from attacking or destroying his critical resources, thereby hindering our ability to be effective in spiritual warfare. So, he wants to prevent us from gaining access to his forces, and he wants to keep us from accessing our own critical supplies.

What are the enemy's key resources that he is determined to protect? Paul names some of them as "principalities, powers, rulers of darkness, spiritual wickedness in high places" (Ephesians 6:12) and "strongholds" (2 Corinthians 10:4). These are Satan's power base; they are strong, experienced and they hold their authority directly from Satan himself. No human weapon is effective against them. They rule hearts, minds and nations. They have gained control over the minds and actions of many political leaders and have infiltrated throughout the government, educational, financial and entertainment structures of our entire society. They even confront God's angels and are capable of withstanding some of them (Daniel 10:13).

It should come as no surprise that Satan, the father of lies (John 8:44), uses the lie to convince us that these spiritual powers are not even real, that they are just old-fashioned myths with no place in modern, sophisticated minds. Denied access. He wants us to think that there is no such thing as an architect of evil, wickedness personified, who is personally committed to our destruction. So why should you be on guard against something that really isn't there? Again, denied access. Well, they are real enough that God created a special place for them (Matthew 25:41).

Humanly speaking, these forces are untouchable, however God has given us two great weapons that are capable of not only defending against them but of actually defeating them. These, of course, include the armor of God described in Ephesians 6:10-17 and the authority of the Name of Jesus. I think that we miss some of the point of what the Holy Spirit is saying here. He is saying that the mere presence of genuine truth, righteousness, peace with God, faith, salvation and the Word of God, held in the authority of Jesus, has the same effect on Satan's powerhouse as penicillin on bacteria. It kills it, eradicates it, pushes it away. Satan's forces cannot overcome it, nor can they resist it. Of course, Satan knows very well how effective these weapons are, so he will do everything in his power to deny their use in the hands of believers. So, he will mingle our truth with his lies (wrong believing), taint our righteous walk with sinful habits (wrong living), shake our peace by sowing fear and lies in our minds (wrong thinking), weaken our faith by planting doubts (wrong trusting), convince us to let go of the blessings of victorious living by turning a deaf ear to the Holy Spirit (wrong worshiping) and lead us to relax our grip on God's Word by simply not reading it (wrong priorities). He will use busyness, crises, finances, friends, schedules, success, failure ……. whatever it takes to get our attention and weaken us in the middle of battle. If he succeeds in this, he has denied us access to the only weapons that could assure us of victory. Remember the penicillin analogy mentioned earlier? Well, bacteria don't come to the penicillin; it works the other way around – the penicillin has to go to the bacteria before it can do its job.

<u>From our perspective</u>, we want to disrupt Satan's plans and movements, prevent him from being able to use his forces effectively against us, and we also want to make our own critical assets "off-limits" to him.

We have already touched on the armor of God, but sometimes I think that we automatically take up a defensive posture with it; we use it to defend ourselves when Satan attacks us. That's good, but no army ever won a battle by staying on the defensive. That armor of God, and the authority of Jesus' Name to use it, is intended to be used in attacking Satan's forces. That's how we tear down his strongholds (2 Corinthians 10:4). We must intentionally target his supply lines, his messages, his broadcasting machinery, his agenda. They are not hidden today as they might have been at one time. His plan has become well advanced throughout our schools, our governments, even our churches. Our minds have been pried open with human philosophies of political correctness and "tolerance" to the point where wickedness of every kind demands entitlement and has become the new "normal".

That brings us to one of our weak points. We have failed to deny the enemy access to many of our most critical assets. Like letting the enemy poison our water supply, we have left the back door open in too many places:

- Our children (and their parents) are being thoroughly brainwashed through the combination of an education system based on atheistic humanism and an entertainment universe filled with every form of blasphemy, indecency and perversion,
- We have sold ourselves to materialism and hopeless bondage to debt,

- We have seen the Holy Spirit driven out of churches and denominations that once were fortresses of Biblical strength,
- We have forgotten what it means to have a God-centered home, where we practice accountability to the Lord and live out a holy fear of a coming day when all of our works will be judged, and so we have forfeited our authority to confront wickedness in the very places where Jesus should be Lord.

It's hard to imagine that we can be effective on the battlefield when we are so weak where it counts the most. Could it be that we have allowed ourselves to become deceived, imagining that we are accomplishing something for God with our religious activity when, in fact, we are living in defeat? The outward signs of zeal, no matter how powerful, are meaningless if they are not inwardly genuine (1 Corinthians 13). What will it matter if we battle the devil for the whole world but fail to lift our shield of faith over our own household? Is the applause of the crowd more important than the final approval of God?

It's time that God's Prayer Warriors adopted a new policy of denying the enemy access into our lives, our homes, our churches and our institutions. Let's begin with some house cleaning to get back to a firm foundation. Here are some suggestions of things that we can do individually and together.

1. Set a date. I remember that, in my childhood home, Monday was laundry day. Seems that everybody else in town did the same thing on Monday, every Monday. There is nothing Biblical about Monday being laundry day, but it made sense. So, why don't we pick a day each month when we will clean house with God, renew our commitment to His Lordship over our home, ask for His wisdom in the decisions we make, and renew our promise to look to Him as our Provider.
2. Pray against the enemy's handiwork in your home, claiming freedom from guilt, freedom from spiritual fear, freedom from doubt, freedom from weakness and ask God to bring the blessedness of Romans 8:1-2 right into every room in your home.

3. Remove or ban from your home things or conversations that dishonour God or send a message to others that conflicts with your testimony as believers.
4. Renew your dedication of your home to God and pray or sing it out loud. Deny the enemy entrance to your home (Joshua 24:15).
5. Check your prayer list and make sure that your family members are right at the top, then make sure that you hold them up before the Lord every day. Pray in your authority as a spouse, parent or grandparent, raising your shield of faith over those loved ones and breaking the claims of the enemy over them. Command the powers of darkness to leave them now.
6. Pray directly against the enemy's plans and schemes that are aimed at your loved ones. Pray that the devil's agents will be confounded and confused and that their efforts will fail (Psalm 70:2, 71:13, 83:17).
7. Pick a school in your area and begin to pray that God would place a hedge of protection (Psalm 139:5) around it so that every ungodly spirit and influence would be removed and prevented from returning. Pray that God will send Christian teachers.
8. Pray for your church leaders, asking that they would be anointed by the Holy Spirit as capable watchmen (Ezekiel 3:17) and workers (2 Timothy 2:15).

Let's be more determined to make sure that our enemy has not gained a foothold where he does not belong; make sure that these places are strictly "off-limits". Slam the door in the face of the intruder who is trying to steal, kill and destroy (John 10:10) in your back yard.

Remember, Satan does not want us to possess the things that God has laid up in store for us, the very riches that Jesus has purchased for us. So be bold to take possession of every blessing that has been laid up for you in Christ and *refuse to be denied* by the lies of the evil one. The riches of God are not just reserved for Heaven, but are revealed for us to possess now (1 Corinthians 2:9-10, Romans 9:23, Ephesians 2:10, Psalm 31:19).

Mission 52

Move Out!

The D-Day invasion of Europe on 6 June 1944 took seven months to plan. Three countries (Britain, the United States and Canada) worked secretly to orchestrate the largest amphibious invasion in history. From five different launch points in England, 156,000 men set out for five landing zones on the Normandy beach. A few hours before the main force left England, another 20,000 paratroopers had flown into the countryside immediately behind the beaches where the main force was about to land. After all those months of preparations, it all came down to one final command to "Move out". None of those troops had come to England to stay; their one and only purpose was to be ready to move out when the command was given.

Prayer Warrior, we have been trained to be prepared for something for which heaven has been waiting for a very long time. Earth is about to be invaded for the second time; the first invasion came at the defeat of Satan in his battle in heaven against God's angels. The result of that battle saw Satan and his demons cast down to this world (Luke 10:18, Revelation 12:7-10). This was an invasion of evil. Our present spiritual warfare is all about fighting against that demon force and its influence in this world. When Jesus began His earthly ministry, He announced that God's Kingdom had arrived, but Satan's kingdom was still very much in place and was not about to walk away. For over two thousand years we have seen the clash of these two kingdoms.

Scripture tells us that, as we approach the end of this present age, we are to expect a dramatic increase in the intensity of demonic activity (2 Timothy 3:1-9, 2 Peter 3:3). Of course, that means that our spiritual warfare will also increase in intensity. All of this is a signal that the second invasion of planet Earth is about to take place; the return of Jesus to call out His redeemed ones (1 Thessalonians 4:16, 1 Corinthians 15:51-54).

So, Prayer Warriors, we now stand in the midst of the greatest spiritual battle this world has known and on the threshold of the return of Jesus. The command to "Move out" is both a call to complete the Kingdom work to which we have been ordained and to be ready for evacuation at any moment.

The call to complete the Kingdom work while there is still time (John 9:4) is an urgent call, and there will be many who will turn a deaf ear to that call. The call to be evacuated out of this world will not be up for discussion; like the unprepared bridesmaids (Matthew 25:1-13), many will find themselves shut out. Fooled into thinking that they controlled the time to make the commitment to God's Kingdom, they will discover too late (Matthew 7:21-23) that the timing was always under God's sovereign control.

The Bible gives us many warnings about being unprepared and unwilling to hear God's call on our life. Of course, Satan is working hard to keep us unprepared and unwilling. Here are some of the things that will cause even many professing believers to turn away from God's urgent call to settle the question of Jesus' Lordship in their life:

1. *Entrenched in the world.* Paul described it as being entangled (2 Timothy 2:4). If we dig our roots deeply into this world, letting go will become impossible. Answering God's call will become impossible. Having committed and spent our life for our own pursuits, we will have nothing left with which to serve God. The truth is that we have only one life to spend; after it is spent or mortgaged to this world, we have nothing left. The choice we are being called to make is critical and the time is now (Matthew 16:25). Lot knew the difference between righteousness and corruption, but even at the end he was so entrenched in Sodom that he had to be dragged away by two angels just to save

his life (Genesis 19:15-17). God will not drag us into Kingdom commitment.

2. *In love with the world.* This love affair is always fatal. Selling ourselves to the glitter of this world makes us an enemy of God (James 4:4), filling us with emptiness and false hope (1 John 2:15). If we have given our heart's love to this world, then there is no room to love God. Don't fool yourself into thinking that God will be satisfied with a little piece of your love; with Him it's all or nothing! And while you're thinking about it, or maybe deciding to make one last trip on the world's merry-go-round, you will run out of time. No second chance.

3. *Unsure of the value of God's Kingdom.* If you haven't taken the time or made the effort to listen to Jesus' words about God's Kingdom or haven't bothered to search God's Word for the many descriptions of the treasures laid up for His children, then you might wonder what all the fuss is about. But, of course, that is exactly what Satan wants you to think. He knows how gloriously beautiful heaven is, but he doesn't want you to know that. The thing is, you have no excuse. The responsibility lies entirely with you. You choose. You settle the question of the worth of God's Kingdom.

4. *Out of contact with the Lord of God's Kingdom.* Unfortunately, this carries with it the rider that you are very much *in* contact with the god of this world. Out of contact means to be without communication. We're talking about prayer. Sadly, many of us know what it's like to drop the ball when it comes to real prayer, but we can be thankful that God has graciously brought us back to a much better place. Many professing believers never know the reality of prayer; oh, they make the usual pleas when trouble hits close to home or when they desperately need something, but that's all there is to it. Some will go so far as to acknowledge the importance of prayer, but their way of dealing with that is to "farm it out", asking others to pray for them and their loved ones as a substitute for doing it themselves. Here's the simple truth: you cannot be passionate about someone or something with whom you have no connection. You cannot love and long for God's Kingdom

without being in contact with the Lord of that Kingdom, Messiah Jesus.
5. *Unwillingness to break ties with this world.* Sometimes this may involve the pleasures of this world to which we have become accustomed and to which we are addicted. Or it may involve memories or special relationships which we are enjoying (or have enjoyed) in this world, and somehow, we feel that we will be throwing them away if we place Jesus as the Lord of our life. To be sure, not even our dearest loved one can sit on the throne of our life if we want Jesus to be Lord. Satan wars against our soul and mind by trying to confuse us about the difference between memories and Lordship.

Now here is where it gets tough if you are still undecided about God's call of Lordship over your life. It is much later than you think, and most of your opportunities to make a real commitment to Jesus and His Kingdom are in the rear view mirror. Gone. None of us has the promise of tomorrow as a time to make up our mind; tomorrow may come, but the same devil that kept you from making that commitment today will certainly do the same thing tomorrow. One day, it will be one day too late.

On the eve of the Normandy invasion, General Patton (who was not known for his gentle speech!) spoke to the troops who were about to embark on the landing craft. It wasn't meant to be a comfy cozy speech; it was a harsh reminder that war was about to come into their lives in a hard way. He told them that only about 2% of them would be killed in the battle, but that those who survived would be able to tell their grandchildren that they had taken part in one of the greatest battles in history. I guess he figured that knowing the truth about how bad it could get was the best way for each man to do everything possible to make sure that he was among the 98% who were expected to survive. Truth is a great reminder of reality.

Today is the day to start to make a difference in the spiritual battle raging around us; today brings us one day closer to our evacuation call! Today is the day to make that critical decision about Jesus' Lordship in your life. It isn't the first decision you have made in your Kingdom walk, but it is the most important one you are facing that will determine how well you walk tomorrow.

Jesus' response to your commitment will be both instant and eternal. The instant reward will be indescribable peace (Philippians 4:7). The eternal reward will be fully revealed after the evacuation!

Mission 53

God Has Secrets

I wonder what God knows that He hasn't yet told us.

The fact of our finite understanding, alone, must mean that there is much more "unknown" than "known". In our human way of thinking, it must frustrate God that we place such a limit on what we are able to receive. After all, He is a revealing God, intent on revealing Himself and His wisdom. Creation is His handiwork, just a portal in time and space through which we can glimpse His majesty and glory (Psalm 8:3). Yet, God seems to delight in teasing us with bits of revelation by sharing some of His secrets with us. And He plainly tells us that He has secret places, secret wisdom and secret things that He has yet to reveal.

The biggest secret of all time must be that mystery which God concealed from eternity past. Paul took up the subject in at least four of his epistles. The Romans learned of it as " the mystery kept secret since the world began" (Romans 16:25 NKJV). To the Corinthians he called it "the hidden wisdom which God ordained before the ages for our glory," (1 Corinthians 2:7 NKJV). To the Ephesians he called it "the mystery, which from the beginning of the ages has been hidden in God who created all things through Jesus Christ; to the intent that now the manifold wisdom of God might be made known by the church to the principalities and powers in the heavenly places," (Ephesians 3:9-10 NKJV). To the Colossians it was "the mystery which has been hidden from ages and from generations, but now has been revealed to His saints" (Colossians 1:26 NKJV) and "the knowledge of the mystery of God, both of the Father and of Christ, in whom are hidden all the treasures of wisdom and knowledge". (Colossians 2:2-3 NKJV).

David knew the comfort and safety of God's secret place (Psalm 91:1), a place so close to God that he was hidden from his enemies (Psalm 27:5). He could even say "The Lord confides in those who fear him; he makes his covenant known to them". (Psalm 25:14 NIV). Solomon also spoke of this type of intimate conversation with God where "His secret counsel is with the upright". (Proverbs 3:32 NKJV).

Then there are those many hidden treasures that God has prepared (laid up) for us, waiting for us to claim them. Some of these are for our enjoyment in heaven, but many are for our possession here in this life. For instance

Oh, how great is your goodness, which You have laid up for those who fear You, which You have prepared for those who trust You in the presence of the sons of men!
Psalm 31:9 NKJV

Paul placed great importance on those treasures that are laid up in heaven (Colossians 1:5) and on his own crown of righteousness awaiting him there (2 Timothy 4:8).

Prayer Warriors, this is not a matter of intellectual curiosity. God wants to speak to us, even to the point of revealing Himself to us in special ways. God wants us to be close to Him, close enough to whisper into our ears. It should not be a matter of selfish pride on our part to be made party to God's secrets, but it should be our eager desire to hear as much from God as He is willing to reveal to us.

Sometimes God wants to reveal "things" to us. These are facts, information, understanding. God wants us to become better informed, particularly about His Kingdom and our responsibilities as spiritual warriors in advancing that Kingdom. God's "whisper" to us will almost always involve a deeper understanding of His Word, and will always be in complete agreement with it. Revelations and experiences do not confirm the Bible; it's the other way around! We must rely on the Bible to determine the authenticity of any revelation or experience. Paul's instructions concerning taking the gospel into Macedonia (Acts 16:9-10) were contrary to the Apostle's plans but were so clear that he could not ignore them.

Sometimes God wants to reveal "times" to us. Like hearing God say "Now is the time". We have sensed a period of preparation, and then God announces that those preparations are complete and it's time to move ahead. Joshua had been waiting for 40 years to finally be able to re-enter the Promised Land, and finally he heard God's command that the time had arrived (Joshua 1:2).

Sometimes God wants to reveal "situations" to us. This will often involve meeting certain people or walking into circumstances that quickly speak to our spirits. The widow of Zarephath was preparing to eat her last meal when she met Elijah (1 Kings 17:8-16); that encounter saved the lives of her son and herself and was the means by which her son was later restored from death.

Sometimes God wants to reveal "dangers" to us. These are specific to our situations and are far more detailed that the general Scriptural warnings. God warned the king of Israel through Elisha of a plot to ambush him (2 Kings 6:8-10).

Prayer Warrior, how much time do you spend getting so close to God that you can hear His whisper? It might be a whisper of comfort or warning, but He does have something that He wants you to hear. God has His secrets, but He will never reveal them to the careless or the casual or the disinterested.

For the Prayer Warrior, hearing what God has to say is far more important than getting Him to listen to us! Engage your spirit with the Holy Spirit and begin to draw in the deep things of God (1 Corinthians 2:12).

MISSION 54

Step On It!

After the death of Moses, the servant of the Lord, the Lord said to Joshua son of Nun, Moses' aide: "Moses my servant is dead. Now then, you and all these people, get ready to cross the Jordan River into the land I am about to give to them—to the Israelites. **I will give you every place where you set your foot**, *as I promised Moses. Your territory will extend from the desert to Lebanon, and from the great river, the Euphrates—all the Hittite country—to the Mediterranean Sea in the west. No one will be able to stand against you all the days of your life. As I was with Moses, so I will be with you; I will never leave you nor forsake you."*

Joshua 1:1-5 NIV

For the children of Israel, after their mighty deliverance out of Egypt forty years earlier and all those years in the wilderness, this was finally what God had promised; the Promised Land! The boundaries of the Deed were clearly marked, so all that remained was for them to claim what was theirs.

Now, there were a couple problems. The first (and most obvious) was that all of the promised land was on the west side of the Jordan River; they were standing on the east side of the river! Although there was a shallow crossing place some distance upstream (Joshua 2:7), God wanted to make certain that this crossing was going to be remembered as His work and as His anointing of Joshua as His man (Joshua 3:5-13), so He had them cross at a point where the water was too deep to ford. The promise was going to start with a test of faith. The very instrument that God chose to deliver the promise was the same one that He chose for the test: their feet. They had to take the first step into the water of the river before God made the path clear for them. In a way, God consecrated their feet, the same feet that would step onto the Promised Land.

The second problem was that the Promised Land was already inhabited, and those occupants were not going to walk away easily. Clearly God had already taken that into account as part of the promise He made to Joshua. The Israelites would prevail, but they had to put their faith to the test every time and take the step that would plant their feet on the Promised Land. Five years later, the land was divided up (Joshua 14) and there were still battles to be fought to finish the possession.

Prayer Warrior, we are standing on the east bank of the Jordan in our faith journey. We have heard God's promises to us. We are called to do great works in the Name of Jesus (John 14:12-14). We are called to endure, to persevere, and to claim the crown (2 Timothy 2:3-6). We are told that we can be successful in the great harvest for God's Kingdom (Matthew 9:37-38). We are told that we can use all of God's armor to protect us and to give us the victory in our spiritual battles (Ephesians 6:11). God has laid up immense treasures for us, both in this life and in the life to come (Colossians 1:5). There's just one condition that we must meet in order to make those riches our own possession; we have to step on them! God is not in the delivery business when it comes to these riches. It's up to us to test our faith and to reach out from where we stand. If we don't move our feet, we claim nothing. Nothing now and nothing in God's Kingdom to come.

The time has come. God has prepared us for the first step and His provisions for the next one are waiting for us on the *other* side of this test.

Some lessons from Joshua's experience are worth remembering in the faith campaign that lies ahead of us:

1. God has set the time for crossing over; some time later, when it's more convenient for us, will be too late;
2. This is a real test, and the outcome will determine our future;

3. This is not going to be the last test, but the nature of these tests is to see if we are willing to let God demonstrate His power in us so that we will triumph;
4. Our place in the community of believers is extremely important; we are not a band of independent stragglers;
5. Our enemies are very real and very dangerous. They may even appear to us as giants, but God's promise of victory is not dependent on the size or strength of the enemy;
6. God's presence goes before us, so the first thing that the enemy sees is the Almighty God who is our leader (Joshua 2:6);
7. The enemy knows that we are coming, and he is already filled with fear (Joshua 2:9,24);
8. God's simple promise to Joshua is the same to us; every place we step on is ours!
9. God will give us something to remember this first great step of faith (Joshua 4:8-9).
10. God will sanctify our "feet" of faith in this test.

Now we come to the very personal part. Do you actually believe that you have come to an important turning point in your spiritual life? Are you convinced that this is not just another "prayer Mission", but rather the beginning of the discovery of a depth of God's riches that you have not known before? Has the Holy Spirit planted a new determination in your heart to claim all of the riches that Jesus has purchased for you? Are you ready to step away from the desert and into the place of God's promise?

Mission 55

Kingdom Warfare

We are engaged in the greatest war this world has ever known. It is a war between kingdoms and kings, a people and peoples, light and darkness, the great I Will and the great I AM. This war touches everything and everyone in the world. It is total war.

One chapter in this great war is described in the crossing of the Jordan River by the Israelites as they began to take possession of the Promised Land. They were going to build a kingdom in which God would be their King, and it was God's plan that, through this people and this kingdom, all the people of the earth would know Him. The taking of that Promised Land was just the latest episode in the war that began with the rebellion of Satan and the casting out of heaven (and down to earth) of Satan's defeated legion of angels. God's promise of a man, the seed of Eve (Genesis 3:15), who would ultimately crush Satan's kingdom, was none other than Messiah Jesus; Satan's response to that was to plan the corruption of part of the human race by defiling the genetic lineage so that the promised Messiah could not possibly be completely human. He attempted this corruption through the mating of some of his fallen angels with human women, producing the half-breed Nephilim (Genesis 6:1-5) who were known as giants and renowned warriors. Although most were destroyed by the flood of Noah's day, the Nephilim race survived through Ham's wife, then through their sons Canaan and Cush to produce the Philistines, Jebusites, Amorites, Girgashites, Perizzites, Hivites, Hittites and Canaanites. This Satanic genetic mix now populated the entire region which Joshua and the Israelites were about to enter. These were genetic giants that had been "planted" there by none other than Satan himself. This is where God was going to set up His kingdom. Of course, it is no coincidence that this region constitutes perhaps the most fortified Satanic stronghold on earth even to this day, and it will be the place where the last great battle is fought between Satan's army and God.

It's no wonder that the world is a mess! And it is no wonder that the spiritual war in which we are engaged is so fierce. It did not start with us, but we may well witness its next great turning point with the return of Jesus. Meanwhile, the battle intensifies as that day approaches.

Those enemies of Joshua in the Promised Land, all those "ites", are still well represented in our world and in our society, and they have managed to spread around the world. And they have had a few thousand years of perfecting their tactics and building their kingdom since Joshua's day. These are the enemies we face as we enter the place of God's promises to us, our spiritual Promised Land.

Moses was told by the spies (Numbers 13:22) about the descendants of Anak and his sons (Ahiman, Sheshai, Talmai) who inhabited the Promised Land. In addition to their giant size, these people had certain characteristics that were completely opposed to God's people and His plan for Kingdom living. Their names define these characteristics:

Anak	to choke or strangle, to kill slowly
Ahiman	to block or hinder
Sheshai	to create a false appearance by painting or whitewashing
Talmai	to accumulate or hoard

Taken together, these characteristics constituted strongholds that were put in place by Satan to defeat God's people, not quickly, but a bit at a time. They ultimately led to a mindset to "settle for little", an attitude of materialism and apathy with no effort or determination. All of this, of course, concealing the real motives and strategy of the enemy to infiltrate God's people with these same mindsets. Once entrenched, these attitudes would render His people useless and disinterested in any Kingdom work.

Forty years later, when the Israelites finally entered the Promised Land, they were confronted by a whole new generation of these enemies now entrenched in their own kingdoms in the very place that God had given to His people. In all, there were seven kingdoms, each distinguished by its own "personality":

Jebusites	trodden down, spirit of defeat and condemnation
Girgashites	dwellers of clay or marshy regions, spirit of compromise
Canaanites	materialism
Hittites	spirit of fear and insecurity
Perizzites	open and unwalled dwellings, no boundaries, spirit of immorality
Amorites	spirit of pride, rebellion, self-edification, unforgiveness, bitterness
Hivites	to lie openly without shame, spirit of humanism – exalting man over God

These were going to make great neighbours! And let's not forget how they got there; Satan planted them there not only to corrupt the genetic heritage of man (particularly the bloodline that would one day see the birth of Jesus) but to corrupt the society of which God's people were a part. By simple infiltration, these Satanic strongholds would subdue God's people and subvert God's plan. It's no wonder that God's orders to Joshua were to exterminate them. The last time God saw this move of Satan was in the society of Noah's day, and His response then was to exterminate wicked mankind.

The spiritual counterparts of each of these kingdoms confront us today. Those strongholds have infiltrated and captured most, if not all, of the institutions of the nations of this world; their governments, their education systems, their entertainment networks, their financial institutions, their religions ..... everything. These kingdoms are here to attempt to destroy God's Kingdom and God's people; this is kingdom warfare. This is the war in which we are called to be Prayer Warriors.

Sound easy? Not at all! Are the stakes high? They couldn't be higher! Satan is going for it all, and that includes you, your family, your children's school, your church ..... everything that stands in his way. It is in precisely this situation that God has summoned us to be completely obedient to His call, to be strong and to not fall back. It is altogether too easy to just be carried along with the tide of our society, to enjoy what they enjoy (even if it isn't exactly uplifting), to accept their standards (even if we see that they are contrary to God's standards), to yield to their demands of "equality" and political correctness (even if we recognize the Satanic corruption in it), to become obedient to the "new normal" (even if we know deep down that it violates God's laws of decency and morality), to willingly adopt the bondage of smothering debt and servitude (even when we begin to recognize that these things have mortgaged us away from God's service), to gladly offer up our children to educational institutions that exalt man above God, ridicule any form of Biblical faith and mandate recognition of false gods in the very places that forbid the Bible and prayer. The list goes on, sadly! Or did you not notice? So, we do nothing, or, worse yet, we see nothing really wrong! The "ites" have done their work masterfully well by conquering through infiltration. Large sections of the professing church have, in many ways, adopted the same dreams and strategy of self-kingdom building through accommodation instead of being the watchmen God intends. The light is getting harder to see.

Prayer Warrior let's stop dancing to this world's music. Let us ask God for a new spirit of boldness to know the truth and to live it out regardless of the consequences. And there will be consequences! But, before it is too late, can we not lay hold of God's mighty power to be all that He has called us to be? Holy Spirit power is not optional in this battle, and only those fully equipped with God's armor will be able to make a difference.

Could it be that God, in His sovereign will, has allowed the giants to become so big and plentiful as His way of demonstrating His mighty power through us as we build His kingdom?

Mission 56

Spirit-Man, spirit-Man

How well is your spirit?

Or perhaps I could ask "How strong is your spirit?".

Strange questions to be asking a Prayer Warrior. Strange, yes, but very important.

Let me start by reminding us that God has created us as a triune being, meaning that we have three distinct "parts": body, soul and spirit. We all knew that, of course. We also know that our body is our connection to the earth (literally, and it will return to the earth), our soul is our "life" connection (including our senses, emotions, conscience, will, reasoning, intellect), and our spirit is our connection to God. Our body is definitely not eternal (although believers will receive a new eternal one at our resurrection); we can discuss another time if our soul is eternal, and we know that our spirit is eternal.

Our body is suffering the consequences of Adam's fall, so it must eventually die. Our soul is corrupted by sin and so is tainted and distorted to the point that it is completely untrustworthy (Jeremiah 17:9) as a guide to life. Our spirit is totally dead as a result of being born in a sinful condition and is only brought to life in the new birth (this *is*, in fact, the new birth, as in 2 Corinthians 5:17). It is this alive-from-the-dead spirit which now is able to communicate with God's Spirit. In fact, this is precisely how the Holy Spirit, given to every believer as his/her birthright (2 Corinthians 1:22) when coming into God's family of faith, is able to communicate with us.

Spirit to spirit. From that point on, our walk of faith is determined by the health and fitness of our spirit.

When we are born into God's family, our spirit is that of an "infant". It is God's intention that that spirit will grow in strength as it matures, all the while growing in harmony with and under the tutorship of the Holy Spirit. It is God's plan that we become mighty in spirit as we mature in the faith.

Now here's where we may have gone off the track in our faith walk. Suppose I told you that I wanted to improve my physical health and muscular strength by starting a healthy diet and hiring a personal fitness trainer. That trainer could lift weights effortlessly. Whenever I wanted something lifted, I would call him over to my place and get him to do the job. You're starting to see where this is going off the rails. The trainer's job should be to train *me* to lift weights, not to do the lifting for me.

Now let me use another example. God wants me to grow strong in my spirit, so I call upon the Holy Spirit to act in my place because I think that's what is meant by surrendering to the Holy Spirit. I also think that the Bible tells me to let the Holy Spirit fight my spiritual battles for me, especially the ones with my fleshly appetites and desires. Then I wonder how it can be possible that I hardly ever win these battles! What's wrong with God?

Let me suggest a few things that might sound a bit strange to you, but I believe that you will soon see the point:

1. Your re-born spirit is completely the workmanship of God (Ephesians 2:10) and is not the seat of sin in your life. God gave it new life with a supernatural ability to hear the voice of the Holy Spirit.
2. Your spirit can grow or not, depending on its diet and exercise.
3. The "size" of the Holy Spirit is exactly the same in every believer. The notion that the Holy Spirit may be "big" or "small", "strong" or "weak" depending upon how much we "surrender" to Him is absurd. God doesn't change to "fit" into us.

4. God intends that *your* quickened spirit will take control of your life, that it will direct your soul (your attitudes, desires, ambitions, priorities, etc) and ultimately your whole walk of life.
5. Your battle with sin and sinful desires in your life, like Paul's (Romans 7:14-24), is not a battle between your flesh and the Holy Spirit, but between your flesh and *your* spirit.
6. The work of the Holy Spirit in your life is not to replace your spirit or to substitute for it. His purpose is to be your personal trainer (among other things), bringing you to the place where your spirit (in harmony with and empowered by His presence) is mighty.
7. Your "flesh" (i.e., your soul-driven life) cannot submit to God, no matter how much you "surrender". It is simply impossible for our flesh to become submissive to God (Romans 8:7), and the struggle between spirit and flesh (i.e., *our* spirit and *our* flesh) cannot be pacified (Galatians 5:17). Our "flesh" must be intentionally denied and defeated (crucified) daily (Galatians 5:24).
8. God intends that your life be driven by your spirit (which is intimately in tune with the Holy Spirit), directing your soul in every aspect of life. This is what it means to "walk after the spirit" or to be "spiritually minded" (Romans 8:6). Unfortunately, most of our Bible texts simply (and incorrectly) capitalize every "spirit". God wants us to become spirit-driven people, with our spirit completely in tune with the Holy Spirit and "driving" our life.
9. The more our spirit grows and exercises, the more nourishment it requires to remain strong (Hebrews 5:12-14, 1 Peter 2:2).
10. God is not pleased with an infant spirit in an experienced believer (1 Corinthians 3:1-3).

Prayer Warrior, God cannot send us into battle as children, nor will He put us into situations where he cannot accompany us. He has not come to replace us, but to empower us by growing us up into mighty spirit-men and spirit-women. He wants the fruit of the Spirit (Galatians 5:22-23) to become the fruit of *our* spirit! The Holy Spirit does not have to demonstrate His fruit-bearing connection with God (He *is* God), but **we do.**

Make it your prayer today that the Holy Spirit will continue the work to which He has been sent in making your spirit strong.

MISSION 57

What If Nobody Notices?

If you knew that God had inspired you to compose the most beautiful song ever written, but that nobody would ever sing it, would you write it anyway?

If you knew that God had given you the most powerful sermon ever imagined, but that nobody would ever hear it, would you preach it anyway?

These may sound like hypothetical questions without any real value, but please stay with me.

What is it that gives worth to things (like songs and sermons)? We live in a world that has put a price tag on everything. Consumerism, materialism. But for the believer, surely there is a different answer than the one we get from the world. Is it the song or the sermon or the book, or is it the One for whom we compose or preach or write? As Prayer Warriors, we need to stop and consider the true worth of the *things* we do in the service of God's Kingdom, and that worth should have absolutely nothing to do with recognition or kudos from others around us.

Here is a much more difficult question. If you, as a parent of a young child, learned that your son or daughter had a disability that would very seriously limit their life, how would that affect their value in your eyes? Or what if we knew that our son or daughter would never be famous, or win recognition of any kind? What if that boy or girl were in someone else's family? We are so used to reducing the "things" in life to a value, how well do we do when it comes to valuing people?

Prayer Warrior, sometimes we can get carried away with the whole question of value or worth; sometimes we may have a hugely inflated view of how important we are, or we may have just the opposite view that we are worthless. Both views are wrong, and both may cripple our effectiveness in the spiritual warfare to which we are called.

In Mark 12:41-44 we have a short episode in the life of Jesus. This is the story of the poor widow who put her two small coins into the offering box. Jesus said that those two small coins, worth next to nothing in the world's estimation, had enormous value as far as He was concerned. Our lesson from this is that the value of *things* depends completely on how God sees them. But there is another lesson here; that poor widow was nobody special as far as anyone could tell, and quite possibly there were many among the respectable crowd of church goers that day who thought that she was worth very little. Maybe nothing at all. But again, Jesus picked her out of the crowd as being someone of remarkable value in His sight. Our second lesson here is that God is the only true judge of the value of *people*. True spiritual warriors must have Jesus' eyes and heart not to miss real value in both things and people.

Again in Luke 12:6-7 Jesus picks out the commonplace to give us a lesson in worth (and humility!). God places worth on even the most common little bird, but infinitely more on just one person. God's perception of worth is not obscured by size or public applause.

An unforgettable portrait in self-worth, or the lack of it, is found in the story of the Prodigal son (Luke 15:19). His confession of a broken heart and a broken life was summed up in the sentence that he was practicing to deliver to his father: "Father, I am not worthy..". He knew what money was worth (he had spent lots of it), he knew what "friends" were worth (he had lots of those as long as he had money), he knew what popularity was worth (he enjoyed that as long as he could keep up his lifestyle), but now he knew what it was like to feel worthless. His father, a picture of God in this story, saw through the ragged clothes and downcast spirit a great worth in his son, a value that was undiminished by that son's failures and disappointments.

Prayer Warrior, do we value what we do in service in God's Kingdom according to how much people notice? Do we see our own value in proportion to how much recognition we receive? Do we value other people's contributions, and other people, that way too? If so, then we really need to step aside and take a lesson from our Master. He's the One who came to serve instead of being served (Matthew 20:28).

Now that we've got our vision corrected, let's take another look at ourselves.

What are we holding onto that is worth so much? We would do well to model Paul's attitude:

> *However, I consider my life worth nothing to me; my only aim is to finish the race and complete the task the Lord Jesus has given me—the task of testifying to the good news of God's grace.*
>
> Acts 20:24 NIV

> *What is more, I consider everything a loss because of the surpassing worth of knowing Christ Jesus my Lord, for whose sake I have lost all things. I consider them garbage, that I may gain Christ.*
>
> Philippians 3:8 NIV

In the place of those "worthless" things that we once treasured so highly, we ought to build up those qualities that are valuable in God's sight:

> *Your beauty should not come from outward adornment, such as elaborate hairstyles and the wearing of gold jewellery or fine clothes. Rather, it should be that of your inner self, the unfading beauty of a gentle and quiet spirit, which is of great worth in God's sight.*
>
> 1 Peter 3:3-4 NIV

Prayer Warrior, if today you are having difficulty seeing your true worth before God, please put yourself into the shoes of that Prodigal son for just a moment and now listen to the Father's words to you as you try to explain your worthlessness. He's not listening to your tearful confession because he already saw you coming home and that said it all! Now He wants you to hear what He has to say to you, because while you were practicing your confession, He was putting together the long list of riches that He now wants to put on you. Undeserved? Surely, but that's why it's called grace.

And, Prayer Warrior, if you want to accomplish something worthwhile in this spiritual battle, pay no attention to the world's measuring stick of success or poll ratings; do it for God even if He is the only one watching. He is the only one who can see the real value in what we do and in who we are. Spiritual warfare isn't all about fighting; it is also about discovering the beat of God's heart.

Go ahead; compose that song that only God will hear!

Mission 58

Surrender Theology

Truly I tell you, if anyone says to this mountain, 'Go, throw yourself into the sea,' and does not doubt in their heart but believes that what they say will happen, it will be done for them. Therefore, I tell you, whatever you ask for in prayer, believe that you have received it, and it will be yours.
Mark 11:23-24 NIV

Prayer Warrior, there is probably not another verse in Scripture that is better known or less experienced than this one. Who has seen a mountain literally cast into the sea in answer to prayer? Even when we broaden the conversation to include all those other "whatevers", not including mountains, in Jesus' words, we are still left feeling that our own experience (much of the time) comes far short of the possibilities promised in Jesus' words. Why is that?

Well, that's our starting point, but I want to lead our thoughts in a direction that you may not have considered. This would be a good time to go back and quickly review Mission 56, especially the part that tells us that God expects *our* spirit to become mighty. We understand that this strength is not apart from the work of the Holy Spirit; in fact, it *is* the Holy Spirit who makes us strong, but the point is that it is *we* who must become strong.

Back to the question I asked above; why is it that much of our experience in seeing this kind of supernatural power falls so far short of our expectations?

If you ask that question in many so-called Christian churches today, you might hear the answer "Miracles like that don't happen today", or something amounting to the same dismissal, that we cannot expect God to deliver first-century performance in the twenty-first century. I hope we know that is nothing short of a lie of Satan. People who believe that will have difficulty convincing God (or anyone else) of their salvation.

If you ask around your Prayer Warrior friends, you will hear suggestions like "Not enough faith". We cannot argue with this answer since Jesus Himself pointed out the absolute necessity of faith in Matthew's account of this same conversation (Matthew 17:14-21). But that sort of begs the question "How do I get that kind of faith?".

We will soon hear the suggestion that such miracles require more "surrender" on our part. Surrender to God. Surrender to the Holy Spirit. This is where I want us to look carefully in this Mission.

We certainly do recognize that we must surrender our life to the Lordship of Jesus. Absolutely. Continually. But surrendering is like deciding to do something; until we take the next step of action, nothing happens. Sometimes our "spiritual" sounding language can be allowed to substitute for action. Sometimes we can fool ourselves into thinking that when we have "surrendered", we have done all that needs to be done. More surrender must mean more power! No!! That's the deception!

Satan does not fear our decisions or our surrender; he fears our action. He knows that, if we become strong in our spirits, strong in faith, moved to action strengthened by the Holy Spirit, then he has a lot to worry about.

Back to the mountain. Jesus did not challenge His disciples to have enough faith to believe that *He* could move a mountain; He told them (and us) that *they* (*we*) could move a mountain.

So, how do we make "surrender" the start instead of the finish, since clearly "surrender" alone accomplishes nothing? Like the person who looks into the mirror and sees the truth (revelation), how do we then not simply turn away and forget what we saw (James 1:23)?

First, we must *quickly* follow revelation with commitment. We must engage our mind and will to move us off the starting block. Satan will waste no time in trying to snatch away the vision, dilute the enthusiasm, bring doubts and sow fear (Matthew 13:19). The "living sacrifice" (Romans 12:1) is far more than surrender; "living" suggests ongoing actions beyond the initial point of surrender. "Living" says that *we* have to be the point of power, not simply the point of expecting God to swoop in and do the heavy lifting for us.

Second, we must exercise all the faith that we have if we want to receive more. Like physical development, increased strength comes only from disciplined exercise (Hebrews 5:14) starting from where we are. We cannot wait until we are somehow strong before we start to lift weights. We become strong by starting to lift the weights.

Third, we must be willing to risk taking the first step into the unknown. Imagine how you would have felt if you were the first priest to put your foot into the Jordan (Joshua 3:8). What about being in Peter's shoes when Jesus invited him to walk on water (Matthew 14:29)?

Fourth, we must expect that the Holy Spirit will lead us to the tough work of spending much time in the Scriptures, in praying, in studying, in sharing our faith …… in other words, it's going to take a lot of effort on our part, all of which God will use to sharpen and strengthen us. In this business of growing us up to become strong, God never works in a vacuum; He works with what we have put into His service. Nothing in …. nothing out!

I'm afraid that much of our praying for God's power in us is mistakenly hooked to the surrender theology that says we must surrender to God and wait to be overtaken (or possessed) by the Holy Spirit, who will then do those powerful acts using us as His hosts. I have deliberately used the language here that should start to remind us of the Biblical examples of demon possession (or at least demon empowerment) in New Testament times. Satan had introduced his counterfeit model of spirit control through demon possession (Mark 5:1-13, Matthew 4:24, 8:16, 9:32, 12:22, 15:22, 17:14, Luke 4:33, 4:41, Acts 19:13-16, 8:4-7, 16:18), manifesting itself in supernatural strength, absurd behaviour, inability to speak, blindness, seizures, convulsions, spiritual impurity such as vulgar and morally perverse speech and actions, outbursts of speech and annoying interference with the preaching of the gospel. Nowhere in Scripture are we told to wait on God to be "possessed" or "inhabited" by any spirit, and certainly we are not told to expect the Holy Spirit to have this kind of relationship with us. Paul's teaching and his own experience with the power and giftings of the Holy Spirit are well summed up in 1 Corinthians 14. The coming of the Holy Spirit to indwell us, as powerful and miraculous as it is, is that of the Comforter, Teacher and Enabler, always marked with grace. He has not come to us to replace our spirit or to do the work for us; He has come to empower *us* to do the work.

If we carelessly (and mistakenly) surrender ourselves to be "possessed" (thinking that this is the means by which the Holy Spirit works through us), we are actually leaving ourselves open to Satan's legion of impersonating spirits, those who come to deceive and mislead by claiming that their actions are those of the Holy Spirit. Our only truth test must be the Word of God, and that alone must be the standard by which we judge any spirit or any spiritual work.

Prayer Warrior, we must live in constant surrender to the Lordship of Jesus, but that surrendering must always lead us along the path of discipleship. Surrender is not the end of the path; it is just the beginning. Consider the Israelites as they were about to cross the Jordan (Joshua 3:5); first they were told to consecrate themselves on the day before the crossing. We might consider this to be their dedication, their surrender to the Lordship of God on the eve of their crossing over into the Promised Land. It was important enough that God gave them clear instructions to make sure that it was done. But that was on the east bank of the Jordan, and the next day they were to put their dedication into action by stepping out into the Jordan. If they had been unwilling to take that step, then they would never possess a square inch of God's promises to them, even though God Himself had given them clear title of ownership. Same goes for us. Surrender without feet is meaningless, and God had told them that it was by their feet that they would possess the land (Joshua 1:3). And, although they were often reminded of the need to re-align themselves with God's agenda, they were never told to go back to revisit the east bank of the Jordan to do it all over again.

So, Prayer Warrior, where are we?

We know how important it is to be fully surrendered under the Lordship of Jesus. That's the *beginning*. We also know that it is the *next* steps we take that are the real test of our faith. Possessing the land starts with surrender, moves to commitment and then executes with action. God always works through men and women of strong spirit in action.

Be strong and work on that mountain! Maybe start with an anthill.

Mission 59

How Much Is "All"?

The fundamental basis for all military orders is that they must be clear and unambiguous; they cannot mean one thing to one person and something different to another. The second fundamental principle is that the orders carry the authority of the one who issued them.

Those same fundamental truths must apply to the orders we receive, and under which we operate, as spiritual warriors.

Words are important, especially so if they are the words of God and if they are directed to us. That makes it personal. And sometimes it isn't the biggest words that carry the most weight; sometimes the importance of the word is hidden in its small size.

Consider the tiny word "All", or its twin "Every". We easily understand that those words convey the meaning of some quantity, but exactly how much is "all"? How big is "Every"? And when we see it in Scripture, did God actually intend to use that word and not some other? Could He have meant to use *exactly* that word?

Let's cut right to the chase. One of my favourite Psalms is Psalm 103:

> *Bless the Lord, O my soul; and all that is within me, bless His Holy Name.*
> *Bless the Lord, O my soul, and forget not all His benefits.*
> *Who forgives all your iniquities,*
> *Who heals all your diseases.*
>
> Psalm 103:1-3 NKJV

How much of what is within me? All.
How many of His benefits? All.
How many of my iniquities? All.
How many of our diseases? All.

Prayer Warrior, are you fighting in a battle with the absolute certainty that God intentionally used that little word in every one of those cases? You can be certain that Satan wants you to wonder if it really means ALL, or if there could be some exceptions. You'd better be sure that you're sure.

Here are a few more that we should all remember:

- And God is able to make *all* grace abound toward you, that you, always having *all* sufficiency in *all* things, may have an abundance for *every* good work (2 Corinthians 9:8 NKJV)
- to know the love of Christ which passes knowledge; that you may be filled with *all* the fullness of God (Ephesians 3:19 NKJV)
- strengthened with *all* might, according to His glorious power, for *all* patience and longsuffering with joy (Colossians 1:11 NKJV)
- I can do *all* things through Christ who strengthens me (Philippians 4:13 NKJV)
- For our light and momentary troubles are achieving for us an eternal glory that far outweighs them *all*. (2 Corinthians 4:17 NIV)
- Love the Lord your God with *all* your heart and with *all* your soul and with *all* your strength (Deuteronomy 6:5 NIV)
- Trust in the Lord with *all* your heart and lean not on your own understanding; in *all* your ways submit to him, and he will make your paths straight (Proverbs 3:5-6 NIV)
- And we know that *all* things work together for good to those who love God, to those who are the called according to His purpose (Romans 8:28 NKJV)

So why is it so important to our enemy that he wants to make us miss the importance of those little words?

First, these are God's words, and every one of His words is flawless (Psalm 18:30). We cannot discover more truth by eliminating even one of God's words.

Secondly, Jesus Himself reminded Satan of the importance of every one of God's words (Matthew 4:4). Satan knows beyond any doubt that God's words are life to us.

If we are willing to concede that "all" might not mean exactly "ALL" in some instance, then there is a crack in our faith, and our enemy will use that crack to weaken us in battle. He wants us to begin to think that God might not be completely trustworthy in *every* situation, especially when everything seems to be going wrong. He wants us to begin to doubt that God really has His eyes on us (Psalm 33:18), especially when it's so dark in our circumstances that we cannot see our way ahead. He wants us to consider the possibility that we might not have access to all grace (2 Corinthians 9:8), that we might not actually accomplish all things (Philippians 4:13), that we might finally grow too weary to finish the race (Isaiah 40:31), that God cannot make all things work for our good (Romans 8:28), that Jesus might not really be the One before whom every knee will bow (Isaiah 45:23).

It would be a great exercise for us, as Prayer Warriors, to remind God of our confidence in His words (even the small ones). Speak these verses to Him as an expression of praise. When your night seems long and dark, press into God and allow Him to remind you that He means every word He has spoken, and especially the ones that you need to hear right now.

MISSION 60

Burn The Boats

In 1519, Hernan Cortés arrived from Cuba on the coast of Mexico with 11 boats, 600 men and 16 horses. They had come to conquer the Aztec empire and to seize its legendary treasures. Instead of immediately setting out on the conquest, Cortes kept his men on the beach while inspiring them with predictions of golden cities and glorious conquest. Then he gave the order "Burn the boats". No turning back! Now it was victory or death.

The tactic succeeded, and Cortés became the first man in over 600 years to conquer the peoples of the Yucatan Peninsula.

A thousand years earlier, Alexander the Great landed in Persia where his Greek army was vastly outnumbered by the Persians. Faced with imminent defeat, he ordered that his ships be set afire, destroying any hope of retreat. Inspired by this act, his army went on to victory.

It is exceedingly difficult to defeat an army that has nothing to lose, that knows it has no alternative but victory or death. History has lots of examples where desperation has made up for small numbers. Every soldier in battle comes to a point where he has to weigh the risk of not going home, and in that moment, he may opt for caution or inaction or even retreat in order not to lose that possibility. An army can collapse at times like that. But if that possibility of going home is removed, then the choice is starkly clear; it becomes victory or death.

God has called us into spiritual warfare, but the problem that many professing believers have is that they do not see the spiritual battle raging around them. It's hard to weight the "life or death" consequences when everything around us looks so "normal". It then becomes impossible to see the need for the kind of commitment to this war that demands that we burn our boats. And yet that is exactly the message that Jesus delivered to His disciples when He called them to follow Him (Matthew 8:22, Luke 9:60, 62).

Satan uses comfort and pleasure to keep many from responding to Jesus' call for commitment in the first place, and he knows how to use those same weapons against us when the stakes of spiritual warfare increase. The temptation to leave ourselves a "safety net" will keep us from ever discovering the true power in commitment to God's kingdom. Commitment with an escape hatch is no commitment at all!

The best place to start on the subject of commitment must be with Jesus Himself. He was fully committed to the kingdom of God from the beginning of His ministry (Matthew 5:17, John 4:34, John 6:38), but aside from His words, it was hard for His disciples to see the true depth of His commitment, and without that "sight", it was impossible for them to get a true measure of the commitment that Jesus was expecting from them. Things became clearer, though, as Jesus showed His determination to go to Jerusalem even though He knew that it meant His betrayal and death (Luke 9:51). Finally, in Gethsemane, He passed the last escape hatch when He prayed to the Father that He was willing to drink the cup of judgment (Matthew 26:39, 42). From that point on, there was no escaping the cross. Having willingly taken on Himself the guilt of all men's sin, He could not expect anything from His Father but the just punishment of that guilt: death. He held nothing back, had no "Plan B". Redemption would be won this way or not at all.

Now God certainly does not ask or expect us to repeat the work that Jesus alone could do on the cross. But he does call us to a level of commitment that requires everything we have to give. Mind you, He promises immeasurable blessings to all who will respond to His call, but the measure of blessing will be in line with the measure of commitment, and Jesus made it clear that those who measure out only partial commitment may be fooling themselves into believing that they are in God's kingdom when, in fact, they are not (Matthew 7:21-23).

So where do we need to look to measure our commitment, and what are the signs that our commitment to God's kingdom may not be what it should be?

We don't invest all of our faith. We may ask, seek and knock (Matthew 7:7-8) but we may be reserving some of our expectation "just in case" God does not answer. If we fully commit in our praying, what will someone say of us if God doesn't give us what we ask? If we pray for someone's salvation, or healing, or restoration and God does not grant our pleas as we ask, what will someone think of us, or what will we think of ourselves? Maybe we need to stop thinking of ourselves, our feelings, our pride and just fully let God be God. God is fully responsible for His reputation. Remember, the double-minded man (James 1:8) doesn't just receive half of what he asks; he receives nothing at all!

We don't invest all of our heart. We just don't want God enough; we want Him "some", but then we also want room in our heart for loving other things and ourselves. We lack the passion that sees Him as being everything to us, more than anything or anyone else. Our hearts must yearn for Him (Psalm 42:1) and must feel broken when we allow sin to break our fellowship with Him. We must plead for His company, not so we can ask Him for "stuff", but just to feel His closeness. We must yearn for the conversation of the Holy Spirit and desire, more than anything else, that His purposes would be fulfilled in us.

We don't invest all of our living. Our "works", simply put, amount to all the things that we spend our time, talent and treasure doing. That's our "life". You may argue that you are actually much more than that, that you really do have a place for God in your life, but unfortunately you are deceived (Matthew 7:16). God certainly knows that our lives must include all sorts of needful things (like working, food, clothing, etc.), but our problem is that we too easily partition that part of our life as having nothing to do with God (and vice versa), and then God ends up being relegated to only certain activities (like praying or attending church). The next step is when we begin to trade off "God time" against "our time". We must step back and give it all to God, asking Him to be at the centre of everything in our life and asking Him to toss out or rearrange anything that He sees necessary.

We don't invest our dreams. It's one thing to give God our "today", but how about giving Him your "tomorrows"? We grow up as a "soulish" person, directed by our ambitions, desires, plans and dreams. We make our decisions based on our own priorities. Then along comes God, and now we are a new creation in Christ. The problem is that our old nature (our soul) is used to being in control and desperately refuses to relinquish power to our new-born spirit. For many (most) believers, the spirit never becomes strong enough to take control and so the life is lived pretty much the same way as before the new birth occurred, except for the occasional excursions into God territory at church. For the Prayer Warrior, life must be lived a long way away from that place; but even for a Prayer Warrior it may be hard to surrender that "dream" that has been in front of us all our life. Usually, it is something that we have wanted for ourselves, not necessarily a bad thing, but something reserved just for our pleasure or fulfilment. It might be a family, a home, a degree, a job, a toy, financial freedom, travel, etc., etc. Now, it's time to surrender it to God, or maybe a better way to express it is to invest it with God. It's a hard thing to do, because it might have been the one thing that you held in your heart, a hope, that kept you going through the tough times of life. Maybe something that you could never afford but hoped that someday you might. Your dream. Now God asks you to leave it with Him.

Now here is the tough part. God will always test our commitment, usually through a trial. Why does He do that? Because He sees that now He has someone with whom He can work. And because of His great love for us (Proverbs 3:12, Hebrews 12:6, 10). He sees that we are in line for a prize and He wants it to be a big prize!

So, Prayer Warrior, got any boats that need to be burned?

Mission 61

Face Value

*Face value: the value of a coin,
stamp or paper money, as printed on the coin,
stamp or bill itself by the minting authority*

Some deals are relatively easy to understand on their face but hard to accept.

Sometimes it's because the claimed value is simply absurd and is not meant to be taken seriously, or it is a fraudulent statement made by someone hoping to lure unsuspecting victims. This is the uninvited letter from some poor widow in Nigeria whose deceased husband stole millions of dollars from a dictator and hid it in a Swiss bank account, and now the widow just wants your help (and your bank account number) to get it out and is willing to give most of it to you for your assistance. We're used to seeing these, so we develop a critical attitude toward anything that looks like this.

Sometimes it's because we have seen so many instances of real value but with extremely low probability of actually winning; this is the lottery ticket.

Sometimes it's because we have seen so many great "deals", only to discover that the "deal" was barricaded behind a mountain of fine-print conditions designed so that nobody could ever win the prize. This is a promise that was never meant to be kept.

So, Prayer Warrior, what do you think of this promise:

> *Most assuredly, I say to you, he who believes in Me, the works that I do he will do also; and greater works than these he will do, because I go to My Father. And whatever you ask in My name, that I will do, that the Father may be glorified in the Son. If you ask anything in My name, I will do it.*
> John 14:12-14 NKJV

This is Jesus speaking to His disciples, and it is one of the most astounding promises to be found anywhere in Scripture. The question is, "How are you going to respond to it?" On its face value, it is an amazing "deal", seemingly too good to be true. Could it mean exactly what it seems to say?

Now here is where Satan is attacking us right now. He also heard that promise of Jesus, and he has experienced some of the results that flowed from it; he wants to put it to an end but clearly he cannot get Jesus to withdraw His promise, so he's doing everything he can to shut it down on the receiving end (that's us!).

At the birth of the church in Jerusalem, with the strong confirmation of Jesus' resurrection, His ministry with His disciples for forty days afterward and the tremendous works of the Holy Spirit that came with (and followed) Pentecost, he had a tough job. Believers just *believed*, and the proof of God's miraculous works were so explosive in Jerusalem and the surrounding area, and then out to the Gentile world through those early Apostles and disciples, that it was hard for Satan to get those believers to accept anything other than the simple truth of what Jesus had said.

Things have changed a lot over the past 2000 years, and Satan has worked tirelessly at his same mission: to move believers away from Jesus' promises, to shake and weaken their faith and to put an end to those mighty works that spoke so loudly in affirmation of the gospel of the Kingdom. He has one main weapon: the lie. He is the father of lies (John 8:44), so it is little wonder that he is so good at his trade. It is amazing how well he has succeeded within the ranks of the professing Christian church, to the point where he has enlisted so-called "ministers of the gospel" into proclaiming those very lies as truths. Perhaps maliciously, perhaps unintentionally, these messengers have spread a "gospel" that directly denies the very power of the gospel that was known 2000 years ago, stripping the strength out of the very words of Jesus.

So, here we find ourselves today, confronted by Jesus' familiar words, and the devil's lies have conditioned many of us to respond with the same attitude as when we received that letter from the Nigerian widow, or the Reader's Digest offer, or a lottery ticket.

Lie #1: That promise was intended only for the original Apostles, but that office no longer exists, so the promise has been completely fulfilled. In addition to the original Twelve, there were many other apostles referred to in Scripture. Paul's strong declarations in Ephesians 4:11 and 1 Corinthians 12:28 leave no obvious exclusion clauses. Besides, Jesus' words in John 14 seem not to have been restricted to a certain few, but to all of His disciples, and that seems to be how it was understood and practiced in the early church where mighty works were widespread among all of the believers.

Lie #2: That promise was intended only for those early believers who experienced Pentecost and the few similar events that followed; again, the promise has been completely fulfilled. The work of the Holy Spirit did not end at Pentecost; it was just the beginning! There was no suggestion in either Jesus' words or in the preaching of Paul or Peter that the mighty works were about to end. Even the prophetic words of Joel 2:28-32 contemplated the widespread, mighty works of God, especially nearing the end of the age. The passage in Joel is often quoted as being prophetic of Pentecost, and it is clear from the passage that it was only *beginning* then!

Lie #3: That promise still applies, but first we must meet certain stringent conditions. Before we can expect anything from God, especially miracles that will affect our everyday situations, we first must "pay our dues". That means that God will not get us out of trouble that we got ourselves into. Sounds fair and just; so, exactly which of our troubles have we *not* gotten ourselves into? Seems there's not much room left for God to work. The real question is "How wide is God's redemption?" Does it include just our spiritual rebirth, or does it reach out to our entire life? Has God redeemed our days, including our past, present and future? Our relationships? Our homes? Our physical health? Our finances? Our strength? As soon as we place some things outside the realm of God's redemption, we begin to limit it, and before long there won't be much left. Miracles and mighty power for us will be "off limits". As soon as we are required to "pay our dues", it becomes hard to find the line where "Jesus paid it all". Satan doesn't mind if we believe the truth of Jesus' promise, as long as we just as quickly move ourselves outside its reach through a spirit of false guilt and condemnation.

Lie #4: *That promise applies only to spiritual works and situations and does not include physical works.* It's hard to imagine how any Bible-reading Christian can accept this lie when it is so obvious from all the examples in Scripture that all of those mighty works involved the physical life as well as the spiritual. Spiritualizing away Jesus' words is a favourite lie of the devil, but check out some of the examples in Scripture to see if God really does bring His mighty works to bear on earthly as well as on heavenly situations (Nehemiah 1:10, Isaiah 44:22, Lamentations 3:58, Psalm 40:2, Micah 6:4, Psalm 107:20). Jesus' own words concerning God's kingdom "on earth as it is in heaven" (Matthew 6:10) should give us a clue that He was certainly including the earthly as well as the heavenly realms.

Lie #5: *That promise still applies but is not available to ordinary believers.* Let's remember that Jesus' followers who heard Him speak that promise were certainly "ordinary" people and, in many ways, quite imperfect both in their understanding and conduct. They were mostly just like us. Yet, Jesus expected *them* to clearly understand His words, take them at face value and to act on them. He was not playing games, a sort of spiritual "blind man's bluff", to get their hopes up only to bring down disappointment on them. There were no secret passwords, no secret signs or handshakes, no hidden clauses, no mumble-jumble legalese escape clauses. Jesus intended to be taken seriously, and He fully intended (and still does) to be called upon to deliver on His promise. He spoke the words so they could be taken at face value. Satan wants us to believe that we don't "qualify"; that's a lie, and he's hoping that you keep on believing it.

Lie #6: That promise still applies, but we must gain a much deeper knowledge in order to correctly understand what it truly means. This one is designed to hit us with a spirit of intimidation, to make us feel that we just don't know the *whole* truth in Jesus' words. Like in the Garden of Eden when Satan challenged Eve's knowledge of what God had said (Genesis 3:1). He says that what we really need is a few degrees in Theology before we can know the whole truth, or maybe some special courses or workshops or extraordinary experiences. Now, please don't get me wrong; those tools can be very helpful, but they are not a prerequisite to understanding Jesus' promises; they may help us understand them better, and the Holy Spirit can certainly anoint them as a blessing to us and others, but He will never elevate them to a place where they actually are a barricade against knowing God's truth.

OK, I think we've seen enough; the list of lies could go on, but here's the point. Spiritual warrior, what are you prepared to risk *solely on the face value of Jesus' words*? Have you fallen for even a piece of the lie? I'm sure that we can all see a time in our life when we were a victim of those lies, but now we're here and we have to make a choice.

Here's what I want you to do. Read John 14:12-14 over several times out loud. Then pray for the Holy Spirit to open your spirit and mind to the absolute truth of those words; dare to believe, just for a few moments, that Jesus intends for you to accept them at 100% face value. What possibilities has the Holy Spirit just flashed into your heart? What might He be prepared to do *through you* if you simply accepted those words and began to act on them?

Satan will try his hardest to get you to dismiss those words, trying to get you to fall back upon the lies. Now get tough! **REFUSE** to let go of the truth; tell Satan out loud that you will not quit asking or believing, that you refuse to accept the lies any longer. Tell God reverently but stubbornly, as Jacob did (Genesis 32:26), that you will not leave without the blessing. Remember that we are not wrestling against God for His blessing; He wants us to receive it, but He needs to see that we are prepared to do anything to get it, even if it means wrestling all night.

Mission 62

Night Vision

Seeing what "cannot" be seen; that's a necessary qualification for a soldier fighting against an enemy who can hide in the darkness or shadows. Why? Because what you don't see *can* hurt you! In the case of spiritual warfare, the hidden enemy wants to destroy you, your family, your home, your marriage, your testimony …… just everything about you. Your life. It is that serious!

Spiritual warrior, you **must** be able to see in the dark!

Deep darkness is all around us, but more frightening than that is the realization that, without Jesus, every person is *filled* with darkness, the without-God kind of darkness that is Satanic and evil in its origin and deadly in its intent. Satan wants to drown the world in his darkness, and he wants to flood that darkness into our lives any way that he can. Failing that, he wants us to be blinded to the reality of what's going on in the spiritual war we're immersed in and to simply not see through the darkness. To not see the connection between this spiritual war and our life circumstances. To not see him at work in our family, our jobs, our relationships, our health, our finances, our schools, our governments, our churches. Like the demons in the two men in Matthew 8:28-33, Satan wants us to leave him alone, to not confront him, to look the other way and to go somewhere else, to just go about our business and not get involved. Until it's too late and our homes are destroyed, our children are prisoners of the god of this age, our society has become the willing servant of the enemy of God and the weeds of the love of money and the cares of this world have strangled the life out of the last would-be disciple. Until our patient heavenly Father, the Creator, says it's time to end it all in terrible judgment.

But God's present work is not yet finished, because it is in the very depths of this Satanic darkness that He will perfect His Kingdom, redeem the lost, heal the broken and reveal His mighty, glorious power in us which He demonstrated in the resurrection of His Son from the grave.

We must see through the blackness because, in spite of the growing kingdom of darkness, God has assigned us the task of being His co-workers in extending His kingdom. We are kingdom extenders; God has placed us on the frontier between light and darkness. This is a kingdom of light and redemption, and we are told not to walk in the darkness that surrounds us and fills the lost. We are children of the light (1 Thessalonians 5:4-9) and we are to expose what our enemy is doing under the cover of darkness (Ephesians 5:4). God is not afraid of the darkness, because He has already confronted it (John 1:5).

Now we kick it into high gear! **God is not on the defensive in this spiritual war, and He does not intend that we should be either.** Darkness around us? For sure! But this is the day for which He has prepared us. Perhaps not others, but He has called out our names. He has handed out the supernatural night vision equipment, so we can see what human vision can never see, but even more than that He has given us wisdom to grasp what human understanding cannot comprehend and power to walk where human strength cannot go.

> *What no eye has seen,*
> *What no ear has heard,*
> *And what no human mind has conceived" –*
> *The things God has prepared for those who love Him –*
> *These are the things God has revealed to us by His Spirit.*
> 1 Corinthians 2:9-10 NIV

Did you catch that? Eyes that see through Satan's darkness, ears that hear through Satan's noise, understanding that penetrates Satan's confusion.

Spiritual warrior, those are things to pray for because, like the armor of God, we cannot be effective and mighty without them.

I used to think this passage referred to our heavenly home, and it certainly must be true that heaven is all of those things, but I now think that God intends for us to recognize the present power of these verses. In fact, He makes it clear that this revelation is the present work of the Holy Spirit. Seeing what no human eyes can see, hearing what no human ears can hear, understanding what no human intellect can comprehend ….. that describes the supernatural working of the Holy Spirit in us - powerful, glorious, wonderful, awesome, mighty, effective – just as Paul described it to the Ephesian believers

> *Now to him who is able to do immeasurably more than all we ask or imagine, according to his power that is at work within us*
>
> Ephesians 3:20 NIV

That's what I'm aiming for – "**immeasurably more**", something that far exceeds my asking and my imagination, because I see that's what God intends for me and I won't be satisfied with less.

So, Prayer Warrior, what do you see? The enemy has been telling you to look the other way, to not see, to not confront him. God says to pick up, stand up, rise up, speak up! Let's start with this:

- Seek God's face to let you see through any dark areas in your own life (Psalm 139:24)
- Recognize that God will always use His Word to shed light into the darkness (Psalm 119:105), so dig into the Bible as you pray
- Ask God to show you the connections between your earthly circumstances and the "unseen" spiritual conflict that is affecting them
- Confront the spiritual forces that are the cause of the battles you are facing in your life

- Ask the Holy Spirit to place someone special on your heart, and then ask Him to give you the eyes, ears and mind of God to be able to reveal Jesus and His redemption to that one for exactly their situation
- Ask the Holy Spirit to give you a new conviction and assurance of His power at work in you, and through you to others
- Ask the Holy Spirit to plant an amazing, impossible dream in your spirit, something that only He could accomplish and for which only He could take the credit
- Dare to believe and refuse to give up, just because we have God's Word on it

MISSION 63

Exam Time

Go therefore and make disciples of all the nations, baptizing them in the name of the Father and of the Son and of the Holy Spirit, teaching them to observe all things that I have commanded you; and lo, I am with you always, even to the end of the age.
Matthew 28:19-20 NKJV

I've been a student nearly all of my life, and I have learned that the most important part of being a student is being able to pass the final examinations. As an engineering student, as well as an engineering teacher, I learned that examinations were all about solving problems. If you cannot solve problems, you cannot be an engineer. You must understand the theory, but, in the final count, the only proof of your knowledge is your ability to correctly solve problems.

Throughout my undergraduate years, the business of writing examinations was aided by the fact that the library kept copies of all the previous years' examinations, so it was possible to actually see what one might expect when we sat down on our examination days. The library copies would never tell us what questions were on this year's exams, but by looking through several years of history we could tell what kind of questions we might expect, and it gave us an important heads-up as to what the professors were expecting from us. We could actually practice writing those old exams, and that practice taught us how to solve the kind of problems that we would face and how to do it within the allotted time. You see, the only way to learn how to solve problems is by actually solving problems. No engineering examination ever asked me to explain a theory, and if I didn't really understand the theory I'd be lost for sure, but it always came down to passing the examinations by actually solving the problems.

Spiritual warrior, are you getting ready for your exams? Maybe you thought that your school days were (thankfully!) over. Got news for you; there is an exam coming up for all of us, but the good news is that we already know what the question will be. It's quite clear in the final instructions that we received from Jesus in Matthew 28. The question will be

"Where are your disciples?"

That's it! Not how many spiritual battles we fought or won, not how many powerful prayers we offered, not how many sermons we preached or how many books we wrote. Jesus told us to make disciples and, by reading all the way through the text, we can see that His intention is that our disciples would make more disciples and so on. We cannot baptize or teach someone who is not first a disciple.

I think that we can also see that the point is not to become expert at the *theory* of making disciples, but to become practiced in the real business of *actually discipling others.*

Spiritual warrior, your crop of disciples will not just pop up like mushrooms out of the ground after a rain; disciples are a cultivated crop, one that requires a lot of time and patience. Our spiritual warfare is not about protecting ourselves or our treasures; it must be about rescuing the lost and discipling them so they can reach and disciple others. The warfare to which we are called comes about because those we are trying to reach are locked behind walls of darkness and are chained to death by the very one who opposes us and God's kingdom. Simply put, Satan doesn't want us to make disciples and he really doesn't want us to make disciple-makers.

We need to get seriously to work preparing for that exam, and what we need is a way to measure our progress and someone to whom we can be accountable. We must keep in mind that the business of discipling is a marathon, not a sprint. And it is God's business; kingdom construction is always God's business, and it must be done in His way.

As we arm ourselves for battle today, let's start by praying that God will direct us to someone whom we can disciple. Once God has made it clear to you who that person is, one of the best things you can do is to tell another Prayer Warrior and ask him/her to keep you accountable in your progress.

Let's pray for each other that when we are asked by God to present our disciples to Him, there will be a mighty crowd behind each of us.

Our mission today is to find that disciple!

MISSION 64

Situational Awareness

Situational Awareness is the ability to identify, process, and comprehend the critical elements of information about what is happening to the team with regards to the mission. More simply, it's knowing what is going on around you.

> *I must work the works of Him who sent Me while it is day; the night is coming when no one can work.*
> John 9:4 NKJV

Jesus had Situational Awareness. He completed His mission exactly as planned.

The five foolish virgins didn't have it and were refused entry to the marriage feast (Matthew 25:1-11).

The self-appointed "believers" don't have it and will be refused entry into God's kingdom (Matthew 7:21-23).

Every soldier needs Situational Awareness in order not to be a liability to himself or to others.

Prayer Warrior, do you have Situational Awareness? Do you know what time it is on God's clock? Do you have a sense in your spirit that something big is going on beyond the scope of human vision or understanding? Can you sense the approaching day of which Paul spoke to the Thessalonians (1 Thessalonians 5:4-5)? The Holy Spirit, through Paul, said clearly that the children of the day do have that sense. There is much more going on around us than can be seen with human eyes.

I believe that we are living in a special time, the time near the end of the great open door of the Philadelphian church (Revelation 3:8) and just before the rich, fatally lukewarm Laodicean church (Revelation 3:16-17). What is in the past does not require Situational Awareness, but the present and future do. We need to know where we are and what lies ahead.

What lies ahead is, in some ways, not difficult to describe because the transition from present to future is usually gradual and there are often warning signs of more abrupt changes. I believe that we can expect much more rapid changes and some very abrupt ones. We've seen how the overnight collapse of banks and economic alliances can catch everyone off guard and we can easily imagine that we could awake some morning to a radically different political and economic landscape in which all of our familiar security would no longer exist. But what about the church, the subject of this part of the Revelation?

I believe that we are living at the end of the Philadelphian era, a time in which God has held open a wide door, a time characterized by the resurgence of the key of David where the power of the early church is once again lived out and the authority of the church to wage spiritual warfare for the expansion of God's kingdom has been rekindled. A time marked by a keen awareness in some that the open door is about to close, that the time of harvest is about to become a time of trial and trouble (Revelation 3:10). A time in which we can already see the Laodicean tares coming to bloom among the wheat. Almost a time of two churches; one, like the wise virgins, ready and prepared and in tune with the voice of the groom; the other, like the foolish virgins, going about living their lives for themselves with no regard for their accountability to God or of the shortness of time in which to put things in order.

The Laodicean future is strange; it will be a time of worldwide trouble (Revelation 3:10) but the picture here of the Laodicean church seems to be one in which they considered themselves to be financially secure and therefore "safe" in every way. As if ignoring the situation would make it go away. This is a picture of surpassing idolatry filled with worship of wealth and worship of self. God's prescription of letting go of the wood, hay and straw (1 Corinthians 3:12) in exchange for true wealth, and the recognition of the all-importance of godly righteousness in place of the shameful nakedness of self-righteousness falls on deaf ears. Compromise may win the tolerance of the world, but it draws God's ultimate rejection (Revelation 3:16).

The Laodicean music is already being piped into today's churches, and many professing believers are swept up in its rhythm. Meanwhile, the true church is hearing more clearly than ever the anthem of the Kingdom calling us to commitment, discipleship and spiritual warfare. Our Situational Awareness lets us hear both tunes, recognize the terrible danger and be reminded of our mission.

So, what kind of a church should we be in this special time? Certainly not one engrossed in our self-satisfaction, trying to build a religious empire patterned after the world's model of success and largesse. Maybe we should be building refuges for the lost, the hungry, the broken; places where the power of true Kingdom living could touch the lives of those who need redemption, healing, love and care. A place close to the highway so we can see and welcome the returning Prodigal sons and daughters whom God is bringing home. A place where we could expect to see Jesus walking and ministering every day. A place where we could expect Jesus to return for His true bride.

Prayer Warrior let's include in our praying a sincere plea to God that He would let us see where we are and where we're going. Let's also ask Him to show us the dangers that surround us and our loved ones so that we may direct our spiritual warfare where it will count the most.

Mission 65

Complacency

Definition: A false sense of safety in a situation of grave danger

Perhaps the greatest example of complacency found in the Bible is the account of Noah. For 120 years, Noah sounded the warning of coming judgment (Genesis 6:3) and for about 75 of those years he constructed the ark on dry land, a testimony to his strong commitment. It all fell on deaf ears. More than that, it seems to have had absolutely no effect on the lifestyle of anyone except for Noah and his family. Of this event, Jesus had a chilling summary:

> *For as in the days before the flood, they were eating and drinking, marrying and giving in marriage, until the day that Noah entered the ark, and did not know until the flood came and took them all away ……..*
> Matthew 24:37-39 NKJV

Prayer Warrior, our enemy is trying hard to lull the world into a stupor, a sense that everything is fine and that there is no danger. Believers are not immune to this lie, this Satanic lullaby, and many today are going about life exactly as people were doing right up to the day that God shut the door of the ark. Our spiritual warfare must include tearing down the stupefying strongholds that have been constructed in the minds of unbelievers and believers alike. The same waters that floated the ark drowned absolutely everyone outside; those close to the ark were as doomed as were those many miles away.

What are some of these Satanic strongholds? First, let's understand that a stronghold, as described in 2 Corinthians 10:4, is a thought pattern, mindset or strong conviction that can govern the actions of a person, a family or a community. It is a wall designed to keep out any other way of thinking or believing. Strongholds can keep the gospel of God's kingdom out and can block the minds of everyone within that stronghold from accepting the message of God's light. To those barricaded behind a stronghold, the words of the gospel simply do not penetrate; they bounce off. Hence the absolute necessity of demolishing the strongholds in order that the word of God can enter in and do its work.

A spirit of complacency is a huge stronghold, and within its dungeons are held many of the lost *as well as many professing believers!* The terrible irony is that every one of these prisoners is completely oblivious to his/her true situation or of the awful consequences which are about to fall upon them. Consumed with their own satisfaction and all the cares of life, they have set aside any and all concerns for any message of alarm. They have believed the devil's lies and are set against anything that would interrupt their living life according to their own rules. Lies are the mortar that holds together the bricks of the walls of complacency. Lies make Satan's kingdom work.

So, what are some of these lies? More particularly, what are some of the lies that have fooled so many complacent believers?

There is no reason to be alarmed; there's nothing to fear.
Consider this simple truth: we must all stand before God to give an account of our life (2 Corinthians 5:10, Romans 14:12). For the believer (like Paul who wrote these words), this cannot be an accounting for the price of atonement, because only the death of Jesus could accomplish that. This leaves the BIG question of how we have stewarded our gift of life, and whose kingdom we have built up. If we have built our own kingdom of comfort, pride and idolatry, this is a chilling warning (1 Corinthians 3:12). The glory of God's kingdom is ours to lose! There is good reason to become alarmed.

And beyond our own personal standing before God, there is the matter of Satan's invasion of every aspect of our society including governments, schools, entertainment and public policy. Satan's henchmen have hijacked nearly every part of our society, and we think there is no reason to be alarmed? How will you react to discover that a Satanic, worldwide, anti-Christian cult has dictated how your children are educated TODAY, right in your friendly neighbourhood school? Not in Syria or Iraq, but right here. Nothing to fear, you say? We need to sound the alarm because the kingdom of darkness has already come to our towns and cities. Everything we know and take for granted is about to change, and not for the better. Alarming? You bet!

We've got lots of time.
Let's remember the reason why Jesus told the Noah story given in Matthew 24; it's precisely because there is not lots of time. Time is running out. Our time is running out, and this world's time is running out. Peter warned his readers of the lie of those who scoffed at the idea of an end to this world as we know it (2 Peter 3:3-9). You don't have nearly as much time as you think, and not nearly enough to get ready on the plan you have. Satan is working overtime to use every moment to spread his kingdom of darkness. He knows that his time is running out, so he is doubling his efforts while telling all that there is lots of time.

We've got the bases covered; we've got the church basics ("accept Jesus", baptism, membership, etc).
There is not a single thing in the "church basics" that is sufficient to guarantee a place in God's Kingdom. Absolutely not one. You can wrap up all of your traditional ceremonies, religious rites, faithful practices (good or bad); not one of these things (or all of them together) can guarantee one's salvation. The only acceptable proof of God's saving work in a life is the transformation that has taken place in that life. Not possible by human means, this transformed life is uniquely the work of the Holy Spirit given to every believer at the moment of becoming God's child (2 Corinthians 1:22). Apart from the ongoing testimony of the Holy Spirit within us (Romans 8:16) and the evidence of life-change, any reliance on "church basics" is a foolish deception, another name for a lie.

God is a God of love, so He wouldn't bring us under judgment.
This lie is meant to blur out God's true character behind a big, fuzzy cloud called "love", making every other consideration simply disappear. God is much more than love. The truth is that God loved us so much that He brought His own Son under judgment in our place (2 Corinthians 5:21). God does not hold us above His own integrity; He assures us that He will judge *all* sin, either on Jesus' cross or in the lake of fire in eternal judgment. The real question is whether you have really come into God's salvation. If you're riding on the thin edge of thinking that you can live life by your own rules and that God cannot judge your sin, then you will lose. God's message of love to you is to come to Jesus' cross in true repentance.

You don't have to take Jesus so seriously; no need to become radical.
It's impossible to read Jesus' call to His disciples as being anything short of radical. Leave your family and home. Get used to hardship and rejection. And it wasn't just the Twelve who got this invitation. Little wonder that most of those early listeners opted out of discipleship; it was simply too demanding for what they had in mind. For us, the hard truth is that a low view of this thing called discipleship indicates that we have a low view of Jesus. We cannot redefine Lordship. No Lordship, no Lord. Now that's serious! Your casual view of Jesus' call on your life says that He is simply not your Lord. You see, true discipleship doesn't come in two sizes ("radical" and "regular"); there is only *one* size! Radical? Call it what you will, but Jesus demands to be taken seriously.

God will accept all levels of commitment, and there will be some heavenly reward for everyone, so there's no need to strain for the head of the line.
Our level of commitment is a true reflection of our view of Jesus' Lordship in our life. And, no, Jesus is not giving points for partial commitment, any more than God could be partly pleased with partial surrender to His authority. Paul had no reservations about his salvation, but he realized that his call into God's Kingdom meant more than absolutely everything else, so much so that he was willing to spare no effort to accomplish and claim every prize that had been laid up for him (Philippians 3:13-15).

So, Prayer Warrior, if the fog of complacency is drifting your way, now is the time to act. You know that you have been called to come against the very strongholds of Satan. You have been given a sense of the shortness of time, and of the terrible threat that hangs over ever soul being held in the devil's stronghold of complacency. You have also been given eyes to see through the enemy's lies. Together, we are part of the army of God.

As you start your praying today, ask the Holy Spirit to give you clear vision and a true awareness of the urgency of the day.

Mission 66

Take Cover!

We all know what that means. As a soldier, that command is instantly understood, and I imagine that there is never any discussion on the matter. Of course, it means that an attack from the enemy is imminent, usually in the form of an artillery barrage or bombardment. It is an attack that cannot be met by simply standing in the face of the onslaught. Common sense and good military tactics dictate that the only appropriate response is to find shelter in which you can survive the deadly effects of the barrage.

Spiritual warrior, do you know when to take cover? Or perhaps you think that you must stand exposed in the face of the enemy's attack. Some attacks must be met with face-to-face combat, but others cannot be met that way. The soldier's armor was not designed to withstand that kind of an attack. So, do you know the difference between an attack that must be met face-to-face and one from which you are supposed to take cover? And that raises a couple other questions: what shelters has God prepared for us in which we can take refuge? What does God intend to be accomplished when we are in the refuge?

So let's take a look at a refuge.

Doesn't look like a battlefield, does it?

If we go back a few years, those trees were short shrubs and there were no flowers or other plants. There was also no brook, no birds or other animals living there. But today, the trees are filled with all kinds of birds that nest there. The shrubs and brook provide food, water and shelter and there is lots of room for them to move around freely without danger. They have become familiar with it and now they show up in increasing numbers each Spring. It's a refuge for them.

There's something else in this refuge; those two chairs spent years folded up and unused, stored in the basement, but this year they have a new Summer home. When you sit in those chairs, you can hear only the waterfalls, the birds, and the silence. And if you are quiet in your spirit you can hear God. You can sit there for a few minutes, a few hours or an entire afternoon and come away refreshed and renewed. It's a refuge. David described it this way in Psalm 23

"He restores my soul"

Spiritual warrior, there is a difference between being tired and being weary. When we are tired, we need rest. When we become weary, we need to be restored in our soul; we need a refuge.

Weariness is a common result of prolonged spiritual warfare and attacks from the evil one. We have all seen the sad case of a child of God who has been the victim of Satan's terrible, prolonged attacks; maybe we have been the victim. Our enemy loves to get his victims alone, separated from other believers by a thousand excuses, and to beat them into defeat while blinding them to the need to seek the shelter of the refuge. Like standing shell-shocked in the open in the middle of an artillery barrage, the victim is relentlessly pounded, unable to raise even a prayer other than to ask "why?", or perhaps to fixate on how they should have been able to change the circumstances of their disaster.

God wants us to know when to take cover, and He expects us to take advantage of it.

God Himself is our refuge (Psalm 46:1, 9:9, 59:16, 144:2 and many more). He will protect us if we run into His shelter. The enemy cannot trespass into that refuge. But we must seek His safety, and the more often we do that, the more familiar we find it. Like those birds and animals that now return regularly to my garden, we must learn to come often and quickly into God's refuge.

We are blessed when we take refuge in God's shelter (Ruth 2:12). The purpose of the refuge is more than a hiding place; it is a place where we are restored, strengthened and prepared to resume the battle. It is a place where we wait upon the Lord, where our strength is renewed, where we are enabled to rise up and run again (Isaiah 40:31).

We become more effective in spiritual warfare after spending time in the refuge. Gideon was strengthened after hearing from God (Judges 7:9), God's people were encouraged and strengthened to rebuild a city when they heard Nehemiah's words (Nehemiah 2:18), David found new boldness when he sought God's face (Psalm 138:3), and (my favourite)

> *I pray that out of his glorious riches he may strengthen you with power through his Spirit in your inner being, so that Christ may dwell in your hearts through faith. And I pray that you, being rooted and established in love, may have power, together with all the Lord's holy people, to grasp how wide and long and high and deep is the love of Christ, and to know this love that surpasses knowledge—that you may be filled to the measure of all the fullness of God.*
> Ephesians 3:16-19 NIV

God wants us to lead others to the safety and shelter of the refuge. Battlefield medics give emergency aid to wounded soldiers on the battlefield, but their immediate focus is to remove the patient to the safety of a hospital as quickly as possible where the long and complicated healing process can take place. Sometimes we try to do major surgery under fire and we wonder why the patient is unable to come to the "starting point" of healing; maybe it's because the noise and panic of the enemy's barrage has made it impossible for the patient to hear your words or to respond to your touch under those conditions. Change the conditions.

God's refuge is not a vacation spot. It's not a place of self-indulgence and laziness. Because God Himself becomes our refuge, any place of God's shelter must be marked by His presence. The Holy Spirit must sanctify and fill the refuge, and He is able to do this in many ways. He may open our souls to the beauty of creation, He may stir our spirits to song and praise, He may fold His wings around us as we weep tears of confession. He may be loud or silent. He is always present in human form in other believers who are themselves spiritual warriors who can pray in power for the healing that is God's handiwork. God has built His true church not only as a fighting army but also as a ministering body.

Satan does not want you to seek God's refuge. He wants you to stand in the open when you should be taking cover. He wants to weaken you with his artillery barrage so that he can then defeat you face-to-face. He uses those big circumstances like sickness, loss, family tragedy, failure as his artillery barrage in order to get close enough to us to attack our minds and hearts with temptation, doubt, discouragement and fear. We pray against those circumstances that are being caused or used by our enemy and we strengthen ourselves with God's armor to win the battle in our heart and mind.

> *He who fears the Lord has a secure fortress*
> *And for his children it will be a refuge.*
> Proverbs 14:26 NIV

Mission 67

Intense

Definition: of extreme force, degree, or strength, having or showing strong feelings or opinions, extremely earnest or serious.

Synonyms: extreme, great, acute, fierce, severe, high, passionate, fervent, zealous, vehement, fiery, emotional

Now, where is your spiritual intensity on this scale? Be honest!

POOR	FAIR	GOOD	EXCELLENT

In order to have a meaningful measurement of our spiritual condition, we must first set the standard of measurement, otherwise we'd all come out "Good" (which means nothing!).

Here are some statements that will help us discover what Jesus sets as the standard for our (and everyone's) spiritual "intensity".

> *But Jesus said to him, "No one, having put his hand to the plow, and looking back, is fit for the kingdom of God."*
> Luke 9:62 NKJV

> *Then Jesus said to His disciples, "If anyone desires to come after Me, let him deny himself, and take up his cross, and*

follow Me. For whoever desires to save his life will lose it, but whoever loses his life for My sake will find it.
Matthew 16:24-25 NKJV

No one can serve two masters; for either he will hate the one and love the other, or else he will be loyal to the one and despise the other. You cannot serve God and money.
Matthew 6:24 NKJV

Not everyone who says to Me, "Lord, Lord," shall enter the kingdom of heaven, but he who does the will of My Father in heaven. Many will say to Me in that day, "Lord, Lord, have we not prophesied in Your name, cast out demons in Your name, and done many wonders in Your name?" And then I will declare to them, "I never knew you; depart from Me, you who practice lawlessness!"
Matthew 7:21-23 NKJV

What if God's Intensity Scale is more like this?

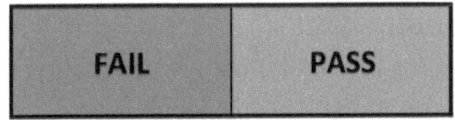

On this scale there is no middle ground, no lukewarm category, no partial credits. On this scale, it's all or nothing. So where did we get the idea that there were so many in-between grades between Pass and Fail?

Satan knows that there are no middle grades. He failed and was judged. He knows that God is completely serious about that. He knows that if we foolishly park ourselves in some middle ground, thinking that we are "good enough with God", that we will fail completely. So, he has sold us the lie that there are many in-between grades that are acceptable to God. He even made up a theology that explained the way that God will deal with "poor performers" by simply giving them lesser rewards in heaven. That way, all one has to do to guarantee a place in heaven (even a small one with less reward) is to "accept Jesus" and then it's a free ride with no demands on our life. We get to have it all here plus we get something "up there". Too bad it's all a lie! All of it. The tragedy is that there are so many "believers" who are actually staking their eternal lives on it.

Here's what the lie sounds like.

- My life is too complicated right now; when things settle down a bit, then I'll focus more of my attention on getting back to God.
- I think that going to church once a week is all that God expects.
- I think that God wants me to put my family first.
- I'm retired now, so that means that I can take all my time for myself.
- God expects me to succeed in my work, so that's all I have time for. He knows that I'm busy.
- I don't think that God expects us to be extreme in our faith; I believe in moderation.
- I'm too young to get concerned with that right now; maybe when I get a bit older.
- I'm too old; that kind of radical stuff is for younger people. Besides, I don't like that music!
- That's OK for you but it's not my personality; God loves me just the way I am, so that's good enough for me.
- That's not how I was raised.
- I believe that I should balance my church life and my out-of-church life; I need both.
- I'm too hurt and disappointed in the church right now, so I need to stay away and get closer to my other (non-believer) friends who support me.

Where do we find in any of Jesus' teachings, or in any of the writings of either the Old or New Testaments, that God will be satisfied with anything short of **radical** discipleship? **Complete** surrender. **Total** commitment. **Intense** praise and worship. **Passionate** service. **Fervent** devotion. **Bold** action. **Extreme** faith. **Fiery** love for Jesus.

Jesus did the most extreme thing that has ever been seen on earth when He allowed Himself to be crucified as a guilty sinner in our place and then arose from the grave. Then, to go even further, the Father gave that same power to us (Ephesians 1:19-20). So, how do you propose to package that into "Mediocre"? And what do you think that God will have to say about it?

Prayer Warrior, it's time to start extreme living for the Kingdom of God. When you hear the devil's crowd telling you to quiet down, you get louder. When they tell you to pull back, you leap ahead. When they call out to you to hold something back, you reach down and give it up for God. When they tell you that you can't expect that much from God, you get on your knees and double your request to the Father in Jesus' Name. When they tell you that God doesn't do that stuff today, you tell them to stand back and just watch what God will do in the Name of His Son. When they tell you that you cannot have that kind of faith and passion burning in your spirit around here, you get up and find a community of believers where that fire is burning in many spirits, because that is where God is.

If we intentionally settle for something less than the full Lordship of Jesus over everything in our life, then we need to see that as a danger sign that we are walking toward failing God's "Intensity Test". Any notion that we have some secret salvation ticket in spite of our lack of discipleship is a false hope, a lie of our enemy. It's a lie that is designed to deliver you to eternal judgment.

Prayer Warrior, it is possible that there will be those who will call themselves "Prayer Warriors" on that day of which Jesus spoke in Matthew 7:21-23. Let's make certain that our efforts as Prayer Warriors spring out of a life that is fully surrendered to the Lordship of Jesus and lived intensely for His glory.

Mission 68

Not Big Enough!

Too big? Too small? Does it really matter? When it comes to faith, it matters a lot!

Let me come straight to the point; it may not be so much that our faith is too small, but that we have not made enough room to put it!

Let's take a look at a little story in 2 Kings.

> *The wife of a man from the company of the prophets cried out to Elisha, "Your servant my husband is dead, and you know that he revered the Lord. But now his creditor is coming to take my two boys as his slaves." Elisha replied to her, "How can I help you? Tell me, what do you have in your house?" "Your servant has nothing there at all," she said, "except a small jar of olive oil." Elisha said, "Go around and ask all your neighbours for empty jars. Don't ask for just a few. Then go inside and shut the door behind you and your sons. Pour oil into all the jars, and as each is filled, put it to one side." She left him and shut the door behind her and her sons. They brought the jars to her and she kept pouring. When all the jars were full, she said to her son, "Bring me another one." But he replied, "There is not a jar left." Then the oil stopped flowing*
> 2 Kings 4:1-6 NIV

Did you miss one of the most important points of this miracle? *The oil stopped flowing when the last vessel was filled.* No wonder that Elisha had told her to "not ask for just a few". Could she have asked for more vessels? Yes. And, if she had asked for more vessels, would she have received more oil from the jar? Yes! Now, as far as we know, she had enough oil, so the point here is not to praise greed. But here is where we can make a very important application to our lives, and here is where bigger is definitely better.

If the jar and oil are a picture of the outpouring and anointing of the Holy Spirit, then what do the empty vessels represent? Surely those are the areas of our life that we are presenting to God for His filling. Now here is the real issue; *when the last vessel is filled up, the oil will stop flowing!* I don't have to tell you what that means; it means that at that point our praying becomes dry and lifeless, our passion for God fades, our joy begins to wither and the holy fire in our heart begins to grow cold. Our vision fades and disappears. Our faith becomes a cold resignation, more just a formality, a recognition of God's existence but not of His real power. Although once filled with the presence and passion of God, the vessel has become just a hollow shell of what it once was.

So, Prayer Warrior, does that describe your life in any way?

Paul tells us plainly that the secret to properly presenting ourselves to God is by becoming "living sacrifices" (Romans 12 :1-2). That's the empty vessel! But what must we do so that the holy oil of the Spirit will not stop flowing? Surely, we must continue to present our empty vessels in the form of our daily sacrifice of ourselves. Stop the sacrifice, stop the flow! No sacrifice, no more anointing. No sacrifice, no more power. No sacrifice, no vision.

So, how big is big enough for God? How full is full enough for God?

And we must realize that God doesn't fill us up just so we can enjoy the experience; no, His filling is for the purpose of equipping us for Kingdom work. This isn't an amusement park where the Holy Spirit is performing for our entertainment; this is spiritual warfare, and the outpouring of God's Spirit is all about guiding, strengthening and encouraging us in that war, and an important part of that warfare is being able to see what God is doing and to hear what He is saying. Vision. Without that, we're just wandering around, really on our own (or our imagined) agenda. That's not Kingdom work, nor is it really God's work.

Prayer Warrior, I'm thinking that we're running out of time on God's calendar. I believe that the Holy Spirit is about to begin a final, mighty outpouring, and I believe that in many places He has already begun to do that very thing. We need to get all the empty vessels we can, and "not ask for just a few"! I believe that He is giving us a big vision, a big heart, a big faith. And I believe that God is challenging us to imagine BIG, to pray BIG, and to believe BIG.

I think that if we have a vision and we can imagine how it might be fulfilled, then that's not the vision that God wants. I think that it's time for a vision of the impossible, something that stretches not just our understanding but pushes beyond the limits of our very imagination! Listen to Paul as he prays

> *For this reason, I kneel before the Father, from whom every family in heaven and on earth derives its name. I pray that out of his glorious riches he may* ***strengthen you with power through his Spirit in your inner being****, so that Christ may dwell in your hearts through faith. And I pray that you, being rooted and established in love, may have power, together with all the Lord's holy people, to grasp how wide and long and high and deep is the love of Christ, and to know this love that surpasses knowledge—**that you may be filled to the measure of all the fullness of God**. Now to him who is able to do immeasurably more than all we ask or imagine, according to his power that is at work within us, to him be glory in the church and in Christ Jesus throughout all generations, for ever and ever! Amen.*
>
> Ephesians 3:14-21 NIV emphasis mine

Immeasurably more than we can ask!

Immeasurably more than we can even imagine!!

The only limiting factor seems to be *us*! All that God will do in us is proportional to the power that is *at work within us*! Surely, the bigger the empty vessel, the greater will be the measure of that power at work within us.

Want a big vision? Get a bigger vessel! Get lots of them!

If it's small, it's too small for God. If it's possible, it's not difficult enough for God. If it's imaginable in our understanding, then it's not grand enough for God! If we think we can do it, then God isn't in it. If we think we have enough resources to accomplish it, then that's not God's plan for us. We need more empty vessels, bigger empty vessels! Someone has to take God at His word, to trust Him to fulfil every promise that He has made to us.

What if *we* are that someone?

Mission 69

Defeating A Strong Man

In the days when battles were fought hand-to-hand, it was common for the opposing armies to bring out their "biggest and best" in order to intimidate the opposition. That's why Goliath was so effective even *before* the fighting started; he was over nine feet tall! It also explains why so much effort went into knocking down that "strong man" in order to turn the tide of the battle. Once the big guy went down, the rest of the army would soon lose heart and retreat.

Satan is a master tactician, and he certainly knows how to play the "strong man" card, usually by trying to dishearten us with his lies and attacks using the spirits of defeat, weakness, fear and false accusation. That is intended to put us on the defensive, to cause us to forget the power that has been given to us (2 Timothy 1:7) and to paralyze us, with our eyes on the problem instead of on the solution. So our enemy knows how to play the bully.

But we must also understand that Satan knows his opposition. That's us. And he knows who are the "strong men" standing to oppose him. That's us, the Prayer Warriors. So, we can expect that he will put special attention on knocking down the "strong men (and women)". So, how does he do that?

The obvious first line of attack is to tempt us into some sin, but that usually has only a temporary effect since the Holy Spirit jealously guards us and immediately brings conviction; that should bring us to confession of our sin and restoration of our fellowship with the Father (1 John 1:9). We certainly cannot treat this lightly, and God never gives us grace as a license for sin, but this is probably not the enemy's most effective weapon to disable the strong man in the long term.

As strange as it may seem, the most effective weapon may be other believers! Now, let's be very clear that other believers are *not* our enemies, but sometimes the real enemy, Satan himself, can use the words and actions of others to knock us down or to at least deflect our attention away from the real battle.

Let me introduce the subject of judgment and judgmentalism. Our immediate reaction to those words is certainly negative, probably for good reason. But let me press on a bit further.

We know that the warfare in which we are engaged is a spiritual warfare, not a physical one, and the real enemies are also in the spiritual realm, not in the physical one (Ephesians 6:10-13). Spiritual warfare comes to *every* believer, although not every believer rises to the challenge to become an effective spiritual warrior. Still, spiritual warfare is not an optional part of Christian faith. So, we are told to become strong in the Lord, to be filled with spiritual power, to recognize who our enemy is and how he works, to make full use of the armor that has been given to us, and to actually engage in the battle first-hand.

Furthermore, we are told a great deal about the enemy we face, the Devil and his demon spirits. This is where we lose a lot of believers; it's starting to sound personal and dangerous. It *is* personal and dangerous! And it is especially difficult because the enemy is so cunning and deceptive. We cannot see him with our physical sight, so must rely on our spiritual senses; that's an area in which we may not have much practice, and so we are at a double disadvantage. We'll talk more about that training later, but for now let's focus on what it means to be able to accurately detect and identify the enemy. It means being able to make accurate decisions based on spiritual observations. It means being able to use the Scriptures to test what we "see". It means being able to seek and find the wisdom of the Holy Spirit. It means being able to correctly "judge" situations for the purpose of determining who the enemy is and what he is trying to do.

To judge a situation means to examine it carefully, to sift, to enquire, to scrutinize, to investigate using all the means available. Scripture tells us that we must become judges (1 Corinthians 2:15, 1 John 4:1) in spiritual matters. We must make judgments. This is not being judgmental; that amounts to fault-finding, and that is certainly not what we are instructed to do.

Now here is where the enemy wants to blind us, to steal away our ability to "see" in the spiritual world, to keep us from detecting the "hidden" truth that would reveal the real enemy and his handiwork. Here is where he tries to knock down the strong man or woman by using the opinions or ideas of others, even other believers.

We hear the enemy quoting (actually misquoting) Scripture into our minds:

1. "Judge not, lest ye be judged" (Matthew 7:1 NKJV)
2. "Or how can you say to your brother, 'Brother, let me remove the speck that is in your eye,' when you yourself do not see the plank that is in your own eye? Hypocrite! First remove the plank from your own eye, and then you will see clearly to remove the speck that is in your brother's eye." (Luke 6:42 NKJV)
3. "He who is without sin among you, let him throw a stone at her first." (John 8:7 NKJV)
4. "For with what judgment you judge, you will be judged; and with the measure you use, it will be measured back to you." (Matthew 7:2 NKJV)

Clearly our first responsibility is to examine our own hearts and motives; better yet, ask God to do that for us (Psalm 139:23-24). Then we are told to reach sound decisions based on correct judgments. Spiritual discernment requires sound judgment. We can see why Satan tries so hard to keep us away from spiritual discernment, and he usually does it by scaring us away from engaging in the process of making sound judgments. It shouldn't surprise us that he will use Scripture to accomplish his goal; he did exactly that when he tempted Jesus in the wilderness.

Now let's understand one very important thing first of all; God has never deputized us to make judicial pronouncements concerning someone else's innocence or guilt before God. We cannot *declare* (to cause it to be so) someone as being either lost or saved before God; only God has that right. We cannot dispense the blessing of salvation or the curse of damnation. But we can make a judgment, based on what we see (both spiritually and physically), as to whether or not someone's conduct (including our own) is consistent with Biblical standards. In fact, we *must* do so if we are to be at all helpful in the ministry of restoration and reconciliation toward that brother or sister. Paul tells us that God has given us that job as part of our responsibilities (2 Corinthians 5:18). We simply cannot do it unless we are willing to make sound judgments.

Satan's use of this line of attack actually involves accusing spirits. In the case of Jesus' temptation, the accuser was Satan himself. In our case, it can be other demonic powers that deliver the messages of accusation whenever we are about to get into the action of making a sound judgment. Of course, the accuser(s) know all about the guilt in our lives, and they are counting on the fact that we, too, have not forgotten our past failures. They will attempt to get us diverted into the comparison game of measuring someone else's failures against ours, until we finally drop the whole exercise or come to some compromise "solution" which may be far from God's standard. *We must counter those accusations by recognizing that they are lies*, based on the completed work of redemption on Jesus' cross (Romans 8). The "truth" of our guilt has been forever expunged by a greater truth, the judicial Word of God on our behalf; that's called justification, and it is all about God's grace.

So, spiritual warrior, have you been the target of the Devil's attempts to knock you down using these accusing spirits? Here's what we must do:

1. Pray for God to reveal anything in our lives that should be brought before Him. Do what He asks you to do. Confess. Restore. Reconcile. Forgive (including yourself).
2. Ask God to give you a discerning spirit that is sensitive to the voice of the Holy Spirit. You cannot reach sound judgments if you do not recognize the voice of God's Spirit.
3. Re-invest your time and love in God's Word. That is the truth against which all judgments must be measured.
4. Ask God to renew your heart's sensitivity to His mercy. In seeking sound judgments, we often become fixated on truth, but *both mercy and truth are needed together* to see God's purposes accomplished (Psalm 85:10, 86:15, 89:14, Proverbs 3:3).
5. Re-read Romans 8 and declare it before your accusers.
6. Get back up on your feet where you belong (Ephesians 6:13).

Mission 70

Flying Blind

How to keep going when you can't see anything outside. It's called instrument flying.

Pilots need special training to be able to fly in clouds, darkness or in any situation where one cannot see the ground. The reason is very simple: it takes only a few seconds to become completely disoriented once you lose sight of the ground. It's called loss of spatial coordination. You literally cannot tell which way is up (or down), and gravity will see to it that you eventually go down. On average, an untrained pilot will lose control of the aircraft within 178 seconds of losing spatial coordination; more than 75% of those cases end in a fatal crash.

The fact is that instrument flying is definitely *not* flying blind; the aircraft instruments are functioning perfectly well, and a trained pilot is able to safely fly the aircraft by relying only on those instruments. The problem is that an untrained person cannot (*or will not*) believe what those instruments are telling him, choosing rather to depend on faulty vision or other senses.

So, what does this have to do with Prayer Warriors? Well, if we are operating as we should, we are completely dependent on God's Word and the reassurance of the Holy Spirit. Our communication channel is prayer. We stay in constant contact with God and He provides guidance. When everything is "normal", we have the feedback of actually sensing God's movement in our lives, plus we have the reassurance from fellow believers who are on the same journey with us. It's like flying along on a sunny day when we have a clear view of the ground, and controlling the aircraft is quite easy. All of the instruments are working perfectly, but we rely mainly on what we can see out the window.

But what happens when something comes along that suddenly blinds our view of the ground? Like flying into a thick cloud. That is when panic usually sets in. And to make things worse, sometimes in these situations we cannot hear God's familiar voice and it seems that our calls to Him are going nowhere. What are we supposed to do then?

First, we must understand this: *an easy faith is of no interest to God.*

I believe that God wants our faith to be a tested faith, so He brings periods into our lives that are designed to toughen us spiritually. Prayer Warriors must become tough, and there is really only one way to get there. It's called trials. God will never abandon us, but there will be times when He will stretch our faith to its limit, because He wants it to become bigger and stronger. There will be times when God puts us into situations that force us to rely on His "instruments", without the usual reassurances from our "sight".

I am convinced that God insists, demands, that we take hold of this thing called faith with both hands, when we feel like it, but especially when we don't. When we hear His voice, but especially when He seems to be silent. He insists that we engage our wills, our stubborn determination to call out to Him simply because He has told us to do so, not just to acknowledge His sovereignty, but because we absolutely refuse to give up seeing His hand at work in us. And to keep on calling even when it seems to be taking a long time for Him to answer. God wants our tested faith (like that of Job 19:25-27), and that doesn't come without a price. Like Paul (2 Corinthians 1:8, 4:7-9), we must arrive at home with the scars and bruises of battle, but unbroken and more assured than ever of God's eternal faithfulness and power on our behalf. No shiny sword or un-dented shield, no unworn armor. No untested faith.

David knew what it was like to endure those silent times when it seemed that God was far away (Psalm 77:1-3). This was not a broken fellowship due to David's sin; it was a test, designed to stretch David's ability to navigate through the clouds until the ground became visible again. David wept but he did not panic. He lost sleep but he didn't lose confidence. Finally, he took control of the situation by determining that he would focus on the great works that he had seen God do on his behalf (Psalm 77:10-11), those miracles that reassured him that God was still able and that He would come through for him again (Psalm 77: 14).

Prayer Warrior, our enemy waits for those testing times to try to confuse and destroy us. He wants us to panic, to quit, to fail, to crash.

- He whispers into our ears the lie that God has deserted us.
- He whispers into our ear the lie that we are condemned sinners and that we don't deserve God's attention, let alone His forgiveness and comfort.
- He tells us that we might as well give up because our calls to God are falling on deaf ears.
- He tells us that our situation is surely hopeless, that we are beyond God's reach and rescue.
- He tells us that our faith is all a delusion, a powerless myth.
- He tries to discourage us by telling us that our efforts are futile, that nobody is paying attention and that we might as well quit now.
- He tries to convince us that reading the Bible is pointless and that prayer isn't going to change anything.
- He tells us that, if there is a God, then He has surely failed us and we cannot trust Him.
- He tells us that this is the end of God's anointing on our life and ministry.

Enough of the Devil's lies! Here is God's truth. Take hold of this with both hands and with all of your heart and mind:

- You are a child of God and you have an eternal citizenship in His Kingdom
- You are not condemned, nor can you ever come under condemnation

- God is eternally faithful, and His Word is true
- We may not always see God in our lives, but He never loses sight of us
- We certainly do not understand all about God, but He has told us all we need to know to be able to trust Him completely
- God Himself is our Provider, our Rescuer, our Defender and our Father
- We are not in bondage to fear and defeat; we have been given power, love and a sound mind
- We are not the conquered ones; we are more than victorious because Jesus is our champion
- We are destined for glory

So, Prayer Warrior, here are some things to keep in mind:

1. Times of testing will certainly come (Hebrews 12:7). God's silence is often a part of that testing. When that happens, our first response must be to ask Him if there is anything in our life that we should confess before Him. When we have done that, we can be assured that His silence is not a broken fellowship due to sin in our life (1 John 1:9).
2. Our enemy is searching for us and he will certainly find us during these periods of testing (1 Peter 5:8). When God is silent, Satan will accuse us and attempt to bring a spirit of condemnation against us, telling us that we are unworthy of God's attention or blessing and that God no longer loves us. Our response must be Romans 8:1, 31-35. We have not been separated from God's love.
3. God's "instruments" are in our hand and He intends that we will use them to stay on course. His Word remains true (Psalm 18:30) and we can depend upon its promises. Prayer is still reliable although we may not "hear" a response; God hears us (Psalm 18:6, 34:15).
4. There is no reason to panic, although the enemy will do everything in his power to drive fear, uncertainty and panic into our hearts and minds. This is a perfect opportunity to pray on the helmet of salvation (Ephesians 6:17) because Satan is attacking our minds.

5. Refuse to be alone. Satan will try to convince you that you are alone in this time. Remember that God often speaks through other believers, so when we cannot seem to hear Him directly, it is often the case that He wants us to learn to discern His voice being spoken through others.

Mission 71

Remove Before Flight

One of the first lessons that every student pilot learns is how to do a proper pre-flight inspection of the aircraft. It's a skill that must be learned and practiced religiously. It's one of those disciplines that is designed to save your life, and possibly someone else's, too. It works like this: at the conclusion of each flight, the aircraft is prepared for the next flight, and the ground crew (or pilot) goes around the aircraft and attaches a red ribbon to every pre-designated inspection point. These are the parts of the aircraft that *must* be in proper working order, the inspection points that must be inspected by the pilot immediately before the next flight. The ribbons are big enough to be easily seen, and it is meant to make it almost impossible to miss any of them. In some cases, the safety ribbons are attached to interlock pins, making it impossible for parts of the aircraft to operate until the pin is removed.

The pre-flight inspection is intended to keep the pilot from becoming careless, inattentive or lazy. Taking things for granted; it worked well last time, so it should work well again, right? Wrong! The whole point of the pre-flight inspection is to develop a new habit that forces one to pay attention and that won't let one take any shortcuts. No exceptions. You always do it the same way, in the same order, every time. Boring? Maybe, but the day will come when you will be very grateful that you learned that habit.

Prayer Warrior, it's too bad that we don't have safety ribbons attached to us. Something to keep us from starting our days without preparation, maybe with something dangerous that we should have taken care of before our next "mission". Maybe something that could cripple our performance or be a danger to someone else.

Some practical examples:

- Leaving for work after an unresolved argument with your spouse,
- Going about your day without reading God's Word or praying,
- Developing a lifestyle that leaves out regular church attendance,
- Getting careless in the areas of stewardship of money,
- Making important decisions when your fellowship with God is cold.

We can add many more examples to the list, but I'm sure we get the picture.

I believe that it's time for us to figure out how to do a better job of preparing ourselves for our life missions. A way to help us be battle-ready before the fighting starts. We know that our enemy is cunning and very observant and will take advantage of every weakness and every crack in our armor. So, here are some red-ribbon items that we need to check before we start another day; any one of these could spell disaster for us and those around us:

- Anger, bitterness – the enemies of God's grace, these will isolate you to a life of darkness and loneliness
- Resentment and unforgiveness – you will strangle yourself, an inmate inside your own prison
- Envy and greed – falling out of love with God, your heart will fill itself with the poison of idolatry
- Pride and arrogance – forcing God to turn away from you, and therefore losing His direction and power for your life
- Prayerlessness – you might as well try to take off with no gas in your tank!
- Lack of time in the Bible – leaving home without a compass, a sure way to soon get lost and a guarantee of a difficult time getting back home

- Cold heart and lack of sacrificial living – unable to receive the life of the Spirit, a quick way to extinguish the fire and passion in your faith
- Unconfessed sin – unable to receive the nourishment of God's fellowship, you will soon grow weak and starve

So, how can we build safeguards into our lives to ensure that we have not overlooked some of these critical items? That's a fair question, and I think that, after a few minutes' consideration, we have begun to realize that the check list has become somewhat longer than it used to be. That's to be expected as we progress in our walk of discipleship and disciple-making. It takes much longer to go through the pre-flight checklist for a Jumbo jet than for an ultralight. It only makes sense! I think it is also obvious that the stakes become much higher when we consider that the safety of many other people is attached to our own care and attentiveness to details.

Prayer Warrior, God is concerned about your spiritual safety as well as that of all those others who are following in your steps. You may not have noticed, but someone is probably imitating your "pre-flight" conduct; they will imitate your shortcuts, and that will probably mean that they will imitate your failures.

Pre-flight inspections can be measured, and that's the objective. Every point is printed and numbered, with a checkbox beside every point. When you are finished, you must have exactly the same number of red ribbons in your hand as there are checkboxes.

Discipleship can be measured, too. There are disciplines that must be learned and practiced (like Bible reading and prayer), and there are ways to help us honestly measure our progress. There are new priorities to which we must commit ourselves (like stewardship of our money, including God's money, and regular church attendance). There are new life goals that must replace the old ones (like becoming involved in building God's kingdom instead of creating our own empire). There are new lifestyles that we must adopt as our new "normal" under the Lordship of Jesus (like servanthood instead of self-gratification).

We need a "checklist" to help us not overlook something important, and to show us what will be expected from us in the next stage of our growth as a disciple. There's always a next stage, right up until we "graduate" into God's presence. I wonder if He's keeping the checklist!

This kind of living works best when we don't try to do it alone. We need help, and sometimes it's that other person whose attention will keep us from mistakes and laziness. It could save our life, or someone else's.

If you are part of a regular prayer group (and you should be), this is a great place in which to put these principles into practice. They all operate through the vehicle of prayer. It's also the best place in which to ask for help in overcoming a particular weakness on your checklist. The group checklist puts everyone on the same team, same rules, same goals. Some may not wish to "sign up", but that cannot be your excuse for not moving ahead.

Start your checklist, pray over it, and ask someone to help keep you accountable. If you tell them where the red ribbons are, they will tell you if any have been overlooked the next time you prepare for a "mission".

Mission 72

Eagle's Wings

who satisfies your desires with good things so that your youth is renewed like the eagle's

Psalm 103:5 NIV

Grey, windy days on the river where I live are often not what I prefer when I look out in the morning. On this particular grey, windy morning I looked up above the river and saw an eagle gliding effortlessly around against the sky. I guess it was a very good day to be an eagle. I thought of Isaiah 40:31.

But some days I don't really feel very eagle-like!

Lord, it seems that the answer I've been praying for hasn't come; I was hoping that it would be here this morning, but I cannot see it. Sometimes I wonder if You really notice my situation, if it really matters to You. It seems that my circumstances have just dropped out of Your attention, or maybe they're just not important enough to You. What will I do if they are too big for You?

Why do you complain, Jacob? Why do you say, Israel, "My way is hidden from the Lord; my cause is disregarded by my God"? Do you not know? Have you not heard? The Lord is the everlasting God, the Creator of the ends of the earth.

Lord, maybe it's just that You are tired of hearing me pray for the same things over and over again. I know they are important to me, but have You become weary of hearing my pleas for help? I don't understand how all this waiting can be good for me. I wish that I could make You understand how I'm feeling right now.

He will not grow tired or weary, and his understanding no one can fathom.

I'd like to be able to say that I feel strong today, but the truth is that I don't. I feel very helpless and weak. I feel worn out. Weary. I can handle physical tiredness, but this feels like I'm weary in my soul. I know that I'm expected to be able to lift others up, but today I hope that no one is counting on me to do that. I see that my enemy is strong, and he has noticed my weakness; I guess it's going to be one of those days. Lord, I need You to give me some of Your strength, just enough to get me through today.

He gives strength to the weary and increases the power of the weak.

I notice that I am no longer a youth, nor do I feel youthful most days. But I also notice that others around me, many of whom are younger than I, are also tired and some of them have stumbled and fallen down. I know what that's like; stumbling and falling down is not reserved just for old men. Lord, surely You are not counting on the strong to perfect Your Kingdom, to do all that must be done; somehow You must have a plan that includes the tired, the weary and the fallen. Don't You?

Even youths grow tired and weary, and young men stumble and fall.

Lord, please help me to lift my eyes to You. Please renew my hope, my assurance, my stubborn conviction in You. Somehow, I must become strong again, but more and more I realize that this strength can come only from You. I am past the point of being able to fool myself into thinking that I can do this on my own. Even if I must wait longer for You to show Your strength on my behalf, I am willing to do that. Lord, You know that I don't like all this waiting.

but those who hope in the Lord will renew their strength.

Lord, how long before I will once again feel strong? Before I will be able to soar above these circumstances and to look down on them from Your perspective? Will I once again be able to feel the blessing of walking, even running, without feeling my own overpowering weakness? I see so many things that need doing; I wish that I could see those things that I should be doing.

> *They will soar on wings like eagles; they will run and not grow weary, they will walk and not be faint.*
> Isaiah 40:27-31 NIV

Prayer Warrior, maybe this is how you feel today; you're not alone.

Our Father raises up eagles, and He knows how to give eagles' wings to His own.

Mission 73

Warriors Through the Ages

Soldiers surely have looked different through the ages, from knights in armor to camoflaged infantry. One thing remains the same, however, and that is that there is a real person inside each uniform. Soldiers' uniforms may have changed a lot, but the people inside have remained remarkably the same.

What about spiritual warriors? We don't wear uniforms, but have spiritual warriors changed through the ages?

Usually, we look at the world through our own eyes; we see things (and people) in relation to ourselves. We grow up constantly re-defining "normal" as being exactly what we are like. When I was a young child, I thought that people the age of my grandparents were really "old". They were in their forties and fifties at the time! Today I consider that to be "young"! I keep bringing my age scale along with me, although I must admit that I no longer know many/any who are 30 years older than I am today. I guess that means that one day soon I will become "old", or at least there are a lot of younger people who think I am!

Let me get back to spiritual warriors. I tend to think of spiritual warriors as being about my age, having similar experiences to my own, and with about the same "time in service". I sometimes lose track of the fact that there are spiritual warriors scattered through every age bracket. In fact, the Bible describes many of them to us. It may be instructive for us to notice that some of these warriors were very much younger than we are, and some were considerably older.

David was barely a teenager when he tackled a bear and a lion barehanded (1 Samuel 17:34), and then he was prepared to take on Goliath the Philistine (1 Samuel 17:36). His young faith in God's power was simply unstoppable by man or beast; uncluttered by all the baggage of life's ups and downs, David was ready and filled with confidence in his God. We should drop some of our baggage and pre-packaged ideas so we could see how much of the "impossible" God can really do!

John Mark was probably a teenager, or at least a very young man, when we first meet him. His mother was among the first believers in Jerusalem after Pentecost, and her home became a common meeting place for the early church (Acts 12:12). Barnabas was his uncle. Peter and many of the other Apostles were frequent house visitors. John Mark became an enthusiastic convert, so much so that he was asked to go along with Paul and Barnabas on their first mission (Acts 12:25), but he soon changed his mind (Acts 13:13) and returned home. Paul considered him to be a quitter, leading to the breakup of the Paul-Barnabas team (Acts 15:37-39). Many years later, this same John Mark, now a seasoned and valuable disciple, was specifically requested by Paul to join him in ministry (2 Timothy 4:11). The point? That young John Mark may have got ahead of God in his call to ministry back there in Jerusalem, but he had the courage and conviction to head out into the unknown with Paul and Barnabas. And he had the grace and humility to get under the mentorship of his uncle and Peter so that one day he *did* fulfill his calling. We need to re-learn the lesson of youthful abandon to a great cause. And enough conviction to not quit trying.

Daniel is introduced to us as a teenager (Daniel 1:6) as he is brought into the court of Nebuchadnezzar of Babylon. There he survived Nebuchadnezzar, his son Belshazzar, and found himself as the most senior administrator under Darius the Mede (Daniel 6:4-4). Now in middle age, Daniel had not weakened his youthful commitment to God. That commitment to faithfully pray got him thrown into the lions' den. Daniel rose to professional success, but he refused to pay for it with secret compromise of his faith. We need to remember what it is like to refuse compromise in a world that is built on "deal-making", even with God.

Nehemiah is another professional administrator, an exiled Jew in the court of Artaxerxes. He was a Prayer Warrior (Nehemiah 1:4-11). His assignment: oversee the rebuilding of Jerusalem. It was a tough and long assignment, but Nehemiah brought all of his skills to the service of the God he served. We need to have the same commitment to bring everything we have into God's service, holding nothing in reserve.

The **Prodigal's father**; we do not have any details in Jesus' parable (Luke 15:11-32), but enough for us to get a glimpse of his heart. Here is a man in whom the years of waiting, praying and hoping had transformed his anger and frustration at his wayward son into a wonderful grace filled with reconciliation and gratitude. A man no longer demanding answers, he had become accustomed to recognizing blessings in small, incomplete measures, and from a distance. We need more men (and women) in whom that persistent hope and confidence in God never fades.

Caleb was 40 years old when the Israelites were delivered out of Egypt; he was one of only two spies who brought back an encouraging report of the Promised Land. He walked through the desert for the next 40 years, crossed the Jordan River into the Promised Land and fought for the next 5 years to take possession of the land. He is now 85 years old when he comes to Joshua and asks for the mountain territory as his portion, for which he is ready to fight the remaining giants living there in fortified cities. His determination and faith are summed up in his words that he felt as young as when he was 40 (Joshua 14:7-12). This is an 85 year old man saying that he didn't feel a day over 40! And he was taking on perhaps the toughest challenge of his life! I don't think he had a retirement plan, but if he did, it didn't include stepping back from front-line service in God's army. We need more spiritual warriors who refuse to stop dreaming big.

So, what does a spiritual warrior look like? Young, old and everywhere in-between. We need *all* of the qualities that God has invested in His army. Let's not make the mistake of thinking that we are the only ones who are just right for the job.

MISSION 74

Just Ask!

> *This is the confidence we have in approaching God: that if we ask anything according to his will, he hears us. And if we know that he hears us—whatever we ask—we know that we have what we asked of him*
>
> 1 John 5:14-15 NIV.

Sometimes we make things too complicated. Like someone asking us what time it is and we tell them how to build a Swiss watch. It becomes more like a maze. Not that we necessarily mean to do it, but that's the way it sometimes turns out. If we could just find the simple way instead of the complicated one.

Take praying, for example. Sometimes we can make our praying sound so complicated that it has the wrong effect on those who may be listening (including ourselves):

- It may discourage beginners from praying because they think that they don't know how to do it "right",
- It may create the impression that we pray that way to attract attention (like the Pharisees did),
- It may create the impression that heavy duty praying must be left to the "pros" (Don't try this at home folks!),
- It may create the impression that "real" prayer requires access to some secret knowledge of God that is in the hands of only a few "anointed" ones,
- It may discourage people from praying out loud with others for fear of being embarrassed,

- It will have an effect on us, as well, when we begin to lose the beauty of the spontaneity of prayer, and the simplicity and power of just talking with God from our heart.

The Apostle John had the closest relationship with Jesus during His ministry and following the Resurrection he spent the remainder of his long life as a servant of God and the church. In some ways he may have lacked the theological complexity of Paul, but I think that his profound understanding of the character of God was unmatched by that of any of his contemporaries. We read his little epistles and we immediately see that he simply *knew* God. And when he talks about praying, it's wonderfully simple:

* If we ask in accordance with His will, He hears us
* If He hears us, we know that we will receive what we ask

It's the same kind of powerful brevity that Jesus used when He told His disciples (including John) to ask, seek and knock (Matthew 7:7-12).

It's the kind of praying that we hear from the lips of a child who is asking God to make Mommy well again. We don't hear a complicated anatomy lesson that sounds like someone is trying to coach God through a complex surgical procedure; no, we hear the "ask", without any frills, probably without many words. I'm sure that God hears it very clearly. How much more powerful could a prayer be?

Prayer Warrior, we know by now that there are many different kinds of prayer and we are called to become effective in all of them. Truly, some are easier than others, and some come to our lips more easily than others. In every case, there is power in brevity, because the heated passion in our souls should evaporate away the extraneous language and words, leaving us with the distilled cry of our hearts. Maybe we should only start praying after we have spent the time in God's oven just to get all the extra "stuff" driven away.

I sat in the surgeon's office with my Dad as we listened to the results of the tests. He had terminal cancer, something that he had never been told even three weeks earlier. The doctor wanted to know what Dad was willing to have him do. The possible answers were simply "yes" or "no", so the conversation was very simple. Not many words were needed. Everything that needed to be said was said and no meaning was lost. More words would not have added anything or changed the message.

Maybe more of our praying should be done after we have filtered out a lot of the words that we are tempted to use; we probably shouldn't start talking until we are ready to start praying.

I'm imagining that John spent long hours in prayer for the close friends to whom he wrote those epistles, as well as for all those friends he knew through the years since he leaned on Jesus' breast at supper. I imagine that those prayers were very concentrated, boiled down, fervent, tear stained.

We're told of an account in David Platt's book *Radical* in which the ground on which believers knelt to pray was literally soaked in tears, so much so that the prayer circle was clearly visible even after the believers rose and left. I don't think there were too many extraneous words there; I think those tears washed away all the extra "stuff".

Prayer Warriors, we have a lot of praying to do, but let's give God the credit for knowing everything we need ahead of time, so let's concentrate on the "ask". And I think it would be helpful to pause once in a while to let God speak back to us, and to allow the Holy Spirit to do His work with our spirit. If our heart "temperature " is too cool, that's the time when He will turn it up to help distill our prayers into offerings to God.

And did you catch the little qualifier in John's prayer instructions?

We must first seek God's will before we can properly frame our prayer, otherwise how do we know that we are asking in accordance with His will? So, probably our prayers should start with the honest request for the Holy Spirit to reveal His will to us.

Now, let's just ask!

MISSION 75

Warrior Watchman

At 7:00 am on Sunday 7 December 1941, two young Army Privates were manning a new piece of equipment in Hawaii near Pearl Harbour. The equipment, called radar, was intended to detect aircraft far beyond sight. As soon as they turned the equipment on, the two operators saw a very large "blip", indicating a formation of aircraft, but they had never seen anything like it before, so they called the control centre for instructions. The officer on duty, with only one day of experience, dismissed the call with the words "Don't worry about it".

What the Privates saw on their radar was a formation of over 180 Japanese bombers, 136 miles from their targets at Pearl Harbour. Fifty-seven minutes later, bombs and torpedoes began to rain down on the American fleet and continued for two hours, leaving 21 ships sunk and 328 aircraft destroyed or damaged along with 2,403 dead and 1,178 injured personnel.

The warning of the radar operators had been dismissed with the comment "Don't worry about it". The consequences of ignoring that warning were terrible.

In Ezekiel 3:16, God set the prophet as a watchman over Israel.

> *Now it came to pass at the end of seven days that the word of the Lord came to me, saying, "Son of man, I have made you a watchman for the house of Israel; therefore hear a word from My mouth, and give them warning from Me: When I say to the wicked, 'You shall surely die,' and you give him no warning, nor speak to warn the wicked from his wicked*

way, to save his life, that same wicked man shall die in his iniquity; but his blood I will require at your hand. Yet, if you warn the wicked, and he does not turn from his wickedness, nor from his wicked way, he shall die in his iniquity; but you have delivered your soul.
Ezekiel 3:16-19 NKJV

Prayer Warriors are sometimes assigned to be sentries, watchmen. It's an important assignment, with critical consequences for everyone.

Agabus was one such watchman (Acts 11:28). His message was to give a warning of a famine that was to sweep through that part of the Roman world; his warning would make it possible for the believers to make preparations for themselves as well as for others in Jerusalem.

I am afraid that we have dismissed the early warnings of the watchmen, and today's watchmen are getting the same response from their audience. The church is looking for a party and wants to hear cheerful news of bigger and better things to come. More comfort. More wealth. More fun. The watchmen's warnings of an approaching storm of trial and trouble are not welcome news.

But the watchman is in a corner; God holds him/her responsible to deliver the warning, and He holds him doubly responsible if he refuses to do it.

Ezekiel had the undeniable vision of God and the word of God spoken to him. But how do today's watchmen receive God's message and their commission to deliver it? It could be like in Ezekiel's case, or it could be quite different. I believe it may have a lot to do with exactly what the message is meant to address. In our case, our whole society is beginning to show the signs of a terrible internal rot. The problem is compounded by the fact that we have become expert at plastering and painting the outside to make it look more and more beautiful. The church has by-and-large bought into the beautiful façade and is, in fact, promoting it.

I believe that today's watchmen have begun to be aware of a growing ache in their spirit, a heaviness, a grief, an oppression. Like hearing thunder rumbling in the distance. Seeing more and more signs that spell together a message of warning and danger that we have not seen before. And a sickening feeling that it may be very late to do anything about it.

That's how Lot felt, but he didn't do anything about it. After all, Sodom was his home, he worked there. His children went to school there and all their family friends were there. What could one expect him to do? Really nothing to worry about.

> ... *righteous Lot, who was oppressed by the filthy conduct of the wicked for that righteous man, dwelling among them, tormented his righteous soul from day to day by seeing and hearing their lawless deeds...*
> 2 Peter 2:7 NKJV

What do you see?

Do you see the schoolteachers and administrators being forced to openly promote homosexual and transgender behaviour in our public schools, even in Middle School years?

Do you see private employers being forced to give time off and to set aside (or create) special facilities for ritual cleansings (i.e. genital washing) in the workplace for anti-Christian religious sects?

Do you see the underpinnings of every one of our social institutions (governments at all levels, entertainment, education, finance) being infiltrated by anti-Christian spokespeople whose agendas are openly against the Christian gospel?

Do you see the results of unbridled greed and consumerism on our financial structure? Have you seen the sure signs of a worldwide economic collapse?

Have you heard the insane and dangerous rhetoric of political leaders around the world?

Have you lost count of the number of atrocities, from beheadings to bombings, being committed every day in the name of a "religion of peace"?

Have you noticed at all that *all* of our Western democracies have become completely removed from their founding Biblical constitutional bases, and have shifted, not to an atheistic position, but to a fundamentalist anti-Christian one?

Have you noticed the crumbling of our social structures (like governments) that were designed to knit people together into an interdependent network for the safety and benefit of everyone, to be replaced by an "every-man-for-himself" mentality that is becoming a threat to everyone?

Can you see just how easily governments could force Christian organizations to hand over their resources for the use of anti-Christian religious groups?

That's enough! We don't need any more examples. If we look, we can surely see them all around us. But what can we do about it?

Maybe first we should look at some of the reasons why most people, like Lot, see what's happening but are not convinced or moved to take any action against it. The status quo is overpowering and paralyzing, and the enemy's message to us is that *we cannot survive without it*. Like plastering and painting the outside of a rotting building, we believe the lie that all this is beautiful, and that it will continue to become more beautiful. The new "gospel" preaches that believers, especially, are in for the best treat of all and that God guarantees it.

Meanwhile, there's nothing to worry about because:

1. All those bad things are happening "out there" in some distant, foreign country, not here at home. Look out; that "foreign country" has come here to stay, and it brought all of its baggage (good and bad) with it.
2. Those Biblical messages about tribulation and troubles are only "spiritual"; they don't affect the "real" world we live in, so, if we

choose not to believe them, then they don't exist. According to that thinking, the "spiritual" and "real" worlds have nothing to do with each other, and so we can simply continue to enjoy the good life.
3. These troubles are unrelated to each other and are only temporary; they will go away or "someone" will fix them.
4. There may be some things wrong with the governments, policies and priorities we have put in place, but there won't be any long-term consequences. Somehow, it will "all work out".

Jesus taught that His Kingdom here on earth operates on the basis of reflecting what is happening in heaven (Matthew 6:10). He even explained that He could only perform His miracles by seeing what the Father was doing in heaven and "imitating" them on earth (John 5:19).

Paul taught that the invisible spiritual warfare being waged around us is intimately connected to the events taking place in our world (Ephesians 6:12). They are, in fact, different parts of the same battle.

Spiritual warrior, we must remind ourselves that we do have an enemy. That enemy isn't content just to make us say bad words or to think bad thoughts; he has a plan for our complete destruction, and the destruction of everything that is God-honouring around us. And he has lots of help, from legions of demons to countless men and women whose hearts and eyes are blinded, making them his willing slaves.

Then it's surely time for us to ask ourselves some hard questions.

1. What does God want His church to look like right now, and how does He want it to act?
2. Where should we pour our resources for the benefit of God's Kingdom?
3. Of all that we are building and doing, how much of it is of any eternal consequence?
4. How can we most effectively confront evil?

5. What would I be willing to sacrifice to prove my commitment to God's call?
6. How much of my "security" today is truly God-based?
7. Are we willing to become God's watchmen today?
8. What should we be praying for in this time?
9. Are we acting as if we were actually running out of time?

Now for the great news.

God would not have given us such powerful weapons if the situation did not demand it. The darkness descending on our world cannot extinguish the true light, but *it will try*. We have the power of the Holy Spirit within us that is more powerful than the power at work in the world, *but it will try to defeat us*. We are told to expect God's amazing strength to be revealed in us, *but the enemy will try to discourage us with his messages of weakness*. We are told to sound the warning to an unsuspecting and unprepared world, *but our enemy keeps saying "Don't worry about it"*.

God has not armed us as His spiritual warriors so that we can protect our idols, our comfort and our selfish materialism. He really isn't interested in preserving our excessive lifestyle. If that's what you are praying for, you can stop now because God isn't listening, nor will He give you what you are asking for.

But if you are praying for a spirit of wisdom, a discerning spirit, to know the times and power to carry the Kingdom of God into the growing storm, then He's listening. If you are praying for a way to make the all-powerful gospel a reality in the lives of real people in real trouble, then the answer is on the way. God's Kingdom is looking for the darkness in order to show what the Light of the world looks like.

Mission 76

Big, Expensive, Irrelevant

In 1929, France began construction of an amazing series of complex underground fortifications along its border with Germany. It became known as the Maginot Line, and it was intended to act as a barrier against an expected invasion from Germany. It extended over 500 miles and included 22 large fortress complexes, 36 smaller complexes and many supporting fortifications, observation and firing posts. Each fortress was completely self-contained with provisions for more than 1000 soldiers for more than a month. At a time when many of the surrounding towns did not have electric power services of any kind, each fortress was entirely electrically powered, including air conditioning, recreation areas, kitchens, dining areas, barracks, hospitals, supply rooms, electrical generators, telephone communication centres, plumbing and 270 miles of underground electric railway connecting many of the fortresses and surrounding placements. Many included a wine cellar and walk-in freezers for food storage.

The Maginot Line was so impressive that Germany decided *not* to attack it, having already adopted an entirely different form of warfare tactics based on mobile armor and air power. They went around and over it! France surrendered in a few weeks and the troops surrendered the Maginot Line fortifications, most without having heard a shot.

The failure of the Maginot Line was not that it was poorly designed or badly built; its failure was that the thinking behind it was flawed. It was built to fight a war the same way that WW 1 had been fought, using trenches and big guns; the fortresses were simply a bigger version of the trenches. It was built to make up for greatly reduced manpower, lack of morale and failing commitment on the part of the country as a whole. The reality was that warfare had dramatically changed at the end of WW1, and the French generals had failed to see the new reality. The Maginot Line was not small, cheap or weak; it was big, expensive and irrelevant.

Wars are not won by building strong defences; they are won by concentrating on taking the offensive against the enemy. A nation that is building up a strong fighting force is not planning on defending itself; it is planning to attack. A nation that is building fortresses is not planning on going anywhere.

So what does this have to do with spiritual warriors and spiritual warfare today?

Well, as we take a look around us at the state of much of the professing church today, we can see some alarming similarities to the fortress mentality of 1929.

- In many parts of our world, the church organization has been more intent on building fortresses and bunkers (we have another name for them) than on recruiting a strong army of committed volunteers,
- We see a commitment of huge amounts of money and effort going into making these fortresses as comfortable as possible for those who are already inside, with absolutely no provision for the many who are outside,
- We see a mindset that rejects the idea of going on the offensive against the kingdom of darkness, choosing rather to wait for the darkness to come knocking on their door,
- We see in many places a lack of serious commitment (called discipleship) to God's Kingdom and His work, being far more interested in their own personal success and comfort,
- We see an almost intentional refusal to listen to the message of a coming time of Satanic struggle and attack directed against God's people and His Kingdom values,

- We see a false sense of security among many believers who think that God simply will not allow His people to undergo trials and hardships,
- We see no concerted plan for what the church should look like in the end times, and instead a stubborn insistence on trying to reconstruct the church of the last century,
- We find it hard to detect a movement in many parts to see the church in this age as a refuge in which great numbers of the lost and broken of this world can find the security, hope and healing of the Gospel, with a redemption message that touches every part of life,
- We see that, at least in our part of the Western church, so much of what is being built in the name of God's Kingdom is entirely dependent upon the financial and social support structures of this world, with no thought of what it should look like (or how it will function) when these supports are suddenly taken away.

If our understanding of what we see around us is true, we may be forced to the conclusion that most of what the church counts as accomplishments may be simply *irrelevant*. Our enemy, the Devil, may have simply contained the church and most of its resources inside its own fortresses, leaving the world an uncontested battleground. Rather than attacking the fortresses, he is simply going around them while those inside are living in a "dream world" and completely unaware of reality outside.

Sobering? Yes, indeed!

Hopeless? Absolutely not!!

I am convinced that God's promise (Matthew 16:18) of the church that can prevail over all of the Devil's attacks is given for exactly a time such as this day in which we are living. But I am convinced that it will not be the church in a bunker or a fortress, striving for its own comfort. Rather, it will be the church that is willing to abandon its own interests in favour of a wholehearted commitment to God's Kingdom (Matthew 6:33), willing to make good on its words that Jesus must increase even as it decreases (John

3:30), ready to trade in the decorations of this world for the honours that God will bestow in His Kingdom (Philippians 3:8).

It will be the church that has finally "sold out" to Jesus and has put all of its trust in His Gospel, abandoned all of its claim to ease and luxury in this world, and has laid hold of the real power of Jesus' resurrection (Romans 8:11, Ephesians 1:17-20).

It will be the church that preaches, heals, redeems, comforts, rescues, sacrifices and stands.

It will be the church that listens for and hears the voice of the Holy Spirit, that puts on and uses the whole armor of God, that insists on being true light and true salt in a dark and decaying world, and that refuses to run away from the darkness of this age.

It will be many things, but *it will not be irrelevant!*

Mission 77

This Is Not Home

There are many accounts of soldiers fighting far away from home who, after the war is over, decide to marry, raise families and live the remainder of their lives in their "new" country.

Sgt John Robertson, part of a US Special Forces Green Beret operation over Laos in 1968, was shot down, wounded and captured. He spent a year being tortured in a North Vietnamese prison and was finally released when it appeared that his head injuries were so severe that he would not survive. He was presumed dead, until 44 years later when he was spotted as a result of rumours that an American was living in a remote village in the highlands of Vietnam. By that time, he had forgotten his children's names, his own birth date and how to speak English. He had adopted a Vietnamese identity, had married and had raised a family in Vietnam. He had, for all intents and purposes, become Vietnamese and Vietnam was his home.

This may be an extreme example, but it does illustrate the point that, for a variety of reasons, soldiers can forget (or set aside) who they are and adopt the country to which they went with the intention of returning home when their service was done.

So, what does this have to do with spiritual warriors? Just this; there is a powerful force at work to win our attention and affection, pulling us into a love affair with this world in which we are supposed to be only pilgrims. Quite plainly, this is not our home; we are only passing through.

When we develop a case of mistaken identity concerning our "home", several things begin to happen that weaken, and ultimately disable, our effectiveness as spiritual warriors in God's Kingdom:

- Paul describes the entanglement that takes place when we become enchanted by the world and its attractions (2 Timothy 2:4). An entanglement is anything that impedes or interferes with our free movement, and we are ordered to not let that happen. More than our time becomes divided; our loyalties and priorities go up for grabs. So, at what point do we begin to think that it is our right to choose the priorities for the use of time or resources? And when did we start thinking that the time and resources were actually *ours*? What happened to Lordship?
- Then we actually begin to expect that God's plan for us is to make us comfortable and successful here in this world. We use prayer as a means of trying to enlist God's power to fill our private shopping list, all designed to build our little kingdom here on earth. We equate materialism with God's blessing and approval upon our lives. The word for that is "idolatry", and God hates it.
- Our minds and hearts will follow our treasure (Matthew 6:21), and when we remember that it is our hearts that God wants more than anything else, we can see the real danger in this "mistaken identity". Falling in love with the world and the things in the world will quench the love of God in our hearts (1 John 2:15); we may live under the false impression that we are still in fellowship with God, but the truth is that the fire has gone out. That's deadly serious. As in any love affair, the one being loved fills the thoughts of the lover; so, it is with the love of the things of the world, and we are told not to be preoccupied with them (Colossians 3:2).
- It becomes impossible to have the mindset that God says is the evidence of true faith (Hebrews 11:13,14). A pilgrim attitude, nothing less, but you cannot have it as long as you see this world as your home. Fooling yourself into believing that you can have all of this world now *plus* all of God's Kingdom later is simply believing the Devil's lie.

- It also becomes impossible to be a disciple of Jesus Christ, because the priorities of the world have become your master (Matthew 6:24).
- You will not yearn for the return of Jesus, a part of the Christian faith that has always been an earmark of the true believer. Lacking that heart cry, you will not be prepared for His coming; Jesus' parable of the foolish virgins (Matthew 25:1-11) is a terrible reminder of this truth.

So where does this pressure come from that wants to root us in this world? Ultimately it must be the product of our sinful nature, but behind that is a Devilish intent to disable and entangle every Kingdom warrior, reducing him/her to uselessness in Kingdom warfare.

In Greek mythology, the Sirens were dangerous creatures, usually depicted as beautiful, naked women, who lured nearby sailors with their enchanting music and voices to shipwreck on the rocky coast of their island. Forget about mythology; the Devil is real, his enchanting music is powerful, we are his intended victims, and the consequences are fatal.

An urgent part of our praying for ourselves and others must be that God would awaken us to true discipleship, give us a pilgrim attitude and lead us to a deeper experience of the Lordship of Jesus in our lives.

Mission 78

Wounded!

Wars produce casualties, lots of them. And besides the deaths, there are many more wounded; it is these wounded ones who most often must continue to pay the price of war long after the battle has ended.

During WW2, the percentage of wounded soldiers, compared to the total who served, for several countries is listed below:

British Empire	2.7%
United States	4.1%
Soviet Union	43.3%
Germany	33.2%
Japan	11.3%

During the 20-year American Vietnam War there were about 60,000 killed and over twice as many wounded.

Since 1917, every American soldier wounded in battle has been awarded the Purple Heart in the name of the President of the United States; there have been an estimated 1.8 million Purple Hearts awarded.

As tragic as the death count is, it is often the heart-wrenching sight and stories of those wounded "survivors" that haunt us.

A story is told about a soldier who was finally coming home after having fought in Vietnam. He called his parents from San Francisco. "Mom and

Dad, I'm coming home, but I've a favour to ask. I have a friend I'd like to bring home with me. "Sure," they replied, "we'd love to meet him."

"There's something you should know," the son continued, "he was hurt pretty badly in the fighting. He stepped on a land mind and lost an arm and a leg. He has nowhere else to go, and I want him to come live with us."

"I'm sorry to hear that, son. Maybe we can help him find somewhere to live."

"No, Mom and Dad, I want him to live with us."

"Son," said the father, "you don't know what you're asking. Someone with such a handicap would be a terrible burden on us. We have our own lives to live, and we can't let something like this interfere with our lives. I think you should just come home and forget about this guy. He'll find a way to live on his own."

At that point, the son hung up the phone. The parents heard nothing more from him. A few days later, however, they received a call from the San Francisco police. Their son had died after falling from a building, they were told. The police believed it was suicide.

The grief-stricken parents flew to San Francisco and were taken to the city morgue to identify the body of their son. They recognized him, but to their horror they also discovered something they didn't know; their son had only one arm and one leg.

Spiritual warfare produces casualties, too. Wounded ones who are somehow scarred from the battles to which every true believer is called. Why would we expect such a terrible war not to produce some, or even many, wounded?

We can easily recognize someone with a physical injury, and many times we can detect the victims of other forms of battle injury, but how do we recognize someone who has been wounded in a spiritual battle? And then, having recognized them, what are we prepared to do about them? And what if we are one of those wounded ones?

Of course, many churchgoers simply refuse to believe that spiritual warfare is real, so for them the problem just doesn't exist! Just a bunch of extremist "hocus-pocus", not allowed in our church! But I am convinced that most true believers know better. We may not understand it but we know it exists, and we may have our own experiences that convince us of the reality of the wounds. Wounds like discouragement, disillusionment, bitterness, doubt, resignation, fear. The list goes on.

Firstly, let's understand clearly what we're talking about. Things like discouragement and fear are common to everyone, whether or not they are a believer and whether or not they are Prayer Warriors. Unbelievers cannot be spiritual warriors and many believers refuse to take it seriously, but the truth is that every true believer is immediately thrust into spiritual warfare the moment he/she becomes a believer. Those who do not take the battle seriously are likely to very soon become casualties, but even seasoned warriors are not immune from injury. The wounds that we are talking about are those received as a result of taking this spiritual warfare seriously, contending and even struggling against the powers of darkness that are set against us and our families, our churches, our governments and ultimately against everything that speaks of God's kingdom and His kingdom values.

Secondly, let's remember who our enemy is. He is the Devil himself. Lucifer. Satan. He is first and foremost God's enemy, and his interest in believers arises only because we have become God's redeemed possession and the object of His special affection. Satan wants to disable us so that we will be useless in the work of extending God's Kingdom. That's his objective, plain and simple. To make us completely ineffective as Kingdom workers. And, as in physical warfare, a wounded soldier actually takes three soldiers out of the battle; the wounded one plus two more to remove and care for him. The devil's first weapon against us, and the one that works most easily, is to get us snared in sin. We have all been there, but the spiritual warrior knows the chain-breaking power of Jesus' blood when we confess that sin, so then the enemy has to resort to a different tactic, one that will wound and weaken us to the point where we are no longer effective. Wounds like the ones listed above. We all need to take the list seriously, because none of us is immune from injury and all of us know someone who has already suffered one or more of these injuries.

Thirdly, let's be reminded that God is not an outside observer in this spiritual warfare. He is our Commander-in-Chief, and He is also our Medic. He is in the battle with us, and His heart is wounded when we are injured. He loves us and His desire continues to be for our good, as much when we are wounded as when we are whole.

So, let's look at some of these wounds.

Discouragement is losing heart. It comes when the battle is so long that it looks like it cannot end, or that our best efforts seem to be futile. We pray and the answer seems to flee from us. We plead for the healing of a loved one, but healing does not come. We ask for God's deliverance from a situation, but the situation just keeps getting worse. At some point we just wish that we could be on the winning side of the battle but instead it looks like we are losing. **Hope is the antidote for discouragement**, so the Devil wants us to give up hope. He knows that if we would only lift up our spirit to see the hope that God is holding out to us, he would instantly lose his grip on our thinking and then on our life. God's Word alone has His message of hope for us. David was often discouraged, and the Psalms are full of his testimony to the power of God to restore the discouraged warrior. But the Psalms are not reserved only for the wounded; they guarantee a renewed strength even for the strong.

Disillusionment is losing purpose. The cause that once resonated in our heart isn't there anymore. We've begun to think that the cause was a mistake, that the battle doesn't matter and that probably nobody cares. The victory that once seemed so certain, and the mighty army that once sounded so close, now seem far away and we start to think that we might have been wrong about the whole thing in the first place. The vision fades and then vanishes. The Devil loves that! **Purpose is the antidote for disillusionment**, and God wants us to be reminded that He has an eternal purpose; we are part of that purpose, and our battles are also part of that purpose. He has not changed, and His purpose is not in any danger of failing. The victory is assured because the Almighty One has guaranteed it. Our part in the warfare we're in has not gone unnoticed by God, and our part is important in His plan.

Bitterness comes with laying blame. Someone failed you, let you down. Someone is responsible. Someone cannot be trusted, so you're done trusting. Ultimately you conclude that God is to blame; He could have stepped in, but He didn't. The awful truth is that bitterness only grows on the tree of pride, and pride always precedes destruction (Proverbs 16:18). Bitterness always keeps company with anger, troublemaking, confusion, filthy language and hatred (Ephesians 4:31). Bitterness is sin. Bitterness is to the spirit what gangrene is to the body; it is deadly poison that will consume you. Bitterness is an earmark of Satan himself, and he wants to brand you with that same mark. **Forgiveness is the cure for bitterness.** Forgive God for the heartaches that you have charged to His account, and then come quickly to true repentance for your sin of bitterness, realizing that the gangrene spreads rapidly, and quickly deafens us to God's pleas for our rescue.

Doubt is failing faith. There are many causes for doubt, and we've all been there at one time or another. Doubt is not a sin. Doubt means losing confidence in something we once believed. But here's where the enemy trips many of us up; our faith is in our faith. That is a formula for failure. Faith is useless in itself; the strength of faith must lie in the One who stands behind that faith. Just as a contract is a worthless document apart from the strength of the signatory who guarantees it, so faith is worthless apart from the One who stands behind it. Faith will fail, but God will not. Faith in faith is useless, but faith in the living God is all-powerful. The Devil wants you to have faith as some form of "positive thinking", "uplifting energy", or some other New Age foolishness, but the only faith that is worth having is the one that is rooted in God Himself. **God-grounded faith is the antidote to doubt.** Doubt is a faith killer, but God's kind of faith is a devil destroyer.

Resignation is giving up. Surrender; unwilling, but surrender, nonetheless. Resignation sets in when we have stared at the problem so long that we don't expect it to ever change. That's exactly where the Devil wants us to keep our eyes, fixated on the problem and unable to see anything else. **Vision is the antidote for resignation**, but this kind of eye-opening can come only from God. Like for Elisha's servant (2 Kings 6:17).

Fear is the panic, the paralysis that grips us when we lose sight of God. Fear prevents us from thinking clearly, seeing completely or acting wisely. It's the sudden awareness that we must be alone, beyond help and in great danger. It is irrational, meaning that it is not the result of a calculated assessment of a circumstance and all of the possible solutions, and it is one of the enemy's favourite weapons. Fear turned Elijah from being the mighty instrument of God's judgment (1 Kings 18) into a fugitive from Jezebel's threats (1 Kings 19:2-3). **Hearing God's clear voice is the antidote for fear**, and nowhere is His voice more clearly heard than in the words of Scripture. Portions like 2 Timothy 1:7 and Romans 8:15. Stop reading Scripture, lots of it, every day and fear will stalk you like a wolf; that's exactly where the Devil wants you.

So, what are we going to do about these wounds, our own and those of others?

First, we must realize that God wants us to be healed from these injuries, even if that means that we may walk with a limp for the rest of our life here. He does not want us to use these scars as excuses for opting out of the battle, but He knows that we cannot be effective in battle while in a wounded state. We must seek help from a trusted Godly friend who can pray with us, counsel us and walk with us for a while. Maybe we are the one who must pray, counsel and walk with someone else.

Secondly, we need to remember that being wounded is not a sin but refusing to acknowledge the injury or refusing to be healed will lead us on a dangerous path in the direction of sin.

Thirdly, we must pray that God will show us how our wounds can reveal His great love for us. Wounds may come in the form of trials which God is using to shape us more and more into the likeness of Jesus.

Finally, do not lose sight of these truths: God is there with you, God cares for you, God has a failsafe plan for you, God is shaping you through trials, God has given you His forgiveness and His acceptance, and God has deposited immense peace and hope into your account for times like this.

Mission 79

Communicating Clearly

The Charge of the Light Brigade was a charge on October 25, 1864 by British Cavalry, led by Lord Cardigan, in the Battle of Balaklava during the Crimean War. The charge resulted from a miscommunication in the chain of command from the commander of British forces, Lord Raglan, all the way down to Lord Cardigan. Lord Raglan could see two batteries giving fire to his troops and ordered an immediate charge. He dispatched these orders to Brigadier Airey who drafted the order and proceeded to give it to Captain Nolan who in turn gave it to General George Bingham, commander of British cavalry. When the order reached Bingham, it was so vague that he had no idea what battery he was actually ordered to attack. Bingham asked Nolan what battery he was to attack but Nolan had no idea as well and pointed to a set of batteries as the designated ones. The ones he pointed out, however, had only one battery, not two as Lord Raglan had assessed. The Light Brigade proceeded to charge this battery, led by Lord Cardigan, through a valley of concentrated fire from a combination of skirmishers, Cossacks, and the batteries themselves. What occurred was immortalized in history in the famous poem by Alfred Lord Tennyson. The assault ended with 110 killed and 161 wounded for the British with effectively no casualties for the Russians and continued fire from the designated battery. Russian commanders were so dumbfounded at such a reckless tactic that they actually believed the British to be drunk during the charge!

Sadly, this isn't the first, or last, example of communication blunders with terrible consequences.

In 1788 a battle was fought in which one of the two sides didn't even show up. The Battle of Karansebes involved the Austrian army which, after a series of blunders including a detachment getting drunk, accidentally firing a shot to keep some of their comrades away from the liquor and shouting commands in a language that was not understood, resulted in a general retreat by the entire Austrian army with a self-inflicted loss of 10,000 men.

In June 1942 the Japanese lost the pivotal Battle of Midway due, in part, to the radio failure in one of its spotter aircraft sent out to locate the American fleet. The Japanese lost all four of their front-line aircraft carriers, the battle, and ultimately the war.

In September 1944 the British army advancing toward Germany in Operation Market Garden was defeated at Arnhem because not one of the radios carried by the advancing British force worked. As a result, the British advance couldn't be supported and was ultimately defeated.

It seems that the matter of clear communication is not just a modern concern; Paul gives a clear example, complete with military application, in 1 Corinthians 14:8 where he says

> *For if the trumpet makes an uncertain sound, who will prepare for battle?*
>
> 1 Corinthians 14:8 NKJV

In that passage, Paul is teaching not only about the importance of communication but about the *purpose* of communication; in this instance, he was dealing with the confusion surrounding the improper use of spiritual gifts, particularly speaking in tongues.

In the general context of communicating with God (both "transmitting" to God and "receiving" messages from Him), most believers think that it just "happens"; we talk and God hears, or God speaks and we hear. In that case, most believers would be wrong! There is far too much at stake to think that our enemy has not made great effort to prevent and distort that communication link, or to imagine that we have not been affected by his efforts.

Here are some basic aspects of clear communication that apply directly to our communication with God, and in particular the matter of receiving communications from God.

Who sent the message? The identity of the sender is critically important. Of course, in our communications with God, we naturally assume that messages we receive have come from God. That is a dangerous mistake! Satan is an expert at sending us messages, which he wants us to believe have come from God, through *impersonation* (loss of true identity), even appearing to us as an "angel of light" (2 Corinthians 11:14) and *distortion* (loss of true perspective). More than 90% of the thoughts that go through our minds (even while praying) are self-talk, and that includes what we think must be God talking to us. Surprisingly, God's voice sounds a lot like ours!

Is there interference? Intentional interference is called jamming, and the simplest way to accomplish this is by increasing the noise level that will eventually "drown out" the message. Eventually, *any* communication can be defeated by noise. Noise could be the thorns and weeds described in Jesus' parable (Matthew 13:22). The sheer busy-ness of our lives, plus the mistaken belief that our work is so important that it deserves all of our time and attention at the expense of everything else, is enough noise to drown out most messages. Preoccupation with the things of this world, self-interests and the love of riches are deadly noises that will destroy communication with God.

Intelligent jamming is even more difficult to detect, and it is therefore much more dangerous. Imagine that you were entering a traffic police radar going 100 km/h where the speed limit is 80 km/h. Imagine that you have a "smart" jamming device in your car which picks up the police radar and generates a new return signal (to the police receiver) which has been designed to carry the information that you are going 80 km/h. The police cannot tell that you are actually speeding because they believe the false message, but they have no way of knowing that they have been "jammed". That's called "intelligent jamming". The victim never knows he's been fooled. Satan uses the same trick; we receive a message that we assume must be coming from God, but it may be a false message designed to deceive us. John warns us that spirituality comes in two flavours (1 John 4:1)!

Verification. There is a motto in military communication: "Trust but Verify". Modern digital communication systems usually have some built-in provision to self-test whether or not the message has been degraded. This "check-sum" feature can immediately detect whether or not the message is received as-sent, meaning that the message received is exactly the one that was sent. But what can we use to verify the accuracy of the messages we receive, bearing in mind that these "messages" could come in the form of impressions while praying, thoughts, sermons, songs, TV broadcasts, something we are told, etc.?

The first test must be the Bible, and no test is complete without the Bible (Hebrews 4:12, 2 Timothy 3:16). Praying about it is no substitute for finding out what God has already spoken on the matter.

Filling in the blanks. No mystery here; sometimes the message leaves out some information, maybe a detail, so we simply fill in the missing parts so that it makes "sense" to us. We "colour" the message by our assumptions. The problem is that we almost always add in parts that are in our favour, or that support our position. Basically, we hear what we want to hear, when we expect to hear it, and we convince ourselves that the entire message is authentic. It is, of course, tainted at best.

Redundancy. One of the best ways to improve communication is by repeating the message using more than one receiver. This is actually one of the strongest recommendations in Scripture; the principle of affirmation (1 Corinthians 14:27-28).

Filtering. One of the most successful communication techniques is a form of encoding that allows the receiver to detect a signal even when it is buried in severe noise. It's called "matched filtering". We're all familiar with a form of this filtering technique when we're in a noisy room and we are able to "tune in" to one familiar voice. It's easier to detect a message when we already know what the voice sounds like. That's one reason why having a deep familiarity with God's Word is so important, because God will frequently use Scripture when speaking to us, often by affirming the words or thoughts He has placed in our spirit.

Prayer Warrior, our mission is all about communication with God, and it is important enough that our enemy is spending a lot of effort trying to disrupt it or shut it down completely. Everyone naturally thinks that he/she has no problems, but we are *all* affected by his efforts, probably more seriously than we realize.

So, what can we do?

1. If you are not already doing so, quiet down the place where you pray. Turn off the phone, mute your cellphone (better yet, put it somewhere out of sight and hearing) and cut off all distractions. Do not take Face Book into your prayer room!
2. Intentionally refuse to allow any work activity to intrude on your prayer and Bible reading time.
3. Ask God to show you how to de-clutter your life; the pile of "stuff" that you are carrying around in your frantic schedule is smothering your contact with God and you must learn how to unload that burden.
4. Take one or two unplanned breaks during the day (or before the day begins) when you can read Scripture. If at all possible, make one of your daily Bible reading times one where you read aloud to yourself. You will be surprised how much better you will be able to concentrate on what you are reading, and you can smile knowing that Satan hates to hear God's Word.
5. Introduce fasting into your prayer life, specifically for the purpose of hearing the voice of the Holy Spirit.

6. If you are praying about God's leading in a particular matter, ask another Prayer Warrior to pray with you (or at the same time) and ask God to affirm His answer to you both.
7. If you have received a word from God, share it with a trusted Prayer Warrior and ask him/her to affirm it to you.
8. Pray against any interfering spirits that the enemy may be using to confuse or distort what God wants you to hear.
9. Submit to the ministry of the Holy Spirit, asking Him to reveal God's message to you. Ask Him to direct you to appropriate passages of Scripture that will affirm what you believe He is telling you.
10. Be patient in waiting on God. Practice quieting your spirit before Him before you pray (Psalm 46:10). Rushing into His presence with the noise of the world still ringing in your ears is a sure way to get it wrong every time. The first thing that we should hear from Him is that our hearts are ready.
11. Start your prayer time with a season of worship and adoration; this is one of the best ways to cut out the noise and to get our spirit "tuned in" to God.
12. If possible, pray out loud! The sound of your own voice speaking to God will be remarkably effective in silencing those stray thoughts and mental distractions, and it is one more thing that the devil doesn't like to hear.

MISSION 80

Stolen Messages

While working in an engineering company in Colorado I became friends with Bill, another engineer at the same company. One day, while in his office, I noticed a submarine ship plaque hanging on his wall; it was the USS Halibut. I knew the significance of the USS Halibut during the Cold War and now knowing Bill made the history come alive. Of course, Bill wouldn't say anything about the famous missions of the Halibut; he just smiled and referred me to the book Blind Man's Bluff[2].

In 1972, the USS Halibut was a spy submarine. It successfully sailed to within sight of a top-secret Russian missile base in western USSR, located an underwater communication cable in 400 feet of water, sent divers out at that depth (breathing a concoction of gases that would kill them on the surface) to attach a listening device to the cable, spent over a week there anchored to the ocean floor to record military conversations and then managed to escape. They did this not once, but twice, managing to avoid detection both times. The Russians never knew that their underwater cable carrying top secret information was bugged and that the information obtained from that operation was immediately available to intelligence operations in the United States. The cable tap continued to work for the next ten years until a US informant broke the secret to the Russians. The Americans had been "stealing" the Russian messages all that time.

Prayer Warrior, we might want to give some thought to this matter of secure communications. Let me give you a couple examples from Scripture to illustrate just how important communications are to us *and to our enemy*.

---

[2] Blind Man's Bluff, Sontag & Drew, Perennial Press/Harper 1999

In 2 Kings 6:8-12 we are told the peculiar account of how Elisha intercepted the secret war plans of the king of Aram who was plotting against Israel. Undoubtedly, God revealed the secret to Elisha, most likely through the prophetic gift that allowed him to "know" what conversations were taking place with the king of Aram.

In Daniel 10 we have the account of a strange spiritual battle in which Gabriel, who was bringing a message to Daniel in response to his prayer, was detained for twenty one days in a struggle against the Prince of Persia, a powerful demonic being who held authority over Persia as part of Satan's earthly government; this demon was attempting to prevent God's message (or messenger) from reaching Daniel, and he was succeeding until Michael, another archangel, came to assist Gabriel. This encounter gives us an unusual glimpse "behind the scenes", and makes it clear that earthly events, including prayer communications, actually involve great invisible spiritual forces who are actively opposing each other.

In Daniel's case, it is clear that he didn't just pray to God once on the matter and then move on to something else. He fasted through this period, constantly before God, and his whole conduct was one of urgent appeal. It seems that he was unaware of what was going on in the invisible spiritual world, but it is doubtless that his continued persistence before God played a role in the final outcome.

In Elisha's case, although prayer is not specifically mentioned, it is clear that this man operated close to God such that his prophetic gift was his "normal" mode of operation. His obedience as a prophet undoubtedly played a part in his effectiveness in that calling, as can be seen to be the opposite case with other later prophets and priests whose lives were a disgrace to that office.

So, what might have happened to Daniel's answer if he had not persisted for three weeks in his praying? Might the message have been stolen by the Prince of Persia? And what if Elisha had decided that it was just too much to expect that he would walk *that* close to God; might the king of Aram have succeeded in his ambush of the king of Israel?

Let's consider for a moment just what takes place in this matter of communication between God and us.

When we pray, the Holy Spirit immediately expresses that petition to the Father in language that is far beyond human language (Romans 8:26-27). Delivery guaranteed. And, although God certainly knows even our thoughts from afar (Psalm 94:11, 139:2), they do not constitute prayers until we intentionally express them to Him. Thinking about God is not the same as talking to Him. And thinking about God is not the same as hearing from Him.

Even with Adam in his sinless state God used the personal encounter of those evening conversations to communicate. Adam and God spoke and heard words. It wasn't mental telepathy. Something took place between God's words and Adam's hearing (and understanding).

It's that communication from God to us that concerns me, because that's the part that is subject to the attack of the enemy. What might Satan (or one of his demonic powers) do to prevent you from receiving a message from God? To help answer that question, it might be useful to give some thought to what is actually taking place when God sets out to speak to us. How can we know that we have received God's message?

I'm sure that most of us know very well that something which we consider as simple as a cell phone is actually an incredibly complicated device, and that the part that we hold in our hand is just one small piece of an even more complex communication system. Anyone who would think that the voice (and picture) in the phone just appears there by magic is certainly missing the real picture.

So it is with receiving God's message; it does not just appear in our mind (or ear) by magic. Let's understand that this is not some form of spiritual "mental telepathy"! In Daniel's case, it involved the messenger Gabriel who was sent to personally speak God's words to Daniel. Could God use that same angelic delivery for us in some cases? And if so, could there be demonic interference attempting to "steal" our message?

And what part does the Holy Spirit play in this communication? We know that one of His assignments with us is to teach us, even jogging our memories of earlier instructions (John 14:26, 1 John 2:27). This instruction is particularly applicable in understanding Scripture. But even here, it is not clear that the Holy Spirit is our mail delivery service; he enables us to read it, to correctly understand it, but He is not necessarily always the One who carries the message from the Father to us.

And how much of our "mail" is being read by the enemy? Like that Russian underwater cable. The Russians still received their messages, but the Americans were eavesdropping, effectively "stealing" the messages by learning their contents and using that information against them.

Time to get practical. What can we do to make sure that our messages are not being stolen?

1. We must be prepared to persist with God if we have been seeking a word from Him and the answer seems not to be there. Fasting while waiting on God is truly Biblical, and even Jesus taught its importance (Mark 9:29). When it seems that God is silent in the face of our prayers, that's the time to pray against opposing spirits and to intercede for the strengthening of God's messengers.
2. As part of our praying, especially when we are seeking God's directions, we should seal up our praying against the enemy, driving away any evil spirits from our prayer place and forbidding them from eavesdropping on our conversations with God.
3. We should pray a covering of protection upon our loved ones, that the enemy will not have power to steal the words of God from their hearing or understanding.
4. For Jesus, receiving clear instructions from the Father was a matter of seeing what the Father was doing in heaven (John 5:19). "Seeing into heaven" might be more than figurative language; perhaps we should add a "visual" channel to our praying, asking God to let us get a heavenly view of what we are praying about.

5. Communication is very important to God. Unlike the useless, endless chatter of today's social media, God has something important that He wants us to hear. We need to agree with God that His words to us are vitally important; more than agree, we must yearn to receive His messages and we must not be shy in expressing to Him how hungry we are to receive them (Psalm 119:103).
6. The Bible remains God's #1 method of delivering His wisdom and instructions to us. God will not substitute anything in the place of His Word. Expecting that we can "hear" God's voice as a substitute for reading and digesting His Word is a huge mistake. It is much easier for the enemy to mess with voices we think we hear in our heads than to steal the words from the printed pages of our Bibles.

Mission 81

Do Not Cross The Line

We've all seen signs warning us not to pass beyond a certain point, usually at border crossings or at emergency scenes. Yellow/black ribbons. The message is very clear; the signs and ribbons are intended to keep us on one side of the line. There are usually penalties for anyone who defies the warning.

Prayer Warrior, do you see any of these ribbons around your spiritual life?

From one perspective, these warnings are good and are given to us by God for our protection; they are intended to keep us on the "inside", where God's hand of protection and blessing is over us. Like obeying His commandments (Leviticus 26:3, Deuteronomy 5:29, 32-33), and in case you thought that those warnings were restricted to the Old Testament, then check out what Jesus has to say (John 14:15). Yes, there are lines that God commands us not to cross, not to move our lives out of His place of protection, and if we choose to ignore His instruction, then we will reap the consequences. Grace does not excuse us from obedience!

Then there are those lines that are intended to keep us on the "outside", like God's warnings that tell us to stay away from things that will work to destroy us (Proverbs 1:10, 15). Again, this line is given for our protection and ultimate blessing.

Did you know that our enemy also uses "Do Not Cross" lines? He surely does, and they can be remarkably effective in his service! Like the following:

- Materialism (also known as idolatry, loving the world (1 John 2:15), friend of the world (James 4:4), cares of this world (Matthew 13:22), love of riches (Matthew 6:24)). In short, the line that Satan tells us not to cross is the line between selfishness and servanthood, telling us not to give up our "stuff", threatening us not to stop pursuing our own best interests. The insidious side of this "Do Not Cross" line is that Satan tries to put us into a position of pride where God Himself will reject us (James 4:6), and materialism will certainly do that.
- Tribal thinking (also known as walking the party line, not making waves, denominationalism). This "Do Not Cross" line tells us not to defy the group think. Our group doesn't allow *this*, or our group doesn't want us to believe *that*. The definitions of what is allowed are almost always based on some particular interpretation (or misinterpretation) of an isolated Scripture passage; ironically those same passages are used by groups on *both* sides of the line for their own purposes. The enemy hog-ties both groups with one phony line.
- Spiritual blindness (also known as closed mindedness, stubbornness). This amounts to a wholesale refusal of the truth that God wants to bring into our life. The Devil knows that a faith that refuses to grow (or grow up) is doomed to shrivel and die; at best, it cannot bear any fruit and will one day receive the just penalty from the Lord Himself (Matthew 25:14-30).
- Bondage. We know that we are not completely in the right place before God, something is holding us back, but we do nothing about it and quietly hope that He will bring His blessing to us where we are. Abraham understood that, in order to receive God's promise of a new city, he had to first leave the one he was in; God was not going to bring the promise to him.
- Fear. This can be summed up by the words whispered into our mind or heart that say "What will happen to you if you risk everything on God's faithfulness to *you* in *this* situation?". "Can you dare to trust completely in God's promises?". "What if God doesn't come through for you?". This fear keeps us from venturing

out to the edges of our faith *and then stepping beyond that into a place where we have never been.*

Now the Devil knows very well that his "Do Not Cross" lines are lies, but he counts on the fact that we will believe them anyway and that the pressures of our own sinful, selfish natures will do the enforcement for him. We become our own jailers!

Prayer Warriors, what would happen if you walked straight up to one of those phony "Do Not Cross" lines that the Devil has put up around you and boldly stepped across in the mighty Name of Jesus? What if you singled out just one place, perhaps your prayer life, where you could "step across" and know that God Himself would give you the power to do it and would meet you on the other side? What is stopping you right now from saying "OK, Lord, I'm ready to step out!"?

This might sound like God is asking us to start out with giant steps; perhaps He is, but it could be that He wants us to start with small steps in the right direction. Bigger steps will follow.

- Commit to fasting just one meal, and intentionally use that time to spend in God's Word, with the specific request that He would teach you something new.
- Renew your promise to pray through your prayer list of names.
- Prepare for worship service by arriving just ten minutes earlier than usual, and purposely spending that time in prayer and worship.
- Promise the Lord that you will carefully tithe your income as you receive it, not after you have paid all the bills; do this for a few months and see what God will do.
- Prayerfully ask the Holy Spirit to bend your faith, and promise to respond to Him in obedience, not argument.
- Give up one thing for God and put it into His service. That could be an evening that you have reserved for your own agenda or enjoyment.
- Set aside a period of time weekly when you will get on your knees before God, interceding for your spouse, children or grandchildren.

Don't just mention their names; plead for them, asking God to place their burden on your heart.
- Serve someone. Willingly take the place of the servant even though it might be your right to be served.
- Ask God to change your mind about something that the enemy is using to imprison you.

I'm sure that you can add to these suggestions. The important thing is that you don't just agree intellectually that you *should* do them, but that you become convinced and committed to actually *doing* them. **Satan doesn't care about what you believe; he worries about what you are willing to put into action.**

Now reach out and take hold of one of those yellow ribbons and tear it down!

Mission 82

Restore the Glory

Furniture building is one of my hobbies. One thing you soon learn in this hobby is that building fine furniture is not easy; it takes a lot of talent, practice and patience. You also soon learn that there are many pieces of fine furniture that have already been built but which have fallen into disrepair, sometimes to the point where they are scarcely recognizable. Certainly, their damaged condition makes it almost impossible to recognize the beauty they once had. It takes a careful eye to spot the old glory buried beneath the damage, and it takes a lot of skill to restore that piece back to where the old glory is again visible for all to see. Like the table shown in the picture above.

Sometimes I think that Prayer Warriors are a lot like furniture restorers; we're on the lookout to see the hidden glory that lies beneath a covering of neglect, brokenness and shame, sometimes even in pieces that have been tossed by the wayside.

Of course, we're not talking about furniture now. This is about real lives and real people. And the glory is not the beauty of fine wood, but the glory of the practiced presence of God Himself abiding in a quiet heart. Or it may be only the seed of a glory that has never bloomed.

Sometimes the glory has become hidden under a cloak of abandonment. Like the perfectly unblemished piece of furniture that has been buried beneath a heap of other "stuff"; the glory is still there but it is hidden, buried, unpolished. How beautiful it would be if someone would just rescue it from obscurity, lovingly polish it and put it where all could see it and admire it. Our homes and nursing homes have many of these treasures hidden in their halls, convinced of their final worthlessness in God's kingdom-building here. We need to seek them out, for our blessing as much as for theirs. We all need to see the glory of the presence of God who is in them.

Often the glory is one that might have been, a glory that was stolen in its infancy by some circumstance or decision. Like the Prodigal son (Luke 15). The work of grace was done by God, as only He could do it, in the pig pen when the son was turned toward home, but the work of mercy had only begun, for it took a loving father to run down the road to look past the stink and the sin to see the son. That father's glory was in his son, but it had never been seen before; now it would take work, but that glory would finally be seen.

Then there is the glory that seemed lost. Once clear and beautiful, it has somehow become very un-glorious. This is the man or woman who, through pride or foolishness or by a thousand other ways, let their life get away from God's glory. Perhaps it was the lie of seeking self-glory. Whatever it was, it has taken the life that once spoke loudly of the grace of God and has now silenced it. Shipwrecked (1 Timothy 1:19). But God may not be finished with that one, and it may be that the glory of that restored life would far outshine its original beauty. God's restoration work does not hide the cracks; that's precisely where His most careful craftsmanship is made clear. *Exchanging brokenness for glory is God's style.*

Some of that hidden glory might be in us. Would we be willing to put ourselves into the hands of a master craftsman who could chip, sand and scrape away the blemishes and stains that are hiding the glory beneath?

The measure of success in the work of restoration is the degree to which the object can be brought back to the original design of its creator. Not the design of the restorer, but that of the one who created it in the first place. So it is with restoration in Kingdom work; we must be seeking the glory of the Creator, not our own, and we must be willing to let the signs of our scratching and sanding become completely overshadowed by the glory of God being revealed. *We don't get to sign the work!*

Spiritual warrior keep your eyes open for hidden treasures along the way. As we seek new miracles, let's not overlook some older ones that may be hidden close at hand. Those pieces into which God has already invested a lifetime of grace are worth finding, and their restored glory may surprise (and outshine) us all. It will require a full measure of humility, because God may put us to work on a "piece" whose glory far outshines our own. That way, He gets to work on *two* "pieces" at the same time!

Something to pray about:

1. Ask God to go to work on you so that His intended glory will begin to be visible.
2. Ask God for humility to see the hidden glory in others and ask for grace to help in the great work of restoration.
3. Ask God to show you His glory.
4. Ask God to give you a "piece" to work on. Give it your best, because that may be your answer when the Lord asks you "Where are your disciples?".

MISSION 83

Closing Ranks

Closing ranks is a military maneuver derived from the practice of closing the spacing between lines (ranks) of troops, as they are deployed across a battlefield, thereby decreasing the depth of the formation as it faces the enemy side. This practice allowed for the second rank to fire their weapons without movement, sidestepping, and firing alongside, and slightly to the rear of the first rank. This manoeuvre was "perfected" in the "British Square", a tight formation of infantry who formed back-to-back in a square that could fire equally well in all directions and made famous at the Battle of Waterloo in 1815.

The order to "Close Ranks" was given as the military unit was about to come under attack. It was a strong defensive position designed to concentrate fire on the enemy while not exposing gaps in one's own line. Normally those in the front two ranks would fire the weapons while those in the rear would reload and pass the loaded weapons to the front. Teamwork. It goes without saying that it required enormous courage and commitment to stand facing the enemy assault without flinching or turning. In the days when this type of fighting was the norm, the combatants were rarely more than 30 meters apart.

Prayer Warriors, we're in a different kind of battle but the call to "Close Ranks" is just as relevant to us today as it was a century ago. As an army of modern believers, we are seriously "out of rank" and dangerously exposed in many important aspects:

- For many believers, regular attendance at worship meetings of the congregation of which they are a member is taken as optional.

They might or might not be there, depending on a host of excuses, and it clearly is not an issue to them.
- Commitment to participation in a weekly prayer gathering of the church is considered by many as also "optional", and many are unashamedly unwilling to adjust their personal schedules to make place for it. As a result, their spiritual lives are swinging between tottering and train wreck, and their loved ones are being lost and picked off by the enemy.
- Many churches do not have a single, compelling, Biblically sound mission statement that is understood and accepted by all of their members, and which is a rallying point for their service in God's Kingdom work.
- Most church members do not have a rigorous, personal discipline of daily prayer and Bible reading.
- Sacrificial giving of time, money and attention is a rare exception instead of the norm.
- Most church members do not disciple anyone, have no real idea how to go about it and don't see its importance to them personally.
- Many believers have no sense of a Kingdom call on their lives, a purpose for which God has placed them here at this time.
- Many believers have no real sense of "what time it is" in God's calendar, and most have no interest in finding out. Most have no sense of alarm or urgency.
- For many, the concept of Kingdom lifestyle has no practical meaning.
- Many churches, in their routine activities, resemble picnics, parties or club meetings instead of sanctuaries for the broken, lighthouses in the darkness or battlefield hospitals.

The list could go on, but it's time to focus on what to do about it.

Let's start with commitment. Commitment to God's Kingdom. Commitment to Jesus' lordship. Commitment to each other. Commitment to disciplined living. Commitment to a call, *one call*, on our life. Coming to a total conviction that being true to that call of God means everything and is worth anything it takes to meet it.

> *Not that I have already attained, or am already perfected; but I press on, that I may lay hold of that for which Christ Jesus has also laid hold of me. Brethren, I do not count myself to have apprehended; but one thing I do, forgetting those things which are behind and reaching forward to those things which are ahead, I press toward the goal for the prize of the upward call of God in Christ Jesus.*
> Philippians 3:12-14 NKJV

Abandonment of every other loyalty to this world and to the god of this world. Your daily priorities tell the truth about who, or what, is the lord of your life. Make some hard choices, turn your back on some old, misguided loyalties. Seek the lordship of Jesus over your life, give yourself wholeheartedly to it, confess it to Him and speak of it to others.

> *But what things were gain to me, these I have counted loss for Christ. Yet indeed I also count all things loss for the excellence of the knowledge of Christ Jesus my Lord, for whom I have suffered the loss of all things, and count them as rubbish, that I may gain Christ and be found in Him, not having my own righteousness, which is from the law, but that which is through faith in Christ, the righteousness which is from God by faith; that I may know Him and the power of His resurrection, and the fellowship of His sufferings, being conformed to His death, if, by any means, I may attain to the resurrection from the dead.*
> Philippians 3:7-11 NKJV

Determination to be transformed, to see your family transformed, and to see the fruit of true godliness in your own life. This means discipleship. Giving up being the master of your life, your schedule and your ambitions. You must become very unsatisfied with your present state of spiritual maturity and you must ask the Holy Spirit to give you a fire in your gut for life on a higher plane. Recognize that those things in your life that are standing in the way between you and God are, in fact, plainly wrong in His sight and that He will not come close to you until you give them over to Him. "Just as I am" is the right way to come to God, but He will never leave us in that state; His only plan for our life is to transform us completely.

> *And do not be conformed to this world, but be transformed by the renewing of your mind, that you may prove what is that good and acceptable and perfect will of God.*
>
> Romans 12:2 NKJV

> *For whom He foreknew, He also predestined to be conformed to the image of His Son, that He might be the firstborn among many brethren.*
>
> Romans 8:29 NKJV

> *But we all, with unveiled face, beholding as in a mirror the glory of the Lord, are being transformed into the same image from glory to glory, just as by the Spirit of the Lord.*
>
> 2 Corinthians 3:18 NKJV

Become strong in the Spirit. Become a man or woman who is mighty in faith, mighty in prayer and mighty in service. Faith must be exercised to become strong (Hebrews 5:14), and it does not happen overnight, but it needs a first step. We won't always get it perfectly right, but our faith will become stronger the more we exercise it.

Expect darkness and walk in light. Ask the Holy Spirit to show you the nearness of the enemy, how his evil hand grasps to take hold of your children, your friends, your loved ones. Seriously ask God what time it is and be prepared to learn that it is much later than you think.

> *But concerning the times and the seasons, brethren, you have no need that I should write to you. For you yourselves know perfectly that the day of the Lord so comes as a thief in the night. For when they say, "Peace and safety!" then sudden destruction comes upon them, as labor pains upon a pregnant woman. And they shall not escape. But you, brethren, are not*

> *in darkness, so that this Day should overtake you as a thief. You are all sons of light and sons of the day. We are not of the night nor of darkness. Therefore, let us not sleep, as others do, but let us watch and be sober.*
>
> 1 Thessalonians 5:1-6 NKJV

Value the body of Christ. The fellowship of other believers is not here for your convenience; it is here for your health and survival. Treasure it as you would a life raft at sea.

> *And let us consider one another in order to stir up love and good works, not forsaking the assembling of ourselves together, as is the manner of some, but exhorting one another, and so much the more as you see the Day approaching.*
>
> Hebrews 10:24-25 NKJV

"Together" means in the same place at the same time for the same purpose, and did you notice that the passage urges us to *increase* our "togetherness" as we see that Day approaching? Why do you suppose that is so important? Prayer Warrior, this is not so it will be easier for God to find us; it's because God knows that we will soon have to become very dependent upon each other, and the close community of believers will become the centre of life for us and our families. This world is about to become a very dangerous place for true believers, and no place to be wandering alone.

Practice Kingdom living. So, what does that mean? One good place to start is by reading Matthew 5:3-12, and then ask God to show you how you can put those principles into action. Those earmarks of Kingdom living are exactly opposite to what this world says is the way to get ahead. It means servanthood living. Do something sacrificial for someone who is broken or abandoned or hungry.

Start to release your grip on the treasures of this earth; the love affair with this world must end because we simply cannot "have it all" here and expect to have the treasures of heaven too.

Desperately seek the lost. This is the Father's heart, and if it is not reflected in our heart, then we must question our relationship with God. The comfort and convenience of the saints are of no importance as long as there are lost loved ones still outside the fold of safety. Reach as far as you can, and strengthen the hands of those who are able to reach where you cannot.

Prayer Warriors now is the time to "Close Ranks". Urgently. Quickly.

Mission 84

Open Immediately!

Some messages cannot wait; they must be read and heeded immediately. The consequences of not listening to the message or of not taking it seriously could be severe, even life or death.

I have gathered four examples of men and women who have sounded warnings, but whose messages were disregarded, all with terrible consequences.

In April 1912 Cyril Evans was working as the telegraph operator on board the SS Californian on a voyage across the Atlantic. On the night of April 14, 1912, the Captain of the Californian brought the ship to a halt as it had entered a wide ice field with many large icebergs and came into the wireless operator's room and ordered Evans to warn other ships in the area of the ice. Evans proceeded to do just that, sending out wireless warnings to other ships in the area that they were approaching ice. In the wireless room aboard the Titanic, operators Jack Philips and Harold Bride were trying to get through a backlog of private messages they were to send from the ship to the United States, the destination of the Titanic on her maiden voyage. Philips received Evans' ice warning message, but because the Californian was so close to the Titanic and Evans had his set turned to full power, he almost blew the headset off Philips head. An angry Philips told him to get off the air and Philips never passed along the ice warning to the bridge or to the ship's Captain. Evans felt he had done what he was ordered to do, switched off his radio set, and went to bed. A short time later the Titanic, heading at full steam west toward America, came upon the ice Evans had tried to warn them about, struck an iceberg and sank with the loss of over 1,500 people.

Katsuhiko Ishibashi is a well-respected professor and seismologist at Kobe University in Japan. Since the early 2000^s he has been warning Japan that the country's many nuclear power plants are in danger of serious damage or even a melt down because they have been built in earthquake-prone areas. In 2006, he was a member of a government committee that was to revise the national guidelines on making Japan's nuclear power plants more resistant to earthquakes. He proposed that Japan review its standards for surveying and assessing the danger from active faults, but this proposal was rejected. Ishibashi also stated that Japanese engineers were overconfident in their predictions of plant engineering and safety design to withstand an earthquake. Ishibashi warned of the danger of an earthquake-induced nuclear disaster at an International Union of Geodesy and Geophysics conference held in Sapporo but no one took his warnings with any sense of urgency. All of Ishibasi's fears came true on March 11, 2011 when a huge offshore earthquake and resulting tsunami damaged the Fukushima Diiachi nuclear power plant, resulting in a level 7 International Nuclear Event Scale disaster – the highest-level nuclear disaster possible.

When Brooksley Born took over as head of the Commodities Futures Trading Commission (CFTC), a government agency empowered with the task of monitoring and regulating the commodities exchange in the US, she very quickly discovered something that shocked her. An entire branch of the commodities market known as Over-The-Counter commodities (OTC commodities) existed that was totally unregulated. Worse, the government (which was supposed to monitor and regulate commodity trading) didn't even know these types of commodity investments existed. Huge sums of money were being traded as OTC commodities called "derivatives," with no regulation and nobody even aware it was taking place. On Wall Street they called it the "Black Box" of trading; only those involved knew the details and they wanted it to stay that way. Born had other ideas. The more she learned about OTC commodities and the derivatives markets, the more frightened she grew that something terrible would happen to the US and world economies. Born believed that it was the job of her agency to investigate and prosecute such fraud and when she tried to move to regulate OTC derivatives for the first time, she was met by the full force of the financial industry lobbying effort. She and her agency were crushed by political power and Born eventually resigned. But the warnings she had made about the unregulated OTC derivatives market becoming far too large and posing a threat to the very structure of the US and world economy did not go away. By 2007, just before the crash, the OTC derivatives market was valued at a mind-numbing $595 trillion. It was a house of cards of financial debt waiting to fall, and all it needed was a triggering event. And the collapse of the housing market did just that. In a matter of months, the huge load of debt triggered an almost complete collapse of the US financial market.

In the 1980s Roger Boisjoly worked as an engineer at Morton Thiokol, maker of the solid rocket boosters used in the space shuttle program. In 1985, a year before the space shuttle Challenger disaster, Boisjoly had been warning Thiokol that the joints used to seal the sections of the solid rocket boosters could fail if they became too cold before launch. The space shuttle used two solid fuel rocket boosters and a central hydrogen tank, to fuel the engines for launch. The different sections of the solid rocket boosters were sealed to one another with a rubber material or gasket called an "O-ring." Boisjoly and other Thiokol engineers had found that in cold weather conditions, the rubber material in the O-rings became brittle and did not seal the sections into place. In this case, the O-ring would fail to prevent the flames from reaching the rocket's metal casing. If this happened, the flames could trigger a huge explosion of the hydrogen fuel tank located right next to the boosters. On January 27, 1986 the space shuttle Challenger was on the launch pad set for launch the following day. The weather forecast for Cape Canaveral was to be unusually cold, with temperatures dropping below freezing. All of that evening and into the morning hours of January 28, Boisjoly and other engineers pleaded with NASA to delay the launch. Senior managers at Thiokol and NASA officials rejected their argument. NASA insisted the shuttle would launch the morning of January 28 as scheduled, even with the cold weather. Only a minute after taking off, the o-ring on one of the solid fuel rocket boosters failed just as Boisjoly had predicted it would. The flames shot out from the booster and hit the hydrogen tank, which exploded, killing all of the astronauts on board.

All of these people who warned of danger were simply people who understood what they were talking about, and their warnings were ignored by self-serving organizations and people to whom power, wealth, political acceptance and prestige were more important than the consequences of which they were being warned.

Ezekiel was a prophet to Judah and Israel, and his warning to the nation came from none other than God Himself. His message was one of imminent judgment as a result of widespread wickedness. But his message was refused by nearly everyone, and especially by those in places of religious and political authority. Even when they could not deny the charges brought against them by the words of God, they refused to accept the urgency of the warning.

> *And the word of the Lord came to me: "Son of man, what is this proverb that you have about the land of Israel, saying, 'The days grow long, and every vision comes to nothing'? Tell them therefore, 'Thus says the Lord God: I will put an end to this proverb, and they shall no more use it as a proverb in Israel.' But say to them, "The days are near, and the fulfillment of every vision. For there shall be no more any false vision or flattering divination within the house of Israel. For I am the Lord; I will speak the word that I will speak, and it will be performed. It will no longer be delayed, but in your days, O rebellious house, I will speak the word and perform it, declares the Lord God."*
>
> *And the word of the Lord came to me: "Son of man, behold, they of the house of Israel say, 'The vision that he (Ezekiel) sees is for many days from now, and he prophesies of times far off.' Therefore, say to them, "Thus says the Lord God: None of my words will be delayed any longer, but the word that I speak will be performed, declares the Lord God."*
>
> Ezekiel 12:21-28 ESV

Judah and Israel saw no reason to be alarmed, thought they had put themselves in a safe place politically and economically, and thought it to be completely unimportant how far their spiritual walk had strayed from God's commandments. They even had a corps of false prophets who preached wealth, health and good times. Finally, through Ezekiel, God said that the "time was up". The judgment that seemed so impossible to imagine was about to fall without further warning. And, so it did!

Not the first time that God brought judgment upon His beloved people, nor would it the last time. These were surely the people whom He dearly loved and whom He desired to bless above all nations, but their open, continual wickedness of idolatry, materialism, violence and immorality was a direct offence against God and a blatant disregard for His authority over their lives and society. From the days of wilderness wandering right up to Ezekiel's time, God's own holiness would not allow Him to excuse even His own people from wickedness any more than it could overlook the sin of Satan, who was the architect of the rebellion of all of mankind.

We may shake our heads at the foolishness of those Israelites in Ezekiel's day, but what about us today?

Oh, you say that it's all been taken care of in the cross of Jesus, and today we have nothing to be concerned about; God will never bring any such judgment upon His church. After all, isn't He supposed to rescue His people out of this world before He brings His just judgment upon planet Earth?

Let's just come to grips with what God has really told us. Certainly, Jesus has taken the penalty of the sin of every believer; that work is eternally final and complete. On that cross He demonstrated His infinite love for us and His eternal contempt for sin. That is why He has spent so much effort to teach us the importance (and necessity) of making Him the Lord of our walk, our work, our speech, our thinking ...... absolutely every part of our life. And we are told that He wants us to live holy lives that reflect His own holiness (Romans 12:1, Ephesians 1:4, 5:27, 1 Peter 1:15-16). We are also told that He is willing to discipline us to achieve that end

(James 1:2, Hebrews 12:5-11). And how can we think for a moment that the present state of pagan idolatry, materialism, violence and immorality in our society (exactly the same things that Ezekiel pointed out), and even in our churches and tolerated among professing believers, will not draw God's judgment? God will separate His own from the world, finally by removal, but probably before that through great trials. He is not taking garbage into heaven!

> *For I do not want you to be unaware, brothers, that our fathers were all under the cloud, and all passed through the sea, and all were baptized into Moses in the cloud and in the sea, and all ate the same spiritual food, and all drank the same spiritual drink. For they drank from the spiritual Rock that followed them, and the Rock was Christ. Nevertheless, with most of them God was not pleased, for they were overthrown in the wilderness. Now these things took place as examples for us, that we might not desire evil as they did. Do not be idolaters as some of them were; as it is written, "The people sat down to eat and drink and rose up to play." We must not indulge in sexual immorality as some of them did, and twenty-three thousand fell in a single day. We must not put Christ to the test, as some of them did and were destroyed by serpents, nor grumble, as some of them did and were destroyed by the Destroyer. Now these things happened to them as an example, but they were written down for our instruction, on whom the end of the ages has come. Therefore, let anyone who thinks that he stands take heed lest he fall.*
> 1 Corinthians 10:1-12 ESV

Paul, that great apostle who taught us more about salvation by grace than any other writer of the New Testament, is saying that these lessons from the Old Testament are given for our warning *today* by way of example. Example of what? That God is willing to use severe measures to separate His people from wickedness, or to remove wickedness from His people. That means that God is saying we should take the warnings seriously. Urgently. Fearfully.

Prayer Warrior, we have every reason to believe that God's calendar has reached the day when He will move that separation to a new level. Certainly, the fuse has been lit that will bring about the sudden and unprecedented collapse of the economic and political kingdoms of this world. So, how should we prepare *today* if that day should come tomorrow, or next week, or next year? Rest assured, it is coming sooner than we may think.

Certainly, we must come to a deeper appreciation of the body of Christ – other believers with whom we are part – as we saw in the last Mission. It also seems obvious that we must discover a new meaning of worship together. Worship with praise from full hearts and empty pockets. Worship with tears of joy and intercession. Worship that lifts up Jesus among us. Worship without pretence or props. Worship that has grown through being tested.

It also seems clear that we must come to a deeper appreciation of the Word of God. What would we do if all of our Bibles were confiscated, including (most easily) all of the electronic gadgets? How much of the Bible would we have from which we could read, preach, teach? How much of it could we turn to for comfort, direction and encouragement? The plain answer is that we would have only those portions which we had written on our hearts through memorization, together with any portions which we had managed to hide away. Sound ridiculous? There are believers today for whom this is a daily reality, and I'm afraid that we will see the day when it will become our reality, too. How much of the Bible would we have collectively as a congregation if we had to reconstruct it entirely from bits and pieces that we had memorized, written down and hidden away?

The good news – the great news – is this; God is ready to reveal Himself to His waiting church in a way that we can scarcely imagine. After all, the only things that have kept us from seeing Him more clearly until now are those very things that He now wants to help us remove. Those are the chains that have shackled us to this world's lies, and He is about to break them all, and in so doing, He will release His power among us in salvation, restoration, reconciliation and redemption.

Prayer Warrior, what should we take away from this Mission? Maybe simply that we must take God seriously and we must take His warnings as urgent messages that demand our immediate action.

Mission 85

Crack of Light

Hope doesn't begin the moment that you discover the answer; it starts the moment you realize there might be one!

Faith often starts out that way. I'm talking about the kind of faith needed to step up to one of God's challenges, especially if the challenge looks like a mountain and God has given you the opportunity to move it. Every other time you've thought of moving that mountain you have immediately dismissed the idea as being ridiculously impossible, but this time it's somehow different. Still big. Still a mountain. Still impossible. But you believe that someone has whispered into your spirit that "with God, nothing is impossible" (Luke 1:37). And, whereas all those other times you thought that it must be someone else who could experience God's power that way, this time, for the first time, it seems that *you* could be the one for whom the mountain would move.

Prayer Warrior, soldiers are not born strong and mighty; they are trained to be that way, and they all started that process from a place of weakness. For every one of them, there was a moment when they first dared to believe that they could become strong. For every Prayer Warrior who has ever seen his/her prayer miraculously answered, there was a moment when they first thought that such a thing could actually happen to them. That first moment of daring faith may have been like the slim glow of light around a door in a dark room, just enough to convince you that there must be more on the other side, and that if you would only swing open the door, you would be flooded with light.

It's the divine persistence of that "vision" that gives it its power; it just won't go away. It keeps daring you to open the door and to step into what lies on the other side. God's call is persistent!

You don't need to be "called" to be ordinary; unfortunately, many people turn away from God's call and settle for ordinary. For them, the vision of the glimmer of light fades and the door finally closes.

What do you suppose was going through David's mind when he stepped out onto the field separating him from Goliath (1 Samuel 17:45-51)? From what we read, he was remembering that God had given him power to kill a lion and a bear, saving his own life as well as that of the sheep. Also, he was firmly convinced that Goliath was a direct insult to God and that *someone* had to put an end to him. Since nobody else stepped forward, David concluded that he was the one to do the job. Maybe his line of thought went something like this:

> God wants the job done
> *Someone* must be called to do it
> What if *I'm* the one to do it?

His conviction was that God's honor would not only protect him but would give him power to kill the giant. What David couldn't have known at the time was that, some years later, others in his army would kill four other giants, among them Goliath's brother (2 Samuel 21:18-22). David's step of conviction resulted not only in the power to kill a giant, but the power to inspire others to follow his example and to do the same thing.

Joshua and Caleb spied out the promised land, saw the giants living there, saw the fortified cities and reported that the land was theirs for the taking (Numbers 13:30)! They were able to connect the dots from the miracle-working God who delivered them out of Pharoah's hand, spared them from the angel of death and took them across the sea on dry land and now was certainly well able to give them this promised land. God had paved the way with miraculous deliverance, and they could plainly see that He would do the same again, no matter how great the odds against them.

Their confidence was not in their own power to win, but in the power of God to win on their behalf. They could see that God had opened a door for them to pass through, and they were willing to do just that. When the Israelites refused to follow God's leading, that door of opportunity closed and then, when they changed their mind and wanted to take the land, they were defeated (Numbers 14:39-45).

Then there was Peter. Out on the lake in a gale wind, and suddenly he (and the other disciples) saw Jesus walking on the water (Matthew 14:28-30). It was Peter's idea that Jesus could give him the power to also walk on the water, so off he went. What thoughts must have gone through his mind as he stepped out of that boat? Possibly it was the assurance that, since Jesus was doing it, so could he. Somehow in the course of a few moments he went from "What if Jesus really means that I can do it?" to "I'm doing it!".

And just in case you were thinking that these challenges come only to the "heroes" of the Bible, consider the lady in Matthew 9:20-21; we do not even know her name, but she stands in the place of all of us who have ever hid in the shadows and secretly wondered if God could bless me, if He could give me just a moment of His attention, if He could call me, if His amazing promises could be for *me*. That dear nameless lady, who didn't want any attention, had a thought, maybe her last resort, that touching Jesus' garment could instantly make all the difference. What if it were possible? What if it could be true for *her*? What did she have to lose?

What do you have to lose?

What if Jesus really means that *you* can do that impossible thing? Of course, you've never done it before, and you may not do it again (Peter never repeated the water walk), but what if Jesus really does mean for you to take that step out right now? It comes down to whether or not you are totally convinced of God's call and of His ability to come through for you.

Maybe God's call to you is more like a small nudge; not moving a mountain but taking a step of obedience and commitment further than you have gone before. Trusting that sudden, tiny glimmer of assurance that He really does have the answers to the struggles you are facing, the healing for your pain, the order to your confusion. Could it really be possible that you could have joy again? That you could see life making sense for you? That you could discover a purpose worth living for?

Yes! Yes! That's it! God is not going to kick the door down and flood you with light; He is more likely to just open it a tiny crack, just enough to make you think for a moment that *this time it might be for me if I will just reach out.* It *is* possible!

God's truth often comes like that. First a tiny shaft of light piercing into the darkness of the devil's lies; if we will allow that first glimmer of truth to find lodging in our minds, more will follow. It is that first shaft of light that announces our freedom from the darkness, because "the truth shall set you free" (John 8:32). Satan operates in darkness, and his kingdom is one of darkness, but God has liberated us from being children of darkness and has brought us into His glorious Kingdom of light (Colossians 1:13).

Lost on a dark night, there is nothing more reassuring and inspiring than to hear someone say "I see a light!". *You* be that someone.

Mission 86

Extraction!

In military tactics, extraction is the process of removing personnel when it is considered imperative that they be immediately moved out of a hostile environment and taken to a secure area. This process is usually the result of urgent calls for help from the endangered force.

Prayer Warrior, we are in hostile territory and we are under attack from our enemy, Satan, and his demonic forces. We are outnumbered (in human terms), we can see the signs of the enemy's success all around us, and sometimes those enemy successes come too close to us, to our loved ones, to our homes. Sometimes it seems that our prayers begin to sound a lot like urgent calls for rescue, even extraction!

The problem is that, if we are spending all of our time expecting to be removed from difficult circumstances through a miraculous "extraction", then we have forgotten that we have been placed here to fight the enemy, not to find a way out of the battle. That means that we are to expect increasingly difficult times, even trials and tribulation such as we have not seen before. It seems more likely that God's miraculous intervention will take the form of victories in the middle of battle than some "extraction" that would never test our faith and courage in the face of the enemy.

At times like this, nothing is more helpful than to be reminded of what God has already told us about our situation, and what we may expect from the plan that He has already revealed to us.

1. **Our present battle situation is exactly as it was predicted by Jesus.**

   In the world you will have tribulation; but be of good cheer, I have overcome the world

   John 16:33 NKJV

   Jesus plainly told His followers that they (and we) should expect increasingly troubling times. He told them to expect to be personally hated by the world (John 15:19). Satan's attacks will be intense, direct and personal, just as they were directed against Jesus, and he will not hesitate to use human agents to do the dirty work, just as he did with Jesus. The battles we face are not the exceptions to the rule, nor do they surprise God.

2. **Jesus specifically asked the Father <u>not</u> to remove us from this battle too soon.**

   I do not pray that You should take them out of the world, but that You should keep them from the evil one.

   John 17:15 NKJV

   It may come as an unpleasant reminder that it never has been God's plan to remove His people from all trouble, and just in case you thought that the plan had changed with the resurrection of Jesus, it hasn't! God's purpose for us includes preparing us for hardship, even suffering. This wasn't just the program for those early disciples; it's the program for us today. The problem that many believers have is coming to grips with the fact that the false gospel of comfort, ease and pleasure that we have come to think is our free, Christian entitlement is, in fact, a lie. We're not on a picnic, we're in a war and we are expected to arm and conduct ourselves accordingly (Ephesians 6:10-18).

3. **Jesus Himself refused "Extraction" at the most critical point in His battle.** In Gethsemane He prayed repeatedly to know if

there could be some way to complete His mission without the cross, but there was none, and He bowed to the Father's will (Matthew 26:36-42). He gave up any possibility of rescue, and by the time that He became sin for every man (2 Corinthians 5:21), even the Father had to turn away from Him.

4. **The Father already has an "Extraction" plan, including a precise schedule.**

For the Lord Himself will descend from heaven with a shout, with the voice of an archangel, and with the trumpet of God. And the dead in Christ will rise first. Then we who are alive and remain shall be caught up together with them in the clouds to meet the Lord in the air. And thus we shall always be with the Lord.
1 Thessalonians 4:16-17 NKJV

This, of course, is the glorious hope of the church; the return of Jesus and the gathering of believers to be with Him. Extraction! But wait; the first verses of the next chapter (1 Thessalonians 5:1-10) describe a time (before the "Extraction") of increasing darkness, confusion and trouble which will be the signs to the expectant believers that their deliverance is imminent. Far from being spared any tribulation, the believers will experience the increasing troubles as the sign of God's stirring wrath and the very signal of their expected "Extraction".

5. **We may be under heavy attack, but we are not losing the battle nor are we about to be overrun by the enemy**; in fact, we are winning, and our victory is guaranteed by Jesus.

The enemy, of course, does not want us to know that. He wants to convince us that he has the upper hand, that his plan is succeeding, that we should be filled with fear and discouragement, and that ultimately his kingdom will prevail on earth. All lies!

But what exactly is it that we are winning? Are we winning the world? Are we expecting to see the imminent collapse of Satan's kingdom of darkness? No, neither! We are seeing the glorious advancement of God's Kingdom right here in the face of the enemy, on his own turf. God is showing His mighty power in us by saving the unworthy, doing the unthinkable, rescuing the unreachable, healing the hopeless, restoring the broken, freeing the prisoner; He is stretching our faith and our imagination; He is demonstrating in us that same power that He exerted when He raised Jesus from the grave; He is raising up a glorious light right in the middle of Satan's empire of darkness; He is perfecting His wheat in the middle of the enemy's thorn field. He will do all of this exactly as He said He would despite everything that Satan can do to prevent it, and when He has completed His plan to perfection, THEN He will take us away, not because He could no longer protect us, but because His plan is then to bring judgment upon Satan's kingdom as final confirmation of His sovereign power. And through all of this, *not one* of His children will be lost (John 10:29)!

6. **Could it be that many of the things that we are "losing" in this war are things that we should not have set our hearts on in the first place?** Our idols will be the first casualties; better that we throw them away now before they become the means of our own destruction. Lot, no doubt, felt that he had lost everything in the destruction of Sodom. Sadly, he was right; he had invested his life, and his family's life, in a city of wickedness. He is a tragic example, one that no one should imitate. Sadly, Lot has many imitators today. The one who gives up his life rather than trying to hang onto it is the one who will, indeed, find life (Matthew 16:25). The wise man is the one who has nothing left to lose, and everything to gain. Satan has little hold on such a man.

"He is no fool who gives up what he cannot keep to gain what he cannot lose"

Jim Elliot

7. **What if it is God's plan that, instead of extracting us at the first sign of tribulation, He keeps us here in order to show to the enemy what His grace and power look like in human form?**

Satan expects us to run away from the darkness, afraid that we will be swallowed by it. He expects that, instead of steeling itself to fight, our army will focus all of its hopes on retreat and extraction, while selfishly enjoying as much of this world as we can in the meantime.

What will he do when he sees us charging *into* that darkness, armed with the power of God, the light of the Gospel and the unstoppable boldness of people who have sold out to Jesus with absolutely nothing to lose and everything to gain? And how can he begin to comprehend that our mission is not to seize territory, but to carry out the biggest prison-break in history? We're not defending turf; we're going after the lost, the hopeless, the broken, the Prodigals, the losers, the prisoners, the condemned --- the very ones that Satan holds in bondage, and we are about to see the greatest extension of God's Kingdom that has ever been seen.

This is not a retreat or even a withdrawal; this is an attack! Don't leave now or you'll miss the best part!

Mission 87

Dinner Is Served!

Very few announcements have as wonderful an effect as the dinner call! At the end of a long, hard day, the thoughts of a waiting dinner are hard to beat; we can almost taste what awaits us!

The home-call to dinner usually means leaving the work behind, at least for a few hours. The meal becomes a sort of retreat away from the cares and trials of the day. A safe place where the threats of the day cannot enter. It comes as no surprise that so many of our fondest childhood memories have something to do with the family mealtime.

Spiritual warrior, we have a dinner call that will one day see us seated together with all of the redeemed of God in the presence of Jesus Himself, but we're not there yet. Today our dinner call is more like the "mess call" of a soldier. It is a meal call, but it doesn't take place *after* the battle is done, it takes place *during* the battle, and it may be far from a safe, comfortable place.

David describes a prepared table surrounded by enemies and trouble, even death.

> *Even though I walk through the valley of the shadow of death, I will fear no evil, for you are with me; your rod and your staff, they comfort me. You prepare a table before me in the presence of my enemies; you anoint my head with oil; my cup overflows.*
>
> Psalm 23:4-5 ESV

This is not a description of a heavenly banquet; here we see the meal of a soldier, or a pilgrim. Someone for whom the warfare has not yet ended. While God has a wonderful future banquet planned for us with Him after our war is over, this meal is not in heaven; it is right here, right now! It should come as a great encouragement that God intends to feed us along the way, not just after we arrive home.

So, spiritual warrior, are you hungry? What's on the menu? Here are some things to consider on our way to the "mess call".

- Our company has already been chosen
  Angels? Loved ones who are already with the Lord? No; it's a bit less glamorous than that. So, who will be eating at the table with you? Look around at your prayer meeting, at your worship time, when you are in the middle of your battles, when you have been praying for a faithful friend. Your dinner partners are the very ones who are in this spiritual war with you. Not everyone who says they believe, and certainly not every believer, but just those who are in the struggle close to you. You see, soldiers in battle usually huddle together in a foxhole or small shelter big enough to hold only a few. Look again at your prayer partners; they are your dinner company! If you cannot see the treasure of their company here, you probably won't find your name on the reservation list at the heavenly table (1 John 4:20-21).

- God has reserved the venue
  Elegant surroundings are rare in the middle of battle. Real soldiers know that! That home living room where you gather to pray, that not-so-church-looking place where you meet to worship, that kitchen table where you pray and weep and laugh together through joys but especially through sorrows, those tough places where you visit the broken and wounded. Your prayer closet. Those are the reserved tables! Please be seated. If you have not learned to find the comfort of walking with a brother who is lonely or broken, then you probably won't get to appreciate the luxuries of heaven.

- Our Lord has chosen the menu
  A banquet? Well, not yet! But it will be exactly enough, and every item will be chosen with purpose. Soldiers are fed a diet that will give them energy and strength. Are you ready for a soldier's meal? It's called a military MRE (Meal – Ready to Eat); that means you eat it just as you find it. You cook it in the bag. You eat it with a plastic spoon. The tray is optional; you may have to eat right out of the plastic bag.

  God adds to that the blessings of holy company. Jesus spoke of food that was not of this earth (John 4:32,34). Paul tells the Corinthians that being unwilling to eat strong spiritual food is a sign of carnality (1 Corinthians 3:2). Peter points out that an elementary diet of spiritual "milk" is for newborn babies (1 Peter 2:2). The writer to the Hebrews notes that being stuck on "baby food" is a characteristic of one who is "unskilled in the Word" (Hebrews 5:13). The message is quite clear: spiritual warriors must become used to strong food in order to be effective in spiritual warfare, otherwise they will quickly become casualties. Our "taste" for the soldier's MRE today will determine where we get to eat when the battle is over.

So, what can we take away from this? Here are some thoughts to hang on to.

1. Learn to place a high value on your proven fellow believers; if you're waiting for better dinner company, you probably won't find it! Surely you have noticed that some of those who once huddled with you in your spiritual battles are no longer here. We must begin to treasure those in the body of Christ whom God has placed close to us.
2. Many believers have no heart for the hardships of spiritual warfare. They are looking for the banquet, but sadly they miss what Jesus said about the price of true discipleship (Matthew 6:24), and ultimately, they may find themselves locked out of the banquet (Matthew 7:21-23).

3. Don't run away! Take every opportunity to get close to where God is, and that will always be where His true followers are gathered together. There are lots of "imitations" but keep looking until you recognize the reality and power of the Holy Spirit in changed (and changing) lives.
4. Seize every possible opportunity. Soldiers in combat do not miss a mess call, not just because they are hungry, but as much because they don't know when the next opportunity will present itself. Is your schedule too full of more enjoyable pursuits for you to attend the "mess calls"? God may be telling you to take another look at your schedule. One day soon, nobody will remember (or care about) all that urgent "work" that consumes every waking hour of our days.
5. Digest God's Word, as much of it as you can lay hold of. It will be the first thing that the enemy will try to take away from us in the coming battles. Memorize it. Write down portions of it. Carry it on pages and scraps in your pockets. Get alone with God and His Word. Treasure it as if it were a personal message from God; it is!

Mission 88

Complaining!

Complaining is a trap; easy to get into but hard to get out!

Soldiers have always found something to complain about. It's an old saying that if the soldier has enough time to complain, he's not being trained hard enough!

I'm sure that we do know that conditions can become very difficult for soldiers, especially in combat situations and over long periods of time. There does come a point where "normal" complaining about the food, the socks, the weather, the lack of support and a thousand other things can begin to erode morale. It's at that point that the fighting unit begins to lose its combat effectiveness; it accepts orders more slowly, cuts corners, loses heart and begins to openly question the authority or wisdom of the commanding officers. That's when casualties begin to mount, and the enemy takes command of the field.

Same rule holds for spiritual warriors.

Prayer Warrior, what does your "Complaint Department" look like? Have you been there lately? Sometimes we even make jokes about our complaining, but did you know that God has something to say about that? Actually, He dislikes it ….. a lot!

The arch-example of complaining in the Bible has to be the story of the Israelites on their way to the promised land. Ten times (Numbers 14:22) before they even got to the wilderness; in fact, the 40-year wilderness experience was judgment for their complaining. If it had not been for

Moses' intercession for them, God would have killed them all right there on the edge of the wilderness (Numbers 14:12) just because of their continual griping and complaining.

So, what's so bad about complaining, and why does God react so harshly to it? After all, wasn't it their complaining in Egypt that prompted God to intervene on their behalf?

Firstly, their situation in Egypt had become truly oppressive. Pharaoh had deliberately imposed increasingly harsher conditions upon them. They had come to Egypt as welcome guests when Joseph was a powerful voice for God's people, but in the following 400 years their favoured status had been reversed and they were now being used as a source of slave labour.

Secondly, deliverance from Egypt was God's plan, including the emergence of the two men at the centre of this drama: Pharoah and Moses. Deliverance did not come as a result of the Hebrews' complaining.

Now God had miraculously delivered the entire Hebrew people, sparing them from the angel of death and even persuading the Egyptian people to give them all of their gold, jewellery and valuables (Exodus 12:35-36). The Red Sea crossing, the annihilation of the Egyptian army, food and water in the desert, clothing and footware, and even God's very Presence in His Tabernacle. Blessing after blessing, miracle after miracle, and the promise that they were only days away from entering into the land that God had promised them. Their response: idolatry, disobedience, insurrection and continual grumbling.

So what did their complaining say to God?

- That God was not treating them well enough
- That God was not paying attention to their predicament
- That God had given them poor leaders
- That God took too long to give them His directions
- That God could not deliver on His promises
- That they refused to be thankful for *anything*

Complaining hasn't changed much since Moses' day. Nor has God changed His attitude toward it!

Complaining comes from putting ourselves at the centre of our world, with the attitude that everything here is for *our* benefit. With our eyes and hearts focused on the "stuff" of the world, we become so self-centered that anything that comes between us and what we think we deserve leads us to complain.

Complaining comes from forgetting our true purpose for being here. If it's all about building a monument for ourselves, our success and our comfort, then we complain when anything (or anyone) interferes with that agenda. Our true purpose for being here is not to take care of our family, not to succeed in our business, not to gain personal prominence or fortune, not to make the most of ourselves. Our priority as believers must be the advancement of God's Kingdom (Matthew 6:33). That's not the same thing as church building, empire building or any other kind of monument building to ourselves. If we have the wrong goal in life, if we are the reason for being here, then everything that interferes with that goal becomes a cause for complaint.

Complaining always causes us to lose the mind of Christ. Servanthood is the mind of Christ; not to be served but to serve (Matthew 20:28, Mark 10:45, John 13:1-17). True servanthood and complaining cannot exist together in the same heart. Choose one.

Complaining kills praise. God has taken the responsibility of supplying all the grace to meet our needs (2 Corinthians 9:8). Praise will automatically stop as soon as we take on a complaining spirit.

Complaining causes us to forget that victory requires sacrifice. Complaining robs us of our long-distance vision; we begin to focus on the temporary things instead of seeing the eternal (2 Corinthians 4:17-18), then we lose sight of the true cost of victory. Endurance is one of those costs; sometimes that means sacrifice. Is it worth it? Only if we can see the value beyond the temporary.

Complaining poisons our efforts to win the lost, the confused and the hopeless. If all they hear from us is our whining over not having more of this or that, things that they probably never had the luxury of enjoying, then we really have nothing of value that would be worth their time in listening to us. Complainers are not evangelists, no matter what gifts you may think you have.

If we have slipped into the shoes of a complainer, we must get out quickly because we have already caught God's attention (and not in a good way!).

The first step is to get a reality check, but don't bother to ask yourself if you are a complainer. If you are far enough along to see it in yourself, it's already very obvious to everyone else. We always rationalize our complaining by giving all the reasons why we are right. It actually has nothing to do with the right or wrong of our claims; it's all about attitude, and that's where God wants to go to work. Your circumstances may need to change, but God is more interested in changing your attitude because it's that complaining attitude that has poisoned your relationship with Him.

The next step is to make it a matter of serious prayer with other believers. This complaining attitude can quickly become a root of bitterness (Hebrews 12:15) and a stronghold of Satan in your life. That's serious stuff!

You must realize that your complaining attitude has already negatively affected others, maybe even to the point of turning them into complainers. Complainers make their own company!

Then one must focus on gratitude to God for all of His good things in your life. Make a list if you must but get your attention on God's blessings. Ask God to reveal them to you and to give you a spirit of thanksgiving.

Eliminate complaints from your praying. You may certainly state your needs but stay away from complaining. It's amazing how easily we can turn asking into complaining.

Recognize that complaining is a pattern of thinking developed over a long time, so it will take some time to reverse that attitude and to fully replace it with an attitude of thanksgiving. Good news: the change will be immediately noticeable by others!

Developing a pattern of complaining comes more easily when we are in a spiritual dry time, so be on the alert for those "down" seasons. Focus on Scriptures that speak of joy and deliverance. When David found himself in such a season, he turned to recall all the past blessings of the Lord (Psalm 77:10-11).

Complaining will become easier to spot (in ourselves) and easier to correct as we realize how seriously God looks at it. He will also be the first to notice the improvement!

MISSION 89

The Enemy's Plan - Part 1

In any war, great effort is made to try to discover the enemy's plans and, more specifically, the tactics that he will use to accomplish those plans. Where will he attack? How great a force will he bring into the battle? When? How does the battle fit into his bigger plan? How long is he able to stay in the battle? What are his strengths and weaknesses? What will be our strongest defence? How can we turn the enemy's tactics against him?

Spiritual warfare is no different; if anything, knowing the enemy's tactics is much more important. We must know and recognize the enemy's tactics if we are to be able to win the battle. To be unprepared or uninformed will always result in defeat. Make no mistake, spiritual warrior; our enemy fights because he believes that he can win. He may know that he cannot win the war, but he does know that he can certainly win many of the battles. And he has already won many battles! If we foolishly think that we need not give the battle much attention or preparation, that somehow God will win in the end and it will all work out, then we will live long enough to see the destruction of our families, our homes, our lives, our churches and our society .... all lost to the enemy's actions. And in the end, we will come face to face with the terrible truth that our inaction (or lack of interest) will have resulted in a lifetime wasted, something with no meaning and that made no eternal difference at all!

So, it's time to study the enemy, learn his tactics and become prepared to defend ourself, even to turn his plans against him. Through the following Missions we will take a look at several of Satan's often-used tactics, the ones that have worked well for him down through the centuries and that are still very effective today. Some of them are small maneuvers, while others are far more complex, but they all have one thing in common: they all work!

Here are some of the enemy's tactics that we will examine:

- He attempts to destroy our standing before God
- He spreads lies, half-truths and doubt
- He distorts and confuses God's Word
- He weakens us in prayer
- He uses intimidation to sow fear and discouragement
- He broadcasts a message of defeat
- He is the master of procrastination
- He is an expert at diversion
- He steals the Word
- He sends false messages and false messengers
- He steals our time, our goals, our dreams and our passion
- He sends the supernatural and the exotic occult to replace the godly
- He attacks our secret places
- He interferes with our progress, leading us to think wrong and to make mistakes
- He enters lives, creates strongholds and hardens the heavens
- He instils a paralyzing fear of death
- He offers a shortcut to the Kingdom of God
- He imitates character, signs and wonders
- He is a genius in the uses of sexual allurement and perversion
- He exploits our anger, pride and selfishness
- He brings persecution, sickness and hardship

So, let's get started. And let's keep in mind that our enemy, none other than Satan and his legion of powers, would much prefer that we didn't do this at all, or that we wouldn't take it too seriously. So, I suggest that we each start with a simple prayer that the Holy Spirit will use these Missions to arm and prepare us for effective warfare against our enemy, remove from us anything that would be an offence against God's holiness, and fill us with a stubborn resolve to finish our course well.

Satan attempts to destroy our standing before God

Satan personally accuses us before God, pointing out that we are unfit for God's presence.

Why start here? Simply because, if we believe the accusations brought against us (even a little bit), then we will lack the courage to stand before God. If we feel so unworthy, then we probably won't come into His presence at all. If we think that God has allowed us to only hide quietly in the corner, then we will not have the boldness to bring our requests to the Father, and we will certainly not intercede for anyone else.

What has God said about this?

> *Now there was a day when the sons of God came to present themselves before the Lord, and Satan also came among them. The Lord said to Satan, "From where have you come?" Satan answered the Lord and said, "From going to and fro on the earth, and from walking up and down on it."*
> Job 1:6-7 NKJV

> *Then I heard a loud voice saying in heaven, "Now salvation, and strength, and the kingdom of our God, and the power of His Christ have come, for the accuser of our brethren, who accused them before our God day and night, has been cast down."*
> Revelation 12:10 NKJV

Yes, Satan has always been accusing God's people before God, and he is accusing you and me daily! Nothing new there. Knowing that our name is coming up before the throne of God this way may not make us happy, nor should it surprise us. Our secrets are being openly listed by our accuser before the Judge, but that's not the end of it because God has foreseen that and He has made a provision for us just when we need it most. We have an Advocate, our defence attorney, who immediately stands in the face of those charges against us.

> *Who shall bring any charge against God's elect? It is God who justifies. Who is to condemn? Christ Jesus is the one who died—more than that, who was raised—who is at the right hand of God, who indeed is interceding for us.*
> Romans 8:33-34 ESV

Notice that we do not say anything in the face of the charges against us; it is Jesus who answers because those sins of which we are accused were taken by Jesus on the cross where He made our sins His own (2 Corinthians 5:21). Satan is accusing us, but we are no longer the owners of that sin; JESUS TOOK OWNERSHIP. That's what He meant when He said "It is finished. *Tetalestai.* Transaction completed" (John 19:28-30). More than that, He is now alive in God's presence to prove that the payment for those sins was completely adequate to satisfy God's perfect justice.

So, what do we have to say about these accusations? We don't answer the accuser; Jesus already has done that. We can confess our deep sorrow for our transgression, acknowledging that it was indeed our sins that put Jesus on the cross in our place, but we must also confess before our Father (and all those who hear us in heavenly places) that we gladly claim His gracious, complete forgiveness (1 John 1:9). Accused? Yes. Condemned? Absolutely not!

> *There is therefore now no condemnation for those who are in Christ Jesus. For the law of the Spirit of life has set you free in Christ Jesus from the law of sin and death.*
> Romans 8:1-2 ESV

> *For I am sure that neither death nor life, nor angels nor rulers, nor things present nor things to come, nor powers, nor height nor depth, nor anything else in all creation, will be able to separate us from the love of God in Christ Jesus our Lord.*
> Romans 8:38-39 ESV

So, what is our true standing before God?

Blessed be the God and Father of our Lord Jesus Christ, who has blessed us with every spiritual blessing in the heavenly places in Christ, just as He chose us in Him before the foundation of the world, that we should be holy and without blame before Him in love, having predestined us to adoption as sons by Jesus Christ to Himself, according to the good pleasure of His will, to the praise of the glory of His grace, by which He made us **accepted in the Beloved.**
Ephesians 1:3-6 ESV

Let us then with confidence draw near to the throne of grace, that we may receive mercy and find grace to help in time of need.
Hebrews 4:16 ESV

See what kind of love the Father has given to, that we should be called children of God; and so we are! The reason why the world does not know us is that it did not know Him. Beloved, we are God's children now; and what we will be has not yet appeared, but we know that when He appears, we shall be like Him, for we shall see Him as He is.
1 John 3:1-2 ESV

We are completely accepted by God, called God's own children, and we have the eternal benefits of Jesus' resurrection and seating at the Father's throne. We have been named (by the Father) as co-heirs with Jesus in God's Kingdom. We have been promised God's eternal generosity. We have been given unlimited power, the same power that raised Jesus from the dead. We have been given eternal life and the promise of an endless future of discovery of the infinite reaches of God's creation and grace. We have a loving Father who has mapped out a life of fulfilment and joy for us (even amid hardships) even before we get to heaven.

And that's just from the first two chapters of the letter to the Ephesians!

So, what about that threat of destroying our standing before God?

CAN'T HAPPEN! Carry on!

Mission 90

The Enemy's Plan - Part 2

Satan steals our time, our goals, our dreams and our passion

We've all seen "street people", those all-too-common folks who seem to have become the sad victims of our society. It's easy to imagine those street people as having lost their dreams and goals, and it may well be true, but Satan has his eye on more than unfortunate street people. He wants to steal our dreams, to turn us all into people who have lost our dreams and passion. And maybe one of the ways Satan is doing that is by getting us to make the mistake of seeing those "street people" as hopeless losers who have no claim on our neat, successful lives, making us forget that Jesus Himself could be sitting there right in front of us (Matthew 25:34-40). Human pride and godly passion don't hang together. We cannot get a right view of our dreams if we cannot see ourselves (and others) as God sees us.

Where is our sense of connection to a purpose, a grand reason why we are here in the first place? A purpose that goes far beyond our job, our happiness, our success, our family, our church, our little group of like-us people; something that is as far above us as the heavens are above the earth. And if there was a day in the distant past when we felt that lofty tug on our spirit, how did we ever come to being so grounded, flightless, earth-tied?

Satan is good at dragging us down. He once moved among the highest reaches of God's creation, but when he raised himself against the Most High One, he was "cast down" to the earth (Revelation 12:9). Eat dirt! And that's what he wants to feed us, too.

He starts by fooling us into forgetting that we are created with a beginning and an end. It's that "end" part that he wants us to put out of our minds, to push off into the future. God says that we have an appointment to keep, one in which we will give an accounting of how well we have spent this time He has given us. We were born with an empty shopping cart; if we get to the end with an empty cart we're in trouble! So, Satan gets us to think that the cart is there so we can fill it up with stuff for ourselves; Jesus (Matthew 6:19) tells us that "stuff" rusts, decays or gets stolen. Paul (1 Corinthians 3:12) tells us that "stuff" is highly flammable! In the end, Satan wants us to find ourselves filled with good intentions and out of the one thing that we cannot ever get back: time. God is reminding us every day that the time to seek Him, do good, love Him and others, serve Him and others is now. We cannot "make time" or "find time"; we can only spend it. We need God to show us what time it is.

Satan makes every effort to dim those dreams of commitment and service. He knows that if we let enough time pass, that fire in our soul will grow cool, then cold. The passion will be lost to just the ordinary. Dreams will become something in the past, leaving us with nothing more than wishful thinking.

Busyness is the enemy of our passion, until busyness *becomes* our passion. From that point on, we are wide open to the enemy's agenda which will gradually bring us to a point where we have filled up our shopping cart with schedules, urgencies, priorities, replacements for right relationships, "stuff" that should satisfy our hunger for success and meaningfulness. Until one day we begin to realize that we are tired, disappointed and further than ever from the goal line. You see, the enemy knows that he cannot dull our enthusiasm by offering us "nothing"; instead, he captures our fire by pointing us in the direction of wrong priorities, even if it means wrapping them in the language of Christian activity. Firefighters understand very well that one of the best ways to ultimately control a strong forest fire is by allowing it to burn up all the fuel, even if it means starting another fire in its path. Satan is good at putting stuff in our path to consume us.

So how does Satan gain a foothold in our dreams and passion?

Usually, he starts by dulling our appetite for reading and digesting the Word of God. Remember the first time you read some of those amazing verses in Ephesians? The incredible power released in us by the working of the Holy Spirit? The brilliant light that flashed in our spirit the first time we really realized what God has prepared for us in Jesus? The breathless excitement and glory of beginning to understand God's plans for us extending far beyond time and eternity? What about coming face to face with the revelation that you could do *all* things through Jesus? All things, all power, all strength, all sufficiency! That's the fire that the enemy doesn't want burning in your spirit. So, get back to God's Word and inhale a high-octane breath of something explosive, and don't leave until you start to feel the heat!

What about the first time you heard God's Spirit speaking into your imagination saying "Come with Me and do something that really matters in My kingdom" --- and you dared to believe that all it took was a radical trust in and surrender to Him! So the enemy's tactic becomes one of reminding you that it's too late. That call from God was then, and this is now. You missed the bus and now there's nothing left! It's time to get back to praying for that call from God, praying for that voice of the enemy to be silenced, listening more intently for the Spirit's voice to once again resonate in your heart. The same God who called into your heart those years ago is the One who still speaks your name; there is still a piece of heaven's windows that remain to be opened in answer to the call of His people (2 Chronicles 7:14, Malachi 3:10).

Then the enemy wants us to keep our dreams to ourselves. You see, believers who talk about their dreams and goals usually have an enthusiasm that is quite infectious; their enthusiasm and commitment are contagious. They pray for vision, then they boldly speak of God's leading. They pray for courage, then they unashamedly declare how God brought them to a higher place in doing things that were way beyond their own ability. They offer bold praise, and we wonder how it is that they keep finding more joy. These people cannot be ignored, and the enemy knows it! Want to be one of them? Then get up and get loud!

Still feel like all the "exceptional" has drained out of your life, leaving you with nothing but "flat"? That's the work of the enemy. It's time to have that conversation with God. Start with something like "I'm sorry, Father; this is all my fault. Please forgive me and restore to me the joy of my salvation. No matter what it takes, I refuse to give up until you get me to the place You have planned for me".

MISSION 91

The Enemy's Plan - Part 3

These two tactics of the enemy deal with what he attempts to do against God's Word. Very understandable that he would devote so much effort in this direction since God Himself places such great emphasis and importance on it:

- It is the sword of the Spirit (Ephesians 6:17)
- It is the means by which the light of God's truth enters the human heart (Psalm 119:130)
- It is eternal (Psalm 119:89)
- It is accompanied by God's own supernatural power (Hebrews 4:12)
- It is the means by which God lights our life path (Psalm 119:105)
- It is the instrument which God uses to expose our deepest secrets (Hebrews 4:12)
- It is the means by which God reveals sin in our lives and enables us to please Him (Psalm 119:9, 11)
- It is our source of strength, especially in times of weakness (Psalm 119:28), and comfort in times of distress (Psalm 119:50)
- It is our source of hope (Psalm 119:114, 147)
- It is our source of deliverance from trouble (Psalm 119:170)

The list could go on and on. God's Word is supremely important to Him and it ought to be to us as well. That is precisely why Satan is working so hard to disconnect us from its power. Here are a couple ways he tries to do this.

He steals God's Word away from the one who has just heard it

This is the famous parable of the sower and the seed (Matthew 13:1-9, 18-23). We all know it quite well. Focus on that seed dropped by the wayside, and Jesus' explanation in verse 19. Here is the enemy at work snatching away the seed, removing it from the hearer's heart and mind, so that it cannot even germinate and spring into life. To human eyes, those seeds were picked up by the birds, but in the language of the parable it was none other than Satan himself at work stealing the seeds. Jesus attributes this to the lack of understanding on the part of the hearer; maybe in the context of our part in planting those seeds (or at least attending to them once they are planted) we forgot that the hearer must be given some "understanding", and maybe that translates into our willingness to carefully explain the message (seed) so that understanding will take place. We must learn that sowing the seed is only the beginning of our mission, but then the battle begins over what will become of that seed. The difference between the wayside and the good ground may have a lot to do with the care with which the seed is nurtured.

He attempts to confuse and distort God's Word

How many ways are there to keep believers out of actually getting to know God's Word? And how many ways are there to actually twist and distort the Word so that it looks like a hopeless jumble?

Satan loves to suggest all sorts of complicated scenarios ("what ifs?"), designed to appeal to the human mind to "unravel" God's "mysteries". Endless winding paths leading nowhere. Making it sound so complicated and contradictory that any hope of actually understanding it is lost. "Wordsmithing", inserting false meanings and innuendos, crafting the language to rob it of its direct meaning and power. Bending (or completely breaking) the meaning of words. Wading around in the pool containing some pieces of God's Word and a lot of other deceptive language. The result: complete confusion.

The truth is that Satan often uses human messengers to do this work, and these "messengers" come dressed in a variety of costumes, all designed to appeal to the audience. Some use Bible language but clearly teach some "other" gospel (Galatians 1:7-9). They usually take the name Christian, but they are far from any form of Biblical Christianity (2 Timothy 3:5), and their "Bible" may be very different from God's Word. Some twist the message (2 Peter 3:16) to suit their own agendas, producing useless emphasis on unimportant points (1 Timothy 1:4). In many cases, these "messengers" find eager and gullible audiences (2 Timothy 4:3), a situation which will drastically *increase* as we approach the end of the age.

What? Churches small and large filled with people calling themselves Christians but knowing little or nothing about God's Word? You bet! Sadly, God's judgment for this wicked situation will fall not only on the heads of those "messengers" but also on many of their followers (Matthew 7:15-23).

Robbing God's Word of its power in your life may be as simple as giving yourself excuses for not seriously reading it. Consistently. Honestly. Prayerfully. Daily. In the end, if the enemy's action produces a lack of fruit in our lives, he wins and we lose. We don't have to join some anti-Bible cult or become wrapped up in some crazy false religion; we simply need to fill up our lives with busyness, leaving no room or opportunity for God's Word to do its work. The birds and weeds will do the rest! What should be a productive, producing garden has become a thicket of weeds and bushes and no fruit!

Mission 92

The Enemy's Plan - Part 4

He spreads lies, half-truths and doubt

It should come as no surprise to us that the "father of lies" (John 8:44) would make such great use of this tactic; we expect it of him. What we don't expect is that *we* could be fooled by his deceptions, drawn into actually believing what he wants us to believe, while all the time thinking that we are following the truth. Satan is counting on the spirit of pride *in us* to keep us from humbly realizing that *our* minds and hearts are as inherently wicked and deceptive as anyone else's.

> *The heart is deceitful above all things, and desperately wicked; Who can know it?*
> Jeremiah 17:9 NKJV

Deceitful. That means that it lies. It lies to others, but mostly it lies to *us*. That's the terrible power of it; it fools us.

So, what has that to do with our spiritual warfare? Well, to put it simply, *everything*! We have an enemy on the outside who is none other than Satan himself, and we have an enemy agent on the inside, in the form of our wicked heart and proud spirit. We need help! And let's get it on the table right up front; if we attempt to deal with this threat alone, we will certainly fail every time. This threat must be confronted with the combined strengths, giftings and grace of the corporate body of Jesus. No one individual, regardless of position in the body, will get it right every time. We must have the checks and double-checks prescribed in Scripture to consistently know the truth at a time when lies and deception are everywhere, even (and especially) within the professing church.

Military deception refers to attempts to mislead enemy forces during warfare.

So what is at stake for us right now? Certainly the battle of truth has waged since the Garden of Eden, but today I believe that we are seeing the final moves on the world stage leading up to what we can call the "end times". Satan has been planning this battle for millennia and has been very carefully planting his ideas and his agents down through the years. What we see as national and international "circumstances" are far from random events; they are situations carefully orchestrated to bring about the emergence of Satan's kingdom here on earth, and ultimately the confrontation between his "superman" and Jesus. Remember that this "superman" will be universally popular, probably elected, and extremely persuasive at precisely the time when the nations and people of the world will be desperate for someone with a "solution" to everything from unemployment to economic Armageddon.

All of the tools are already in place; we use them every day when we pay for goods at the stores, sign on to our computers or use our smartphones. Operating behind the scenes, unseen by most of us, are the gigantic systems, people and governments who are making this system so completely efficient and thorough. What we do see and hear every moment of every day is the bombardment of communications containing the brew of deception and misinformation. And, of course, it would be too simple if we could simply trust the billboards, signs and banners announcing "Truth Here". And how tragic and effective it is when the enemy is able to infiltrate even the believing church and convince it to be his broadcaster. How true is the warning given in Matthew 24:24 concerning these very days in which we are now living?

We fall for the lie, the half-truth, whenever we allow the world's agenda to "piggyback" on the Christian gospel. Our communication becomes no more than part gospel and part propaganda. It may be politically popular, but it lacks all the power of God. It may change some minds, but it will not change any lives. It's the handiwork of the enemy and it is a lie.

Surely one of the most prevalent lies today is the message that there simply is no truth, or that it is too complex to grasp and so may as well not exist at all. Planting seeds of doubt. The removal of certainty. Every idea or philosophy deserves to be given equal standing with every other. Every "gospel" should be treated on the same level as the Biblical gospel. All shades and variations are equally "true". And equally "untrue"! In the end, truth doesn't really matter.

We have been given only *one* truth, personified in none other than Jesus Christ (John 16:6). That means that God has only *one* counter to all of the enemy's lies. He doesn't need political or politically correct embellishments, nor will He lend His credibility to any. Only the unadulterated gospel has the power to silence the enemy's lies and to deliver those held captive by the web of deceit into glorious freedom.

Spiritual warrior, it's time to drop the baggage. Clarify the message. Focus on the one thing that Satan can never defeat – the Truth! And it can come only from God's Word. It's not on the news headlines and it's not in the rhetoric of the leaders of our political, financial or entertainment world. Get to know the Truth so well that the error of the lie will become clear.

Our Saviour is not on the Right or the Left, nor will He come from either. He is not the product of human ideology, and He refuses to be captured by any. He stands completely alone and completely above all others. Only He will be crowned as Lord of lords and King of kings (1 Timothy 16:15, Revelation 17:14, 19:16). In a day when the enemy is spreading his lies and doubts, we must pray for wisdom to see and cling to *the* truth, and for the courage to proclaim it with certainty in the face of growing opposition.

Mission 93

The Enemy's Plan - Part 5

It's very hard to defeat an army that is absolutely convinced that it is unbeatable, where morale is at an all-time high.

But there are many examples of a superior force being defeated after having been demoralized and discouraged. Demoralization is an extremely important part of psychological warfare, and our enemy knows how to use it to his maximum advantage.

He uses intimidation to sow discouragement, fear and anxiety

Doubt leads to fear. Fear leads to anxiety. Anxiety makes us ask "What will happen next?". "Who can help us?". Anxiety is the button that the enemy pushes to demoralize us, but in order for this button to work, there must first arise a distancing between groups or individuals from their common cause or leadership because they no longer believe them capable of offering a solution to their anxiety. To put it briefly, people lose confidence in their leadership and their mission.

The enemy manufactures "incidents", crises, situations that knock us off guard, intended to grab all of our attention and drain our emotional resources, leaving us barely able to focus on any course of action. Job experienced this, and we can see how the experience left him with few answers.

So, what is the point of these attacks of the enemy?

His goal is to separate us from our mission, and even to separate us from each other. He wants to get us "alone" where we cannot hear a word of wisdom or encouragement from God or each other. And he wants to get us, as the body of believers, to turn to someone else for rescue from this manufactured crisis. He wants us to become willing to, at least temporarily, suspend our commitment to the lordship of Jesus and the building of His kingdom and to follow his man to solve this crisis. The problem is, of course, that his "man" is the very enemy of Jesus.

Satan wants to con us into unwittingly joining his cause. He believes that, if the circumstances can be made to seem so critical, uncertain and fearful, that we will turn away from godly leadership and be willing to put him in control of the situation, especially if he imitates godly language to do so.

He broadcasts a message of defeat

During World War 2, both Germany and Japan regularly broadcast radio programs in English in which they continually announced their victories over the Allied forces, of course intended to plant the impression that the war had, for all intents and purposes, been won (by them). That message was hard to counter, especially when the Allied forces did frequently suffer defeat at the hands of their enemies. There was no denying the facts; sometimes the enemy did win battles, and many times it did look like they were winning the war. The broadcasting played on these "facts" and projected the (false) conclusion that Allied defeat (and Axis victory) was inevitable. These broadcasts were designed, not just for the soldiers' listening, but for the ears of their governments, supporters and families at home. The point of it all was to make the Allies give up the fight, to consider the war to be a loss, to count the terrible cost as being too high. Quit now!.

Does anything sound familiar here? We are over 75 years distanced from those days in World War 2, but the tactic of broadcasting a message of defeat was not invented in World War 2. Our enemy, the Devil himself, invented it, and he has been using it to great effect. He has been using it against you and me, and he continues to do so today.

He usually starts with some "facts" which he knows we cannot deny. Facts such as

- We have "messed up" more than once in our life
- We have made more than one bad decision in life
- At least some of our present circumstances are consequences of our own failures
- We know what it feels like to be guilty of sin
- We are imperfect, so we may expect to fail again
- Others know about our failures, and not everyone has forgiven us
- We often feel very weak and vulnerable

Our circumstances sometimes put us in a place where defeat seems like the only option. It may be a sudden loss, a terrible sickness, a great disappointment. It may be at the end of a lot of seemingly unanswered prayers. It always involves something that we do not understand or were unprepared for. It usually comes at night or when we are alone. It leaves us crying out "What do we do now?"

The enemy loves times like that. Our thoughts are captured by the problems; even our prayers seem just another reminder of the crisis.

OK. The list could go on, but we get the point.

God certainly knows that we sometimes feel exhausted and discouraged and He knows that our enemy is the one who is broadcasting that message of defeat. That's why He has taken the care to broadcast a message of His own, a message of hope and assurance. Far from being forgotten and abandoned to defeat at the hand of our enemy, we are in the centre of God's attention and He has made special provision for us:

- God has heard our confessions and He has assured us that His forgiveness is irreversible (1 John 1:9)
- God has explained to us that He did far more than simply "forget" our sins; He did not simply "forget" them. He perfected His plan whereby His Son made *our* sins *His own* sins, and in exchange He

made His Son's perfection *our* perfection. Having done that, He executed His final judgment on those sins by allowing His Son to endure death. Case closed! It's called JUSTIFICATION. (Romans 8:1, 2 Corinthians 5:21)

- God fully understands our weakness; He doesn't excuse us on that basis, but He does completely understand it (Psalm 103:14, Hebrews 4:15)
- If God intended to deal only with perfect people, then His grace would be useless (Mark 2:17)
- Although we cannot see the end of our present warfare, including our defeats, God has assured us that He can (Psalm 139:16) and has made provision for *all* of them
- Our present trials are no accident, but are ordained by God for our good (James 1:2-4, 1 Peter 4:12)
- Our ultimate triumph is guaranteed (2 Corinthians 2:14)

Here is God's prescription for dealing with fear and discouragement.

- Run to God's Word daily and refuse to be prevented from doing so. Start with those passages listed above.
- Make praise a bigger part of your faith walk. Intentionally make room for more praise, not simply for the things that God has done for you, but more importantly to recognize God's qualities and character. Let praise be driven by your will, not your emotions.
- Seek God's presence among other believers. Do not abandon the fellowship with those believers. They are God's lifeline to you.
- Pray more. Not just asking for stuff but pouring out your heart before our Father. Pray alone. Pray with others. Pray expectantly. Pray with a listening spirit.
- Look for God to show up!

Mission 94

The Enemy's Plan - Part 6

Tomorrow
(noun)
The best time to do everything
you had planned for today

<u>Satan is a master of procrastination, and he wants you to be the same</u>

Usually something that we make jokes about, procrastination is actually a very powerful weapon in the hands of our enemy.

Satan understands very well that there are times when we are moved to conviction, even daring, and that in that brief moment we are able to commit to a course of action despite even great opposition. He knows that, in that moment, once we have moved from conviction to action, nothing can stop us. His only weapon is to try to create an interruption, a break between that moment of conviction and the following action. He knows that time alone will dull the urgency of conviction, lowering the probability that action will follow or, if it does, it will be a scaled-down version of what we first thought to do.

The enemy doesn't tell us to *not* follow through on our conviction; he simply tells us to do it *later*.

Pharoah waited one more night with the frog infestation (Exodus 8:10).

Governor Felix, deeply convicted by Paul's preaching, waited for a more "convenient" time (Acts 24:25). That time never came.

Paul warned the Corinthian believers that God has prescribed "acceptable" times for responding to the gospel, hence the supreme importance of acting "now" (2 Corinthians 6:2).

The writer to the Hebrews warns that failure to act today may result in a hardening of the heart (Hebrews 3:13), making it impossible to respond tomorrow.

Spiritual warfare, as in all warfare, requires decisive, timely action. The outcome of many of the greatest battles often hinged upon critical actions taken at precisely the right time. Sometime later is not good enough. God has seasons and so do we; if we do not move in God's timing, we may not move at all. Even Jesus declared that He could only do His miraculous works as He saw the Father doing them (John 5:19), and Luke 5:17 indicates that Jesus' works intentionally coincided with the presence of the Holy Spirit. Jesus Himself warned of an approaching darkness in which not even He could work (John 9:4).

Satan is a master of diversion

A military diversion is a tactic designed to draw the enemy's attention away from the real action; it is a short-term tactic usually deployed immediately ahead of the main attack. The purpose of the diversion may be to cause the enemy to move his forces away from the battle zone, to divide his forces, or even to delay doing anything until it is too late. Sometimes the diversion is built up over a period of time using a series of false alarms so that when the real attack comes the enemy will fall for the "cry wolf" deception and think this is just another false alarm.

Satan is maneuvering his forces into position in preparation for his grand assault in these last days. His forces include those demonic powers named in Scripture (Ephesians 6:12), but they also include the human institutions, governments and agencies that have been infiltrated and seconded into his service. Long before the main battle begins, these infiltrations have been taking place. We can see the evidence in all of our educational, financial, entertainment and government institutions. Bit by bit, one law at a time, one step at a time, our society has been transformed (and will continue to be transformed) until it is, indeed, the enemy's kingdom on earth. Ruled by fear and supreme materialism, people will be held under control by manufactured crises, captivating world events and stage-rehearsal personalities until finally this diversion will end with the unveiling of Satan's "man".

Satan's plan for the believing church is that they won't notice what's really happening, won't put the pieces together, will be too preoccupied, along with everyone else, with the masterful diversions. Until it will be too late.

So why is Satan so concerned with what the church does? Surely the church represents only a small fraction of the world's population, so what's the big deal?

Well, Satan knows all too well that believers have at their disposal the very power of Almighty God, Resurrection power. Believers can know liberating truth and can declare it with supernatural effect. Believers can call God right into the midst of the most intense spiritual battles. Believers can defeat and disrupt Satan's plans. Believers have been given God's armor designed to withstand Satan's weapons. Believers have been given God's plan of putting the body of Jesus into action; not just individual efforts, but supernaturally coordinated actions as believers operating together in the harmony of one body. Believers can see through the enemy's deceptions and can receive on-the-ground wisdom and directions from God.

Believers can be Satan's biggest headache! No wonder that he is going to such great lengths to deceive the church. If only he could fool even some of the church into falling for his lie or, better yet, into unwittingly supporting his program.

Fact is, he is well along in actually accomplishing exactly that.

So, Prayer Warrior, what are we to do now?

Let's start with a few things:

1. God is not surprised, nor is He fooled by Satan's tactics of procrastination and diversion. He saw this day coming and has warned and prepared us in His Word. That's where we must go for the ultimate truth test. We must know God's Word. Deeply.
2. God has equipped the church with a variety of gifts to ensure that we continue to clearly hear and understand His voice to us even in the midst of the Devil's noise. These gifts require that we commit to operating closely together very much as did the early believers after Pentecost.
3. We must loosen our grip on this world. We must wean our minds and hearts from consuming the diet that this world provides, for with that diet comes the deception. We must be willing to step away from the "new normal", refuse to accept the "new truth", and stand against conformity to the "new thinking".
4. We must count the cost of true discipleship.
5. We must prepare to receive the harvest, all of it, even the parts that may be broken and scarred.
6. We must uncover the great resources of God laid up for us for this very time in which we are living.
7. We must become committed to asking and acting in the NOW, refusing to be fooled into waiting for tomorrow to do what we know we must do today

Mission 95

The Enemy's Plan - Part 7

<u>He weakens us in prayer, builds strongholds and hardens heavens</u>

Our lifeline to God is prayer. Without it, we cannot last long. Satan knows that, so he tries everything in his power to interfere with our praying.

Prayer quickly becomes work; serious prayer demands a lot from us, not just our time, but a big investment of our heart. We must believe when everything around us tells us the opposite. We must trust even when we cannot see. We must persist even when the enemy tells us to quit. We must surrender before we can ask. We must let go before we can take hold. Sometimes we must wait and wait and wait. Sometimes we will be disappointed or frustrated. Sometimes our heart will soar and sometimes it will break. But the truth is that absolutely nothing of value in God's kingdom can be accomplished without prayer. It is impossible to see heaven's glory through the clouds of this world other than by prayer, and without it our spirits become heavy, our vision darkens and our faith crumbles.

Satan knows all that, so he doubles his efforts to weaken our praying.

Our prayers are weakened when we simply don't pray long enough.

Our prayers are weakened when we allow distractions to interfere with our praying.

Our prayers are weakened when we pray with unclean hearts or selfish motives.

Our prayers are weakened when we stop seriously reading the Bible.

Our prayers are weakened when we allow our thinking to become clouded by ambition, greed, distrust, pride, fear or any of a thousand other things that our sinful hearts can conjure up. Soon, unseen by ourselves but plainly visible to our enemy, we develop attitudes that harden these thoughts into practice. We build strongholds, patterns of thinking interlocked together like bricks in a wall. This is where Satan builds a base within us from which he can operate at will to influence others and to infect our entire life. He usually reinforces that base by bringing us into contact with other people who share those same thoughts, attitudes and opinions. The stronghold becomes a community of common attitudes and patterns of thinking, all designed to block out the truth.

Satan's strongholds are bases of operation out of which he extends his influence to others. Families. Communities. Church congregations.

Strongholds are Satanic constructions that must be destroyed, and they can be demolished only in the power of God (2 Corinthians 10:4).

It should come as no surprise that communication with God, in either direction, becomes nearly impossible in strongholds. That's exactly what Satan wants; to get us into a place where we are out of touch with God, where attempts to pray are hollow and vacant, where some form of godliness remains but without any presence of Godly power. A place in which other believers are made unwelcome. A place where the heavens become brass. Nothing, it seems, gets through.

There is another way by which Satan tries to cut off our communication with God. He sometimes directly interferes with our prayers. More particularly, he tries to interfere with the *answers* to our prayers. We remember that our petitions to our Father are ensured by the effective work of the Holy Spirit (Romans 8:26-27), leaving no opportunity for the enemy to interfere. God's answer to us, however, can often involve other participants (human or angelic) and that process sometimes presents an opportunity for our enemy to interfere. Daniel's case (Daniel 10:12-14) is perhaps the best-known example in Scripture. But how many times, not recorded in Scripture, have God's provisions in answer to the prayers of His people been delayed or undelivered by the hardening of the hearts of those human agents whom He asked to act but who refused to do so?

To the waiting believer, God's apparent silence makes it seem as though the heavens are, indeed, brass. Satan wants us to think that God has not heard us. He wants us to give up and to stop asking. He wants us to stop believing, trusting and expecting. He hardens the heavens to kill our faith.

But Satan knows that he has only a limited time in which to succeed. It's a battle of attrition; he wants to wear us down before reinforcements arrive. It took three weeks for God's message to be delivered to Daniel, but the breakthrough did come. The night seems long, but morning will indeed come (Psalm 30:5b). God's purposes for us will be accomplished despite Satan's determined efforts to cut us off.

Prayer Warrior, here are a few things that we can all take to heart:

- We will all come under the enemy's attack in the area of our prayer life
- We must expect that Satan will neither stop nor diminish his efforts against us both personally and corporately
- We must be alert to the early signs of his interference with our praying
- We must pray together and *pray over each other*
- We must ask for the discernment of the Holy Spirit to see where Satan is building his strongholds near us, and we must demolish them
- We must pore over those Scriptures that remind us of God's absolute care, faithfulness and dependability
- We must keep asking God if we are the messenger of hope, consolation and provision to someone else who is waiting
- We must pray against the enemy's interference and influence in others whom God wants to use as His messengers
- We must pray against hardened heavens

- God's tests and trials, which He is using to grow us, often put us in a place where we are searching for His presence, needing assurance of His nearness, waiting for His deliverance. He hasn't abandoned us; He is doing exactly what He said He would do, preparing our home with Him, but if we listen carefully, we can hear His footsteps.

MISSION 96

The Enemy's Plan - Part 8

Satan sends false messages and false messengers

We all know the story of the Trojan Horse. Referenced by Virgil and Homer, it is uncertain if it is an historical fact or just an epic tale. Either way, the story continues to have real applications to this day. In the account, the Greeks were unable to subdue the City of Troy; they then resorted to a trick in which they presented a supposed gift to the Trojans in the form of a gigantic horse monument. The trick was that, inside the horse, the Greeks had hidden a force of soldiers who disembarked at night after the unsuspecting Trojans had brought the horse inside their city walls. The soldiers opened the gates and Troy was destroyed by the incoming army.

False messages and false messengers are very powerful, all the more so when they are cleverly disguised as something harmless or pleasing, something so attractive that we would haul it inside our walls. The power of the false message (or messenger) lies in the ability of the lie to replace the truth, or to prevent the truth from being detected until it is too late to do anything about it. Like the Trojan Horse, those few soldiers who were hidden inside could not take the city of Troy, but their job was to open the gates and to let the whole army come in. The false message is just the decoy ahead of the main force.

So the question that we must ask is "*What is Satan trying to conceal from us?*". The logical question that follows is "*What do his false messages sound like, and what do his false messengers do?*". Perhaps the most important question of all is "*What is it that we should be doing that is so threatening to*

Satan that he would go to all the trouble of sending these false messages and messengers in the first place?".

That last question is probably the easiest to answer because Jesus Himself issued the marching orders to His followers; based on His promise to build His church (Matthew 16:18), **Jesus issued ONE command** (Matthew 28:19-20) **that is still in effect today.** The authority for this mission, and the power to ensure that it will succeed, is found, again, in Jesus' own words (Matthew 28:18). Anticipating that there would be fierce opposition from the Devil, Jesus added that even all of Satan's attempts to stop His Kingdom plan would ultimately fail (Matthew 16:18). So that explains why Satan sees the believing church as such a threat to his plan to establish his own kingdom.

Now that helps to answer the first question of what is Satan trying to conceal from believers. Think of this:

- Satan is not original in his thinking; **he opposes what God has spoken.** He was right on the scene when Jesus spoke those words to Peter recorded in Matthew 16. First and foremost, *Satan wants to hide those words from believers.* He wants the church to forget them, to let them slip out of relevance. He wants the heart of the church to stop beating to the passion of Jesus building His church. Anything to get the church to get out of Kingdom business. He wants the church to lose sight of its only true purpose in the world. Concealed. Obscured. Hidden. Out of sight. Invisible.
- *Satan wants to conceal his moves in building his kingdom here on earth.* He doesn't want us to notice what's going on. Oh, look at that beautiful Horse! I wonder what could be inside?
- *Satan wants to conceal the consequences of de-prioritizing God's orders.* Satan knows all about consequences; he just doesn't want us to know. Taking Jesus' command as being merely a suggestion or "optional" will bring consequences, and those consequences will not fall on Satan but on us. Our destruction is Satan's objective; he wants us to become the victims of God's judgment in the same way that he is already condemned to be.

- *Satan wants to conceal the fact that time is running out.* God has a timetable, seasons, set times. Satan knows that. God's sovereignty extends over time and eternity. Our window of opportunity to give ourselves wholly over to Kingdom building is going to close forever. Satan wants us to lose the sense of urgency.

Now we can come to the second question concerning those false messages and messengers. More concealment; instead of appearing in their true form of darkness and destruction, they take on the appearance of light (2 Corinthians 11:14). False enlightenment. Like the kind that Satan offered Eve (Genesis 3:5). Fatal enlightenment that killed us all. Higher "truth". Knowledge beyond wisdom. "Facts" over faith. Humanism over godliness. Manufactured peace and hollow promises (1 Thessalonians 5:3). Political salvation. Economic redemption. All here today; the secret soldiers have emerged from the Horse and the gates are being opened wide!

Spiritual warrior, here is our final "to-do" list:

1. Refresh your commitment to our ONE mission; ruthlessly abandon all others. No substitutes.
2. Reclaim the authority of Jesus that was spoken over us in Matthew 16.
3. Seek wisdom and be prepared to accept it.
4. Redeem the time (Romans 5:16); that means being prepared to pay a price.

Which brings us to the next tactic of our enemy.

Satan offers a shortcut to the Kingdom

Satan is offering a discount ticket to God's Kingdom.

He first offered it to Jesus (Mathew 4:8-9). If only Jesus would accept the offer, He could have a kingdom (including peace with Satan) all without having to pay the full price of Calvary. He's offering the same discount ticket to us; sadly, many have taken him up on his offer.

Think of it; painless discipleship, no-cost membership in God's club, no headaches, endless benefits. All this and heaven too! A great deal. Truly too good to be true. And so it is.

Of course, Jesus did not fall for Satan's offer. There could be no shortcut to His Kingdom, and there was no detour around the cross. There was no peace with God's enemy, Satan, and there was no room for compromise on any point. We understand that, and we cheer for Jesus, for His stand against Satan's temptations, and for His single-mindedness in going all the way through the cross.

Satan cannot change any of that, nor is he trying to do so. He cannot undo Jesus' work on Calvary's cross. He cannot take back Jesus' victory over temptation in the wilderness. He's not foolish; he's not trying to do that. He stopped offering Jesus the discount ticket when He finally rejected it in Gethsemane (Matthew 26:39).

Today he is offering the discount to us! He wants us to buy into the deal.

* Comfort and ease on the way to heaven; First Class travel.
* Toys and pleasures to spare (but nothing wicked, thank you).
* No-fault living; fall down, get up, no consequences, no accountability, no problem. Repeat.
* Behind-the-lines lifestyle; leave that front-line spiritual warfare stuff to those who feel "called".
* Might as well make oneself as comfortable as possible here. Spend. Enjoy. Give a little.
* Don't get involved in the messy lives of the unfortunate lost.
* Go ahead, build a church for your fellow happy pilgrims.

Sometimes it is hard to resist the offer and sometimes it is even hard to see the deception. After all, who chooses disappointment, pain, sacrifice, even hardship?

Well, I guess the simplest answer is that Jesus did make that choice for Himself. Then He told His disciples that He expects them (and us) to make the same choice. He does, however, promise to never abandon us through those choices and through the consequences that will follow those choices. Only to those who confront the power of the enemy will He reveal His surpassing power (1 John 4:4). We are not purchasing our redemption through our choices (Jesus did all of that once for all); we are offering our sacrifice of gratitude through our choices. We cannot prove our worthiness of God's Kingdom (Jesus alone made us worthy – Ephesians 1:6) but there are few other ways to express our willingness to accept His lordship.

Satan offers "answers"; God calls us to faith even without answers. Satan calls us to a lie and death; God calls us to true life and glory! **There is no shortcut; our choices here reveal our true destination.**

Mission 97

The Enemy's Plan - Part 9

<u>*Satan sends the supernatural to replace the godly*</u>

We are naturally impressed by the supernatural!

God created us with specific limitations, in particular that we do not have the special abilities and powers of angels (Psalm 8:5), and yet He has given us the ability to observe those powers when they appear to us. Both Old and New Testaments give many examples of angels being recognized by ordinary men and women. He also gave us the ability to understand the source of those powers. So, we have the ability to observe and (to some degree) understand powers that we do not actually possess. "Supernatural" powers, since they do not appear to follow the normal rules of *our* world. Obviously, we are intended to be impressed by those powers because we understand that there is someone greater than us behind them.

God has also made a way for us to access supernatural power even though we cannot possess those powers in the same way that we can possess physical strength. Prayer is one example of access to supernatural power.

Satan understands our weakness as compared to his power; he knows Psalm 8:5 all too well, and he uses it to his advantage whenever he can. He also knows our fallen state compared to God's original pattern in Adam in Eden. His arithmetic is simple; he sees the addition of our created weakness plus our fallen nature to be equal to a wonderful opportunity for his purposes. He can use his supernatural power to impress us. He might even be able to enlist us into his army by allowing us to use some of those powers! Under the right conditions he might even be able to fool us by those powers.

When it comes to attacking the Kingdom of God (or more particularly God's Kingdom people) here on earth, Satan finds more opportunities in not necessarily revealing himself and his works as being dark and grotesque; that might make horror movie material but it's not necessarily convincing or deceptive. He usually chooses the masquerade of light (2 Corinthians 11:14) or engaging conversation (Genesis 3:1-4).

Now we come to a very important distinction. Reality and truth are not necessarily the same thing. Not all reality is truth. If God alone is truth (John 14:6), then not everything that is real is godly. Satan wants to substitute reality for truth. Supernatural reality for supernatural truth.

The first step, then, is to get us focused on the supernatural at the expense of truth. A bit at a time but gradually our appetite for the supernatural will dwarf our discipline to endure the less dramatic things such as careful Bible study. The Bible, after all, is the touchstone of truth and if Satan can weaken our anchorage in that book, then we will begin to drift, and he can substitute error for truth, and we will not notice. All the more so if the spectacle of the supernatural keeps us convinced that this reality is, in fact, the truth. It's real so it *must* be true!

God has never said that a quest for the supernatural would produce godly character in us. He *has* said that His Word will indeed produce that effect (Psalm 119:9,11,50,105,114,165, Deuteronomy 11:18, Matthew 4:4). It is possible to become well-versed in the supernatural and at the same time to become spiritually weak and blind.

The Bible will remind us that the *purpose* of the supernatural events in the ministry of Jesus and the early church was to confirm the Gospel and to bring unbelievers to faith. The Pharisaical demand for supernatural signs apart from any appetite for the truth was condemned by Jesus (Matthew 12:38-39). We may safely assume that those same ground rules apply today.

Satan's goal is to mesmerize us with the spectacle without letting us look for the Biblical evidence whether these supernatural signs are true companions of God's truth in producing genuine godliness in people. God's presence manifested in His people; that's what we should see. After all, what could be more supernatural than true godliness in a redeemed sinner?

<u>Satan imitates character, signs and wonders</u>

Satan is an imposter; that's just another form of a liar, and he is the father of lies and of liars (John 8:44). But what good is a lie if it is obviously a lie? Surely the purpose of a lie is to deceive, to lead astray, to appear as truth when, in fact, it is the opposite of truth. So, when it comes to the supernatural, we may expect that Satan is able to put on quite a show. He is supernatural (he's an angel), so he was created with powers that we do not possess. And he can demonstrate that power. Miraculous signs and wonders. Real? Yes! But not true, since they do not convey the message of God's truth.

Now we have to tell the difference between God's signs and wonders and Satan's version of signs and wonders! This is not a new challenge.

Pharoah could not tell the difference (Exodus 7:8-13, 22, 8:7) until finally his sorcerers were unable to keep up, by which time his heart was completely hardened. But you must admit that those sorcerers did put on quite a convincing supernatural show. We'll give them second prize!

Then there was Simon as we find him in Acts 8:9-23. He was also a sorcerer and he regularly put on convincing demonstrations of power in order to protect his image as "a man of God". Of course, he was not. It seems that he may have even pretended to become a believer under Philip's ministry, but he made the terrible mistake of trying to buy apostolic power from Peter and John who revealed that his heart was, in fact, poisoned by wickedness. Whatever his true state while following Philip, there came a showdown between God's power and Satan's signs.

It's wrong to give our confidence to someone based only on signs and wonders. Miracles. Clearly the Bible is teaching us that there are different sources of miracles and we are responsible to know the difference.

John takes us to the heart of the matter.

> *Beloved, do not believe every spirit, but test the spirits, whether they are of God; because many false prophets have gone out into the world. By this you know the Spirit of God: Every spirit that confesses that Jesus Christ has come in the flesh is of God, and every spirit that does not confess that Jesus Christ has come in the flesh is not of God. And this is the spirit of the Antichrist, which you have heard was coming, and is now already in the world. You are of God, little children, and have overcome them, because He who is in you is greater than he who is in the world. They are of the world. Therefore, they speak as of the world, and the world hears them. We are of God. He who knows God hears us; he who is not of God does not hear us. By this we know the spirit of truth and the spirit of error.*
>
> 1 John 4:1-6 NKJV

Many spirits. All over the world. Many claims. Many messages. Testing the spirits (including testing signs and wonders done by these spirits) is something that we must learn to do reliably. There is the test of *faith* (Who do they say Jesus is?) and there is the test of *obedience* (Are they willing to follow the truth of God?). A wrong answer to either test is a sure disqualification.

- Do these signs and wonders testify about the redemptive work of Jesus Christ of Nazareth? Do they lead people to faith?
- Do these signs and wonders lead to serious discipleship, humility, cross-bearing and servanthood in the Name of Jesus?
- Are these signs and wonders promotions for some program, campaign or organization?
- Do these signs and wonders exalt any person other than Jesus?

- Do these signs and wonders have true Biblical roots?
- Do these signs and wonders have a purpose beyond themselves?

Those accounts of miracles in the Bible, and those that we have seen for ourselves, all have something in common. We can use it as a test to separate Satan's spectacle from God's hand in action:

Genuine God-powered miracles always spring from obedience and produce obedience in others

Mission 98

The Enemy's Plan - Part 10

Satan attacks our secret places

We've all had secrets; things we didn't want others to know about us. Things of which we are ashamed. Maybe a past life. Maybe a foolish part of our life. Something we've wrapped up in the attic of our life. Maybe an old habit that we revisit once in awhile, and maybe more frequently than that.

Satan loves our secret places, and he knows where all of them are hidden. He uses them the way criminals use blackmail, to make us behave in certain ways for fear of being discovered. He uses them to keep us in bondage, a kind of prison, and he has specific purposes in mind.

Satan uses them to bring us under the pain of guilt. If the secret place is a place of unconfessed sin, then the guilt is real and deserved, and the only cure is to quickly confess it to God, claim His forgiveness and turn completely away from the sin.

But what if we have already confessed it but it still lurks there, waiting to be resurrected again and again by our enemy. Time after time we are dragged into false guilt, defeated, discouraged.

It's time that we took control of those secret places, recognizing that our enemy attaches himself to them in order to build a stronghold in our life. As long as they are secrets, he will use them.

The first step is to recognize what these secret places look like; we may not even know they are there. We cannot begin to deal with them until we are able to see them.

The secret place may be a habitual temptation that always leads to the same sinful behaviour. It could be some form of substance abuse, including over-eating. It could be visiting that porn website. It could be buying stuff that we don't need and cannot afford, running up uncontrollable debt. It could be any one of a thousand things, but there is one in particular that always trips us up. That's the one. Satan knows that once we start down that familiar path, the rest will follow like falling downstairs. Every time. So, he knows that our faith walk can always be interrupted and limited by simply pushing that button.

The secret place may be a private pain that we insist on bearing alone. It could be loneliness or sorrow, disappointment or grief, failure or frustration. It could be a prodigal son or daughter, a shattered friendship, a betrayal. Satan knows that some pains are too heavy to be carried alone, so by leading us to think that we must suffer in private he knows that our hearts and minds will never be unburdened enough to make great progress in our faith walk. He also knows that our minds are incubators in which injuries and offences always grow bigger, more hurtful, more bitter.

The secret place may be a deep need in our life, but one that we refuse to share with anyone else. Maybe we feel ashamed or unworthy to share it and ask for help. Maybe we were taught to never trust anyone with those kinds of things. Maybe it's healing that can only come from God through someone else. Maybe we, like Naaman (2 Kings 5:12), want God's blessing on our terms.

The secret place may be doubt or unbelief. There may be some part of your faith (or faith walk) that you don't understand, or maybe there seems to be something in your life experience that flat-out contradicts what you believe. There may be some part of your faith statement that you simply cannot accept wholeheartedly, and the light of understanding eludes your attempts to gain clarity. You have a faith dilemma. Problem is that you don't want anyone to know about your faith dilemma. Our enemy knows that he can fertilize that first doubt until it grows into a crop of unbelief and cynicism.

The secret place may be a mask or false front. Your words may have exceeded your experience, and you find yourself living in a pretend place, a place where you go through the expected motions but there is nothing in your heart to back it up. Maybe living on someone else's faith. Maybe trying to live into a role that you have taken upon yourself, but which God has not given you. Maybe discovering that the faith that you thought you had was not strongly grounded; maybe it was a childhood faith that never really grew up, and now you find it to be inadequate, weak or even non-existent. The enemy wants you to believe that the whole faith trip, all faith, is phoney and worthless.

The secret place may be a dream, something that God has placed in your heart, a call, something special and wonderful. Problem is that this dream is a secret and you don't want anyone else to know. The danger is that the dream will never become more than that – just a dream. The enemy knows that he has nothing to fear from dreams, but if that dream became spoken into reality by a word of faith, that's an entirely different matter.

The secret place may be a hole, a burrow into which you willingly retreat, a place filled with discouragement, worthlessness and hopelessness. All built on your feeling that you don't deserve anything better, that even God could not care for you. The "hole" sometimes seems like a safe place but nothing good ever happens there. The Devil knows that faith cannot flourish (or even survive) there.

The secret place may be in your mind. Intellectualism, Stoicism, humanism. You may come from a cultural or family heritage that places the ultimate value on self-reliance, education, industriousness, determination, courage, intelligence --- and a dogmatic conviction that every life issue can be solved using these tools. As helpful as these attributes may be, our reliance on them as the strength of life is a grand mistake. The gifts of life were never intended to be the giver of life. Satan knows that; he has all of those attributes and many more, but he learned that they do not entitle him to take God's place. He wants us to repeat his mistake.

I'm certain that you can add many more examples of secret places, but the important question is "What do we do about them?". If they are the strongholds of our enemy, then we must know how to demolish them. We must deprive the enemy of those strangleholds in our life. How can we begin to do that?

1. Start by telling your story to someone else. It doesn't have to be the entire congregation on Sunday morning! It may be with a close, trusted friend. The point is that once you have spoken the secret to someone else, it's no longer a secret and the devil loses his power in holding it over your head.
2. Ask someone to pray with you over that secret, seeking deliverance from the bondage that Satan wants to throw over you.
3. Beware of long periods of being alone, especially if you are preoccupied with a troubling situation.
4. Run to Scripture for reassurance. Start with 2 Corinthians 3:17, Romans 8:15, James 5:16, Galatians 6:2.
5. Ask God to give you a way to turn that secret into a source of blessing to someone else.
6. Continue to pray for an open heart and an open spirit.
7. Take this opportunity to recommit yourself to the lordship of Jesus over your dreams and goals.
8. Keep short accounts with sin in your life. Do not try to tame your sin; you must ask God to kill it!

There IS a secret place that God has provided for us; go there often (Psalm 91).

Mission 99

The Enemy's Plan - Part II

He steals our sense of privacy and security

Even George Orwell could not have imagined the accuracy of his "vision" of the future. Written in 1949, his novel was a dystopian description of a world gone wrong, where Big Brother, under the pretence of protecting society, eavesdropped on every conversation and privacy was a thing of the past.

Welcome to *1984*!

If we could "see" the Internet, it would consist of millions of electronic interconnections between "addresses". Every individual "address" is an IP address; that's a way of saying it's your computer's identification number, but not just your computer, it's every device that can be connected to the Internet, including your smartphone, your watch, your car, your exercise monitor, your pacemaker, your smart TV and practically every other gadget you own or have heard of. In 2015 there were 4.3 billion IP addresses; in 2016, an additional 340 undercillion (that's 430 followed by 36 zeros) IP addresses were created. It's not hard to imagine that every individual address is connected, directly or indirectly, to every other address. Anywhere. Everywhere.

This system is working remarkably well. In 1989, the worldwide web consisted of 50 individuals exchanging a few documents. By 2019 the Internet traffic will hit about 2 thousand million million bytes per year. Data storage capacity is doubling every 3 years and computing capacity is doubling every year.

This is convenient when we want to send an email, place our Amazon order, book a flight or do on-line banking anywhere in the world. But there's another side to this. Let's back up a moment to grasp what we're talking about that makes up this "system". It's not just the hardware parts of the system, but it also includes all the information that is gathered, stored and transmitted over the system.

- Every computer, notepad, tablet, etc
- Every smartphone
- Every wireless device, including some body implants such as some pacemakers
- Every bank and financial institution
- Every retail outlet
- Every government office, police force and security agency
- Every GPS equipped device
- Every webcam, security camera, traffic camera, border crossing camera
- Every email, telephone conversation, Tweet, Instagram or text message
- Every Facebook or other social media post
- Every picture you've taken on your phone, including "selfies" that you hope nobody sees
- Every credit card, debit card and on-line purchase, including the things you looked at on-line but did not purchase
- Every web-search
- Every piece of personal information such as health records, financial records, police records, credit cards, passports, visas, travel records

The list is endless and maybe it comes as no surprise to us. We take comfort in the belief that there are laws to control what data are collected, by whom and for what purpose. Those laws are supposed to protect us from becoming the victims of that system, or of those who would use the system to harm us.

Those laws and safeguards are, for the most part, non-existent or powerless today.

New laws enacted in many countries following 9/11 gave governments and police agencies the ability to bypass all of those safeguards at their own discretion in the name of national security and without your knowledge or permission. This month, a law was enacted in the United States making it legal for your Internet service provider to sell your email and Internet usage history (including all the stuff you thought you deleted). We already know that government agencies have been intercepting and recording nearly every private electronic communication (phone calls, emails, texts, Tweets, etc.) for several years, possibly even before 9/11 made it "legal".

So, spiritual warrior, what is the point of reminding us of all this? Some thoughts:

- Satan was not the inventor of computers, cell phones or the Internet
- Tools and toys like cell phones and the Internet were invented for our convenience, safety, entertainment, etc. and, for the most part, for very well-intentioned purposes.
- People with sinful natures (like us) have found ways to pervert even the most innocently intended tools and institutions
- When the time is right for him, Satan will use all of these tools and institutions to bring in his kingdom on earth
- Every tool needed for Satan's program is already in place TODAY
- Satan has already infiltrated key societal institutions in every major nation; these are the same institutions and agencies that have perfected the power of systems like the Internet
- With very few exceptions, every person on earth is "connected" to this system in many ways, some voluntarily and some not, so that it is virtually impossible to "disappear"
- Privacy, in the basic sense, no longer exists; we may not be "visible" at the moment (because we are not important enough to attract attention) but we can be "discovered" (or "uncovered") at any time by nothing more than a few keystrokes on a computer

- Our homes are no longer private sanctuaries. At least two brands of smart TVs (the ones that include such things as on-screen email, Netflix, web surfing, Skype, video chatting) are equipped with cameras and microphones that can be controlled externally online, meaning that *the camera and microphone can be activated by someone somewhere through the Internet connection to actually watch and listen to you at home without your even knowing it*
- ALL of our basic life support services (including food, finances, transportation, energy, communication, healthcare) are controllable through systems such as the Internet
- Individuals can become "people of interest" to government (and other) agencies based on religious beliefs, political alignment, social expressions, etc and these individuals can be located and followed almost instantly anywhere on earth
- The conditions pertaining to the "end times" described in the Book of the Revelation, things that seemed unimaginable only a few years ago, are now very real. Control of all financial transactions (such as getting money from a bank or buying food) using electronic implants connected to a universal system can be easily done today. Selective access and selective denial are two sides of the same coin. What if access or denial are based on Biblical beliefs?
- Satan wants us to feel exposed and defenceless, with no place to turn for help and safety

The point for us is to do an inventory of our faith. What are we prepared to give up and what things are not to be surrendered at any cost? This is real 21st century spiritual warfare and it is serious business. It is impossible to fight an enemy when we know nothing about him or what he is doing. Satan will not limit his attack on us based on our limited thinking.

Spiritual warriors, when we see all that the enemy is prepared to bring against us and when we see the nations and people crumbling around us, let us remember these things:

- There IS a refuge in the midst of the storm (Psalm 46:1); His name is Jesus

- There IS a safe place where the enemy cannot intrude (Matthew 6:19-20); it is in the presence of God
- There IS a dwelling prepared for us that cannot be invaded (John 14:2); it is called Heaven
- There IS one whose eyes are always upon us (Psalm 33:18); He is the great Provider
- There IS an identity that we have been given (1 John 3:1); we are the children of God
- There IS one who has forever erased our sins (Hebrews 1:3); He is the Lamb of God
- There IS one whose knowledge is infinite (Psalm 33:11); He the Creator and Sustainer of everything
- There IS a power that cannot be interrupted or denied (John 14:14, 16:23); it is prayer with Almighty God
- There IS one within us who is greater than the kingdom of darkness (1 John 4:4); He is the Holy Spirit
- There IS a truth that cannot be removed (John 14:6); it is the living Word of God
- There IS a light that cannot be extinguished (Matthew 16:18); it is the Gospel of Jesus Christ
- There IS an arsenal that Satan cannot defeat or destroy (Ephesians 6:10-18); it is the armor of God
- There IS only one who has authority over time and eternity (Revelation 1:8); He is Alpha and Omega

If we are to be hunted and exposed for what we believe and declare, let it be easily known that we serve the One who cannot be defeated, that we have been given life and power that cannot be taken from us, that we have received mercy and grace in place of our guilt and shame, that no accusation against us will ever stand before God, that we are the light that insists on shining in the darkness and that cannot be extinguished. And that all of this is because Jesus Christ loved us, gave Himself for us and called us to follow Him.

And in God's Kingdom, when death, hell and the Devil have been forever put in their place, we will enjoy our Lord's presence throughout eternity. Guaranteed by the resurrection of Jesus. Post that on the Internet!

MISSION 100

The Enemy's Plan - Part 12

Satan tries to paralyze us with the fear of failure and death

Fear is not a cartoon or a joke. It's not funny.

Fear is used by the enemy to put us on the defensive, uncertain what will happen next, or when. Fear tries to convince us that we will not be equal to the challenge when it comes, whatever it is. Fear says that the enemy is strong, and we are weak. Fear is like the cement that hardens around our feet, paralyzing us, wrapping us in a cocoon that won't allow us to think or act. That's a made-to-order instrument in Satan's toolkit. Something that can keep us from thinking or acting.

Our thinking is very important to God. That's why God places such great attention on our minds (Romans 12:1-2) because out of that renewed mind comes the ability to experience God's leading and wisdom. We must understand that when truth peeks into our life, it enters through our thoughts. Something we see or hear or read --- the pathways are many, but they all lead to our minds, our thoughts.

Fear also enters through our thoughts.

Spiritual warrior, could it be that right now God's Spirit is trying to plant a thought in your mind? Trying to bring you a word, wanting to plant a challenge, a mission, an idea.

That's where the enemy goes to work. He's out to keep that thought from taking root in your mind, keeping you from daring to believe that God's idea could be possible for you. But he isn't content to stop there; he really doesn't want that thought to take root in action. So along comes the thought "What if I fail?". "What will everyone think if I don't succeed?". "Maybe it would be better just to play it safe and don't stick my head up". Another good idea going nowhere. The fear of failure defeated the idea even before it was put to the test.

Now let's be clear; not every fear is demonic or of Satanic origin. Some fears keep us out of danger. We're talking about a kind of fear that is specifically targeted against something that God is trying to do in your life, something that requires you to step outside your comfort zone, something that will stretch your faith. You know that the challenge to step out is of God because you have checked it against His Word, and you have had it affirmed through prayer and godly counsel. Stepping out into that challenge could expose you to risks; maybe financial insecurity, maybe moving away from close friends, maybe making a drastic change in lifestyle. You can see that this is going to require a new level of leaning on God's provision and protection than you have been used to doing. Or maybe it will put you into a public place where you have never felt comfortable, doing things that you feel unsure how to do. It might mean letting go of something or someone very dear to you. It might mean accepting a sudden change in your life, one that you were not expecting and do not particularly like.

Fear is the weapon that the enemy uses to discourage you from following God's leading.

Fear is also the weapon that the enemy uses to drive people where he wants them to go. Panic. Terror. Horrific violence and threats of death. Extreme reality laced with lies and deception, all designed to push whole groups of people and even nations in a certain direction. We can see clearly that the horrific political and social conditions described as the end times in Scripture are intended to provide the stage upon which the Antichrist will appear as a saviour. Those conditions bear a frightening resemblance to the days in which we are living.

We understand the power of the weapon of fear; now it is time for us to understand that Jesus has cancelled fear's authority over us, especially the fear of death (Hebrews 2:15). Still, the enemy lies to us to get us to surrender to his lost power.

Here are some things to remember that will keep us from becoming victims of Satan's weapon of fear:

1. God is still God; He has not lost control of the situation nor is He even surprised at the events that confront us
2. God will never lead us anywhere that He is not prepared to make good on every one of His promises to us
3. God is not the author of fear (2 Timothy 1:7, Romans 8:15)
4. God does not want us to live on the defensive; He wants us to arise in His resurrection power to take charge of the day, the situation, the challenge. We are not victims; we are overcomers!
5. Prayer is the communication channel by which we can stay in close contact with our loving Father
6. The weapon of fear is many times more effective against us when we are alone or separated from godly friends
7. Satan will always reinforce his message of fear through lies and lying messengers (faith killers)
8. God's Word is unaffected by Satan's weapons, therefore turn to the Bible to hear the truth that can expose the enemy's deceptions
9. God's truth will set us free from the paralysis of Satan's fear
10. God asks us to trust Him completely; if we could see the future, we would not need faith
11. Satan's authority is limited to this world. He does not have authority over God's children; in fact, believers have an indwelling power, in the Person of the Holy Spirit, that is greater than Satan (1 John 4:4).
12. At the mighty cross of Jesus, God opened the way out of bondage and fear. In the resurrection of Jesus, He announced the beginning of the end of Satan's kingdom of darkness and fear and the establishment of His Kingdom of light and life.

For you did not receive the spirit of slavery to fall back into fear, but you have received the Spirit of adoption as sons
                                               Romans 8:15 ESV

This is the spirit of the antichrist, which you heard was coming and now is in the world already. Little children, you are from God and have overcome them, for he who is in you is greater than he who is in the world
                                                1 John 4:3-4 ESV

Mission 101

The Enemy's Plan - Part 13

Where are God's cows?

Give me a moment to explain!

Let me begin by reminding us that God alone is the Creator and therefore He owns *everything*; of course, that reminds us of Psalm 50:10 which speaks of the "cattle on a thousand hills", hence the picture. So, what has that to do with the strategy of the enemy? Just this: Satan tries to make us believe that *he* owns everything. He then goes on to try to convince us that he has authority over not only all of the physical resources of this world but also of our wellbeing, our finances, even our health.

This puts us on a collision course between Satan's claims of ownership and God's claims. We must pick which one we really believe to be true because they both cannot be true. So much of what we experience of God in this life depends on our choice.

As you read through this Mission, just keep in mind the question above the picture: "Where are God's cows?".

<u>Satan uses the threat of persecution, sickness and hardship</u>

We may have been so blessed that we have not endured true persecution for our faith, but there are many believers today who are not so blessed. For them, persecution for their faith in Jesus is a daily life and death issue.

I dare say that we all have experienced sickness and some measure of hardship.

Satan claims authority over all of these, and he regularly uses that claim to attack believers. Actually, he uses it against everyone, but he makes a special case of believers as we will see later.

So, is Satan's claim true or not?

I believe that the Bible shows us that there is a measure of truth to Satan's claim, but, as usual, it is at best only a half-truth, which makes it a lie.

God gave Adam complete authority over His creation (Genesis 1:26-28). Adam was, in fact, given lordship over God's creation, but along with that authority came responsibility and accountability. Adam reported to God. When Adam sinned by breaking God's command concerning the Tree of Knowledge of Good and Evil, he traded away his authority. To whom? To Satan. That was Satan's bartering chip with Jesus during His temptation in the wilderness (Matthew 4:8-9) and that is why Paul could refer to him as being the god of this world (2 Corinthians 4:4). Since we have all fallen in guilt to sin, we all come under the penalty of Adam's (and our) sin and so we all find ourselves living under Satan's dominion. So far it looks like Satan's claim of authority is true! And there can be no doubt that our enemy has made full use of his power in the persecution, sickness and hardship department. Not only that, but he holds the threat of even more of the same over our heads in order to control what we think, how we act, and in particular how we respond to God.

This is where a "new" element must be add to the power equation. I say "new", but in reality, it is older than the fall of Adam in Eden, because back there God promised a Redeemer (Genesis 3:15) who was finally revealed as Jesus the Messiah. Now to the great part; that same Messiah Jesus went to the cross where he paid the price of redemption, not only for Jews, but for absolutely *anyone* who would call upon His Name for salvation! Jews and Gentiles alike. That death and resurrection of Jesus has *completely redeemed* us from the entire curse that we fell under when Adam sinned (Galatians 3:13-14). That redemption includes not only the cancellation of the curse of spiritual death but also of every other consequence of violating God's law as prescribed in the Law (the Pentateuch). That must include the punishment of hardship (or poverty) and disease as described in Deuteronomy 28:15-68. Although the specific details of these punishments were certainly fulfilled in the captivity of Israel, in a larger sense the principles of breaking God's commands and the punishments that follow must be the same since God does not change. If Jesus' death and resurrection have made a complete redemption from the curse of the Law (Galatians 3:13-14), then it must include *all* of the curse.

So, it appears that there are two groups of people in the world today; those who are still outside of Jesus' redemption and those who have availed themselves of the offer of grace. Those who are still outside are still "unredeemed", that is, they remain under the curse as being guilty of sin, and they remain under the authority of their spiritual father who is none other than Satan (John 8:44). For those people, Satan's claim of authority is true. But for those who have been redeemed, that claim has been broken because Jesus Himself paid the price of release. That's what redemption means: bought back. Satan, the former owner, has lost his authority because, for the redeemed, sin has lost its power, the curse of the Law has been broken and at the same time Satan has lost his authority. **Satan's claim of authority over God's redeemed people is a lie.**

But Satan is a liar, and he does not want God's redeemed people to know the full truth of their redemption; he does not want us to know that being redeemed is more than simply receiving eternal life. As surpassingly wonderful as it is to receive that gift of eternal life, God's generosity toward us has not stopped there but extends to all of our life both here and hereafter.

So, Satan wants us to go on believing that he still holds that curse over our heads. He does not! But if we are unwilling to act on that truth, the result of bondage is the same as if it were true. The jail cell door in which we have been imprisoned all of our life may be closed, but it is unlocked; if we push on it, it will open. Satan no longer holds the key!

Instead of living under the curse, as if it still had authority over us, we must learn to live into the fullness of our redemption. That fullness includes blessings in this present life as well as in eternity. So, spiritual warrior, if you feel that you are living beneath the full measure of God's redemption blessings, how do we change that?

First, God will see to it that our eternal riches and blessings are fully realized in our heavenly home since Satan will have no place or influence in our eternity there. That just leaves the here and now where persecution, sickness and hardship abound.

Now we get back to those cows! If those cows represent all of God's physical assets in this world, then they must all be here now. I don't know if there are cows in heaven, but if there are, they are not the ones being talked about in Psalm 50:10. I think that all of God's cows for today are here today; if we are in need of a cow, God is not going to drop one out of heaven. In the same way, if we are in need of money or of some other material things, God is not going to drop them from the sky. All of God's cows are on earth today. All of God's money is here on earth. All of those things that we need in life, and to which Jesus specifically referred in Luke 12:29-30, are here. Problem is that our enemy, the Devil, has interfered with the supply line and those cows are grazing in someone else's pastures. All of God's money is sitting in someone's bank account today. God has not told us to go out and rustle those cows or to rob a bank but understanding what is going on should help us in our praying on the matter. We are pleading with God to give us a cow, but He is saying that the cow is already here. Our praying needs to turn to the source of the problem; that would be those principalities and powers and rulers of darkness (Ephesians 6:12). They are the ones holding back the blessing the same way that they held back Daniel's revelation (Daniel 10:13). We need to start exercising our authority over those spiritual forces to release our cows, all of our "hidden" redemption blessings, both spiritual and material!

The Holy Spirit can guide our asking for both spiritual and physical blessings; we should ask for both and then go to battle against those powers that are withholding God's provisions from us. We have been given the weapons of our spiritual warfare; now we have another reason to use them. Those weapons are mighty to see the release of that loved one who is held by addiction, and those same weapons are mighty to release God's blessings into our life. In heaven, we won't have to fight for them!

We have so sadly undervalued the work that Jesus did on that mighty cross. It was there that He secured everything that He intends for us throughout this life and eternity. Immeasurable blessings, unlimited power, complete redemption. Hallelujah!

Listen to this (https://youtu.be/yI_SQrRUOt0) and see if your spirit doesn't leap for joy!

Let's get down to our redemption birthright, redemption living. It goes something like this:

- Don't try to do it alone; God placed us in a body (of believers) and that's where we can most clearly see His vision for us
- Let's agree that we will no longer allow our pride or selfish desires to limit what we are willing to do to put ourselves in the right place before God
- Let's make praise our anthem

- Let's learn together how we can humbly express before each other our real needs and desires to God; we may need help in bringing our requests to our Father, and He values the strength of unity in prayer
- Let's not limit God's generosity; if we need a cow, we'll ask for a cow!
- Let's confront our enemy together
- Let's expect that God will strengthen our faith by teaching us perseverance
- God is the Sovereign of Providence as He is of Creation, and we may expect that our faith walk will teach us that patience comes between asking and receiving, that He is faithful and true, that we must learn to worship Him for who He is and not for what He does for us, until we discover, step by step, that He is truly all we need and, in fact, all our heart desires.

Heavenly Father, I need a cow. Devil, get your hands off of my cow!

Final Mission Briefing

The community of believers is, in this time of waiting for Christ's return, the instrument the Lord uses to spread and display His presence in the world. **If God's presence is to be found in the world today, it must and can only be manifested in the church, that is, the body of redeemed people, such as you and me, who have sold out to the Lordship of Jesus and who are burning with a godly passion for Him.** Not just the church as it gathers for an hour on Sunday morning, no matter how worshipful. Not just the church as it captures itself within the walls of its sanctuary, no matter how beautiful. Not just the church as it perfects the art of becoming listeners of the Word, no matter how well it is preached. No, none of these!

Respectfully, the world does not need to be dragged into our sanctuaries with the hope of coming into the presence of God. God's presence is not in sanctuaries, but in His people! People who are being transformed into the likeness of Jesus, and who wear that likeness outside (as well as inside) of the sanctuary.

If you hunger for God's presence here and now, then thirst for transformation here and now.

So, God's main purpose now appears to be to unmistakably display His presence in this world through His people, who are the church.

And we certainly are in desperate need of that presence.

- For safety and deliverance from our enemy, Satan
- For blessing and fullness in experiencing victorious living
- For commissioning, purpose and mission in Kingdom living
- For praise and worship out of a broken heart of gratitude
- For strength and power in spiritual warfare

Given that so much of our present life includes dealing with the everyday realities of our own weaknesses (flesh, temptation, sin), as well as those of others around us, along with the outright attacks of our enemy (Satan and his legion of powers of darkness, Ephesians 6:12), then the matter of knowing God's presence is, for most of us, a serious challenge. **Like two trains on the same track but going in opposite directions, God's presence collides with my weakness.**

I'm sure that it serves our enemy's purposes very well that this is the case. After all, separating us from experiencing God's presence is certain to weaken us and to render us all the more vulnerable to his attacks against us. **Sin has, as its ultimate goal, the destruction of our experience of God's presence.**

Knowing God's meaningful, practical presence here, in the midst of our everyday life, is a struggle that Scripture aptly describes as spiritual warfare. Experiencing God's presence here, predictably, reliably, powerfully (and drawing others into that same experience) must characterize our walk as disciples of Jesus Christ and it must be the goal of our spiritual warfare. And, of all the spiritual armor described in Ephesians 6, **prayer is the only active means of seeking and experiencing God's presence, that is, the supernatural power of God to reach into my spirit, soul and body and to transform me into a man driven by the purposes of God for the benefit of the body of Christ, of which I am a part. To transform me into an expression of God's nature and character.**

So, if prayer is that vital, interactive connection between God's presence and my experience of that presence, then it (prayer) is something radically different from what I understood when first I prayed that sinner's prayer. Strong praying and a strong realization of God's presence go hand-in-hand. The flip side of that coin is that weak praying and a weak realization of God's presence also go together. And it's not so much that we only know God's presence *during* our praying, but more to the point that prayer is the channel through which God's transformative power flows into our life so that we are continually changed as we get up off our knees.

Prayer becomes much more than a communication link to God; it becomes our exercise yard and our battleground where our faith goes head-to-head with the powers of the devil. It becomes the **presence of God versus the presence of darkness**. Now, if there is a place where spiritual warfare comes sharply into focus, that is it!

Wrestling with Satan to break the bondage of an addiction in a son or daughter requires nothing short of the presence of God.

Praying against sickness or disease in a wife or husband or grandchild requires nothing short of the presence of God.

Battling against the darkness of fear, depression or discouragement requires nothing short of the presence of God.

Seeking God's clear leading in the midst of questions and confusion requires nothing short of the presence of God.

This kind of praying is not the result of the presence of God; it is the *means* by which God's presence becomes powerful and evident in us.

It is the same presence of God that was evident in the resurrection of Jesus and is present in us (Ephesians 1:19-20).

It is the same presence of God at work in us that shows the indescribable power of God to do *immeasurably* more than we could ever ask or imagine (Ephesians 3:20).

It was this conviction of a radically different kind of praying that started me on a journey over two years ago to discover what was missing in my praying, particularly in relation to my spiritual warfare. So, I started to write what I called Prayer Missions. It was a sort of journal of personal revelation in this kind of prayer. Over the course of two years, I believe the Holy Spirit gave me these Prayer Missions in what I called "101 Reasons Why Prayer Is Not For Wimps". My wife, my Pastor and others played an important role in affirming the timeliness and importance of these lessons as part of the experience of our church congregation. It has helped me to experience the presence of God in an entirely new light. It has helped me to see the weakness and inadequacy of much of what my praying used to be. It has helped me to begin to experience God's presence in a more profound and practical way.

Now the question comes to us today: How much do you yearn for the presence of God and the evidence of that presence in your praying, and where will you look to find it?

Index of Scripture References

1 Chronicles 14:10, *66*
1 Corinthians 10:1-12, *233*
1 Corinthians 10:12, *29*, *119*
1 Corinthians 12, *80*, *93*, *98*
1 Corinthians 12:10, *85*
1 Corinthians 12:28, *75*, *157*
1 Corinthians 12:7,18, *113*
1 Corinthians 12:8, *85*, *119*
1 Corinthians 12:8-11, *101*
1 Corinthians 12:9, *44*, *85*
1 Corinthians 13, *127*
1 Corinthians 14, *148*
1 Corinthians 14:27-28, *215*
1 Corinthians 14:8, *214*
1 Corinthians 15:12-16, *122*
1 Corinthians 15:17, *122*
1 Corinthians 15:20, *122*
1 Corinthians 15:22, *39*
1 Corinthians 15:24, *72*
1 Corinthians 15:35-49, *70*
1 Corinthians 15:51, *123*
1 Corinthians 15:51-52, *123*
1 Corinthians 15:51-54, *129*
1 Corinthians 15:52, *75*
1 Corinthians 2:10-11, *41*
1 Corinthians 2:12, *133*
1 Corinthians 2:15, *181*
1 Corinthians 2:4, *115*
1 Corinthians 2:7, *132*
1 Corinthians 2:9-10, *128*, *161*
1 Corinthians 3:1, *61*
1 Corinthians 3:12, *166*, *168*, *253*
1 Corinthians 3:12-15, *62*
1 Corinthians 3:1-3, *141*
1 Corinthians 3:15, *75*

1 Corinthians 3:2, *109*, *243*
1 Corinthians 6:9-11, *120*
1 Corinthians 9:22, *80*
1 Corinthians 9:25, *62*
1 John 1:9, *35*, *180*, *186*, *251*, *262*
1 John 2:15, *130*, *207*, *221*
1 John 2:16, *61*, *119*
1 John 2:27, *219*
1 John 3:1, *40*, *283*
1 John 3:1-2, *252*
1 John 3:2, *69*, *122*
1 John 4:1, *181*, *215*
1 John 4:1-6, *275*
1 John 4:20-21, *243*
1 John 4:3-4, *286*
1 John 4:4, *272*, *283*, *285*
1 John 4:4, 5:4, *49*
1 John 5:14-15, *195*
1 John 5:5, *47*
1 Kings 10:6,7, *104*
1 Kings 17:1, *104*
1 Kings 17:6, *104*
1 Kings 17:8-16, *133*
1 Kings 18, *211*
1 Kings 18:22-40, *105*
1 Kings 18:4, *105*
1 Kings 19:2-3, *211*
1 Kings 3:5, *57*
1 Peter 1:13, 4:7, 5:8, *11*
1 Peter 1:13-15, *99*
1 Peter 1:15-16, *233*
1 Peter 1:8, *101*
1 Peter 2:11, *118*
1 Peter 2:2, *141*, *243*
1 Peter 2:4, *106*

1 Peter 2:5, *106*
1 Peter 2:6, *106*
1 Peter 2:9, *33, 107*
1 Peter 3:12, *87*
1 Peter 3:3-4, *144*
1 Peter 3:7, *8*
1 Peter 4:12, *262*
1 Peter 5:13, *112*
1 Peter 5:6,7, *35*
1 Peter 5:7, *98*
1 Peter 5:8, *186*
1 Samuel 15, *78*
1 Samuel 17:34, *192*
1 Samuel 17:36, *192*
1 Samuel 17:45-51, *235*
1 Samuel 18:20-29, *119*
1 Samuel 28:7, 8-14, *38*
1 Thessalonians 4:13-17, *123*
1 Thessalonians 4:14-18, *80*
1 Thessalonians 4:16, *75, 129*
1 Thessalonians 4:16-17, *239*
1 Thessalonians 4:18, *107*
1 Thessalonians 4:3, *66*
1 Thessalonians 5:1-10, *239*
1 Thessalonians 5:1-6, *228*
1 Thessalonians 5:17-18, *43*
1 Thessalonians 5:3, *270*
1 Thessalonians 5:4-5, *165*
1 Thessalonians 5:4-9, *160*
1 Timothy 1:1, *91*
1 Timothy 1:12, *91*
1 Timothy 1:18, 4:14, *91*
1 Timothy 1:18,19, *90*
1 Timothy 1:18-19, *118*
1 Timothy 1:19, *225*
1 Timothy 1:2, *112*
1 Timothy 1:4, *257*
1 Timothy 16:15, *259*
1 Timothy 4:8, *92*
1 Timothy 6:11,12, *90*
1 Timothy 6:12, *91*
1 Timothy 6:4, *119*

1 Timothy 6:9,10, *90*
1 Timothy 6:9-10, *118*
2 Chronicles 20, *57, 77, 97*
2 Chronicles 20:14, *78*
2 Chronicles 20:21, *58*
2 Chronicles 7:11-16, *54*
2 Chronicles 7:14, *10, 254*
2 Corinthians 1:22, *140, 169*
2 Corinthians 1:3-4, 7:6, *107*
2 Corinthians 1:8, 4:7-9, *185*
2 Corinthians 10:4, *125, 126, 167, 266*
2 Corinthians 10:4-5, *82*
2 Corinthians 10:5, *52*
2 Corinthians 11:14, *214, 270, 273*
2 Corinthians 12:10, *35, 103*
2 Corinthians 12:8-9, *66*
2 Corinthians 2:14, *21, 83, 103, 262*
2 Corinthians 3:17, *279*
2 Corinthians 3:18, *228*
2 Corinthians 4:16-18, *70, 102*
2 Corinthians 4:17, *151*
2 Corinthians 4:17-18, *247*
2 Corinthians 4:18, *69*
2 Corinthians 4:4, *288*
2 Corinthians 5:10, *70, 168*
2 Corinthians 5:1-10, *80*
2 Corinthians 5:17, *120*, 140
2 Corinthians 5:18, *182*
2 Corinthians 5:2, *107*
2 Corinthians 5:21, *169, 239, 251, 262*
2 Corinthians 5:2-8, 68
2 Corinthians 6:14,15, *95*
2 Corinthians 6:2, *263*
2 Corinthians 6:4-5, 11:24-27, *80*
2 Corinthians 6:7, *61, 90*
2 Corinthians 9:8, *150, 151, 247*
2 Kings 21:1-16, 23:24-26, *38*
2 Kings 4:1-6, *177*
2 Kings 5:12, *278*
2 Kings 6:17, *68, 211*
2 Kings 6:6, *72*
2 Kings 6:8-10, *133*

2 Kings 6:8-12, *217*
2 Peter 1:10, *108*
2 Peter 1:11, *108, 110*
2 Peter 1:5-8, *108*
2 Peter 2:19, *109*
2 Peter 2:7, *75, 199*
2 Peter 2:8, *52*
2 Peter 3:1, *11*
2 Peter 3:16, *257*
2 Peter 3:3, *129*
2 Peter 3:3-9, *168*
2 Peter 3:4, *106*
2 Peter 3:8, *107*
2 Peter 3:9, *65, 123*
2 Samuel 21:18-22, *236*
2 Samuel 24:24, *45*
2 Samuel 5, *74, 97*
2 Samuel 5:24, *68*
2 Thessalonians 2:6, *115*
2 Thessalonians 2:9, *115*
2 Timothy 1:6, *91*
2 Timothy 1:7, *120, 180, 211, 285*
2 Timothy 2:15, *128*
2 Timothy 2:3,4, *90*
2 Timothy 2:3-4, *79*
2 Timothy 2:3-6, *135*
2 Timothy 2:4, *75, 130, 206*
2 Timothy 3:16, *215*
2 Timothy 3:1-9, *90, 129*
2 Timothy 3:5, *46, 257*
2 Timothy 3:7, *119*
2 Timothy 4:11, *112, 192*
2 Timothy 4:3, *257*
2 Timothy 4:8, *103, 133*
2 Timothy 4:9-11, *98*
Acts 1:11, *122*
Acts 1:4, *75*
Acts 1:8, *96*
Acts 11:20, *111*
Acts 11:21, *111*
Acts 11:24, *111*
Acts 11:26, *111*
Acts 11:28, *198*
Acts 11:5, *101*
Acts 12:25, *192*
Acts 12:12, *111, 192*
Acts 12:1-4, *111*
Acts 12:25, *112*
Acts 12:5, *10, 49*
Acts 13:13, *112, 192*
Acts 13:2, *112*
Acts 13:3-4, *112*
Acts 13:5, *112*
Acts 14:19-20, *49*
Acts 15:37-39, *112, 192*
Acts 16:24, *57*
Acts 16:25,26, *57*
Acts 16:6, *66*
Acts 16:9, *101*
Acts 16:9-10, *133*
Acts 17:22-23, *119*
Acts 19:13-16, 8:4-7, 16:18, *148*
Acts 19:15, *10*
Acts 2:1-4, *75*
Acts 20:24, *144*
Acts 24:25, *263*
Acts 4:12, *46*
Acts 4:24-31, *19*
Acts 4:36, *111*
Acts 8:9-23, *274*
Acts 9:10, *101*
Acts 9:27, *111*
Colossians 1:11, *151*
Colossians 1:13, *237*
Colossians 1:16-17, *69*
Colossians 1:26, *132*
Colossians 1:5, *133, 135*
Colossians 2:13-15, *72*
Colossians 2:15, *83*
Colossians 2:2-3, *132*
Colossians 3:16, *58*
Colossians 3:2, *207*
Colossians 4:10, *111, 112*
Colossians 4:7-14, *98*

Daniel 1:6, *193*
Daniel 10, *217*
Daniel 10:12-14, *267*
Daniel 10:13, *69, 125, 289*
Daniel 2:17-19, *66*
Daniel 6:4-4, *193*
Deuteronomy 11:18, *274*
Deuteronomy 12:29-30, *119*
Deuteronomy 18:15, *100*
Deuteronomy 28:15-68, *288*
Deuteronomy 31:17, 18, 32:20, *54*
Deuteronomy 34:1-4, *100*
Deuteronomy 5:29, 32-33, *221*
Deuteronomy 6:5, *151*
Ecclesiastes 3:11, *107*
Ephesians 1:11, *73*
Ephesians 1:17-20, *205*
Ephesians 1:19, *94*
Ephesians 1:19-20, *94, 176, 292*
Ephesians 1:20-23, *69*
Ephesians 1:21-23, *69*
Ephesians 1:3-6, *251*
Ephesians 1:4, 5:27, *233*
Ephesians 1:6, *272*
Ephesians 2:10, *128, 141*
Ephesians 2:6-7, *40, 70*
Ephesians 3:14-21, *178*
Ephesians 3:16-19, *172*
Ephesians 3:19, *151*
Ephesians 3:20, *161, 293*
Ephesians 3:9-10, *132*
Ephesians 4:11, *75, 91, 157*
Ephesians 4:11-13, *80*
Ephesians 4:31, *211*
Ephesians 4:7-16, *98*
Ephesians 5:19, *58*
Ephesians 5:23, *8*
Ephesians 5:4, *160*
Ephesians 6:10-13, *33, 180*
Ephesians 6:10-17, *61, 126*
Ephesians 6:10-18, *59, 60, 72, 80, 82, 239, 283*

Ephesians 6:11, *135*
Ephesians 6:11,13-17, *79*
Ephesians 6:12, *2, 33, 68, 81, 84, 115, 125, 201, 264, 289, 291*
Ephesians 6:12a, *81*
Ephesians 6:12b, *82*
Ephesians 6:13, *93, 183*
Ephesians 6:14-17, *33*
Ephesians 6:16, *72*
Ephesians 6:17, *186, 256*
Ephesians 6:6, *66*
Exodus 12:35-36, *246*
Exodus 17, *97*
Exodus 20:3, *95*
Exodus 23:33, *119*
Exodus 33:11, 20, 23, *54*
Exodus 33:20, *69*
Exodus 7:8-13, 22, 8:7, *274*
Exodus 8:10, *263*
Ezekiel 12:21-28, *232*
Ezekiel 28, *39*
Ezekiel 3:16-19, *198*
Ezekiel 3:17, *128*
Galatians 1:7-9, *119, 257*
Galatians 3:13-14, *288*
Galatians 4:6, *35, 40*
Galatians 5:1, *118*
Galatians 5:17, *141*
Galatians 5:22,23, *90*
Galatians 5:22-23, *142*
Galatians 5:24, *141*
Galatians 6:2, *279*
Genesis 1:27, *39*
Genesis 1:28, *81*
Genesis 1:3,6,9,11,14,20,24,26,29, *72*
Genesis 11:1-9, *71*
Genesis 15:2, *65*
Genesis 16:2-4, *74*
Genesis 17, 21, *48*
Genesis 19:15-17, *130*
Genesis 19:16, *75*
Genesis 2:7, 3:19, *39*

Genesis 22, *48*
Genesis 22:14, *26*
Genesis 25:21, *44*
Genesis 3:1, *158*
Genesis 3:1-4, *273*
Genesis 3:15, *137, 288*
Genesis 3:5, *270*
Genesis 3:8, *40*
Genesis 32:24-26, *65*
Genesis 32:26, *159*
Genesis 33:10, *54*
Genesis 6:1-5, *137*
Hebrews 1:3, *283*
Hebrews 10:24-25, *228*
Hebrews 10:25, *93*
Hebrews 11:13,14, *207*
Hebrews 11:19, *48*
Hebrews 11:3, *72*
Hebrews 11:6, *109*
Hebrews 12:1-3, *68*
Hebrews 12:15, *247*
Hebrews 12:5-11, *233*
Hebrews 12:6, 10, *155*
Hebrews 12:7, *186*
Hebrews 13:15, *63*
Hebrews 13:15-16, *58*
Hebrews 2:15, *285*
Hebrews 2:7, *39*
Hebrews 3:13, *263*
Hebrews 4:12, *52, 215, 256*
Hebrews 4:15, *262*
Hebrews 4:16, *252*
Hebrews 5:12-13, *109*
Hebrews 5:12-14, *141*
Hebrews 5:13, *243*
Hebrews 5:14, *72, 147, 228*
Isaiah 1:13,14, *95*
Isaiah 1:15, *87*
Isaiah 14:12-14, *40*
Isaiah 40:27-31, *191*
Isaiah 40:31, *151, 172, 190*
Isaiah 44:22, *158*

Isaiah 45:23, *151*
Isaiah 57:15, *107*
Isaiah 6:5, *44*
James 1:12, *62*
James 1:2, *233*
James 1:23, *147*
James 1:2-4, *262*
James 3:1-12, *120*
James 4:10, *60*
James 4:3, *57*
James 4:4, *118, 130, 221*
James 4:6, *25, 41, 44, 221*
James 4:7, *38, 41*
James 5:13-16, *44*
James 5:16, *72, 93, 279*
Jeremiah 17:9, *29*
Jeremiah 17:9, *140, 258*
Jeremiah 33:11, *53*
Job 1:10, *60*
Job 1:6-7, *250*
Job 19:25-27, *185*
Joel 2:28-32, *157*
John 1:5, *160*
John 10:10, *37, 128*
John 10:29, *240*
John 11:44, *72*
John 13:1-17, *246*
John 14:12-14, *72, 135, 156, 159*
John 14:13, *57*
John 14:13-14, *87*
John 14:14, 16:23, *283*
John 14:15, *221*
John 14:17, *69*
John 14:2, *122, 282*
John 14:26, *219*
John 14:26, 16:13, *85*
John 14:6, *61, 273, 283*
John 15:19, *238*
John 15:26, *46*
John 16:33, *47, 238*
John 17:15, *239*
John 19:28-30, *251*

John 3:16, *109*
John 3:30, *205*
John 4:32,34, *243*
John 4:34, *153*
John 5:19, *201, 219, 264*
John 5:46-47, *100*
John 6:38, *153*
John 8:32, *237*
John 8:44, *125, 157, 274, 288*
John 8:7, *181*
John 9:4, *129, 165, 264*
Jonah 2:8, *29*
Jonah 2:9, *115*
Jonah 3:1-3, *65*
Joshua 1:1-5, *135*
Joshua 1:2, *133*
Joshua 1:3, *148*
Joshua 14:6-13, *49*
Joshua 14:7-12, *193*
Joshua 2:2, *84*
Joshua 2:6, *136*
Joshua 2:7, *135*
Joshua 2:9,24, *136*
Joshua 24:15, *127*
Joshua 3:5, *148*
Joshua 3:5-13, *135*
Joshua 3:8, *147*
Joshua 4:8-9, *136*
Joshua 6:20, *20*
Joshua 7:4, *15*
Jude 1:22, *75*
Judges 6:36, *66*
Judges 7:9, *172*
Lamentations 3:58, *158*
Leviticus 17:10, 20:3, 5, 6, 26:17, *54*
Leviticus 19:31, 20:6, 20:27, *38*
Leviticus 26:3, *221*
Luke 1:37, *235*
Luke 10:1-24, *28*
Luke 10:18, *82, 129*
Luke 10:21, *32*
Luke 10:25-37, *16*

Luke 11, *14*
Luke 11:2-4, *92*
Luke 12:29-30, *289*
Luke 12:6-7, *144*
Luke 15:11-32, *193*
Luke 15:19, *144*
Luke 15:20, *124*
Luke 15:20-22, *108*
Luke 18, *43*
Luke 18:9-14, *44*
Luke 19:10, *115*
Luke 19:11-26, *65*
Luke 22:31, *22, 113*
Luke 22:43, *66*
Luke 22:44, *66*
Luke 3:22, 4:1, 4:14, 4:18, *115*
Luke 4, *95*
Luke 4:1-13, *59*
Luke 4:33, 4:41, *148*
Luke 4:6, *72*
Luke 5:17, *264*
Luke 6:42, *181*
Luke 9, *30*
Luke 9:51, *154*
Luke 9:57-62, *28*
Luke 9:60, 62, *153*
Luke 9:62, *174*
Malachi 3:10, *254*
Mark 1:13, *59*
Mark 1:15, *33*
Mark 10:44, *35*
Mark 10:45, *35, 246*
Mark 11:23-24, *146*
Mark 12:41-44, *143*
Mark 14:66-72, *113*
Mark 5:1-13, *148*
Mark 9, *30*
Mark 9:29, *219*
Mathew 4:8-9, *271*
Matthew 10, *24*
Matthew 12:38-39, *274*
Matthew 12:45, *12*

Matthew 13:19, *12*, *147*
Matthew 13:1-9, 18-23, *256*
Matthew 13:22, *75*, *214*, *221*
Matthew 14:28-30, *236*
Matthew 14:29, *147*
Matthew 16, *270*
Matthew 16:18, *10*, *33*, *114*, *204*, *269*, *283*
Matthew 16:24-25, *174*
Matthew 16:25, *96*, *130*, *240*
Matthew 17, *30*
Matthew 17:1-2, *100*
Matthew 17:14-21, *146*
Matthew 17:20, *24*, *43*
Matthew 18:19, *57*
Matthew 18:19-20, *60*
Matthew 20:28, *144*, *246*
Matthew 21:22, *57*
Matthew 24, *168*
Matthew 24:24, *259*
Matthew 24:37-39, *167*
Matthew 25:1-11, *165*, *207*
Matthew 25:1-13, *129*
Matthew 25:14-30, *65*, *222*
Matthew 25:34-36, *98*
Matthew 25:34-40, *253*
Matthew 25:41, *125*
Matthew 26:36-42, *239*
Matthew 26:36-44, *66*
Matthew 26:39, *271*
Matthew 26:39, 42, *154*
Matthew 28:18, *72*, *82*, *83*, *269*
Matthew 28:19-20, *163*, *269*
Matthew 4:24, 8:16, 9:32, 12:22, 15:22, 17:14, *148*
Matthew 4:4, *151*, *274*
Matthew 4:8-9, *288*
Matthew 5:17, *153*
Matthew 5:3-12, *229*
Matthew 6:10, *158*, *201*
Matthew 6:19, *253*
Matthew 6:19-20, *282*
Matthew 6:19-21, *102*
Matthew 6:21, *206*
Matthew 6:24, *95*, *174*, *207*, *221*, *244*
Matthew 6:25-33, *88*
Matthew 6:33, *96*, *204*, *246*
Matthew 6:34, *85*
Matthew 6:5-6, *87*
Matthew 7:1, *181*
Matthew 7:15-23, *257*
Matthew 7:16, *154*
Matthew 7:2, *181*
Matthew 7:21-23, *95*, *116*, *129*, *154*, *165*, *174*, *176*, *244*
Matthew 7:3, *119*
Matthew 7:7, *57*
Matthew 7:7,8,11, 21:22, *87*
Matthew 7:7-12, *195*
Matthew 7:7-8, *154*
Matthew 8:22, *153*
Matthew 8:28-33, *160*
Matthew 8:5-10, *72*
Matthew 9:20-21, *236*
Matthew 9:37-38, *135*
Micah 6:4, *158*
Nehemiah 1:10, *158*
Nehemiah 1:11, *87*
Nehemiah 1:4-11, *193*
Nehemiah 1:5-11, *79*
Nehemiah 2:18, *172*
Nehemiah 4:15-17, *122*
Nehemiah 8:10, *32*
Numbers 13, *84*
Numbers 13:22, *137*
Numbers 13:26-30, 14:6-7, *48*
Numbers 14, *78*
Numbers 14:12, *245*
Numbers 14:22, *245*
Numbers 14:36-38, *48*
Numbers 14:39-45, *236*
Numbers 22:28, *72*
Numbers 6:25, 26, 12:8, *54*
Philemon 10-16, *108*

Philippians 2:1, *107*
Philippians 2:10-11, *46*
Philippians 3:12-14, *227*
Philippians 3:13-14, *103*
Philippians 3:13-15, *169*
Philippians 3:20, *68*
Philippians 3:7-11, *227*
Philippians 3:8, *144*, *205*
Philippians 4:13, *151*
Philippians 4:7, *98*, *131*
Philippians 4:8, *52*
Proverbs 1:10, 15, *221*
Proverbs 11:2, *119*
Proverbs 14:26, *173*
Proverbs 15:29, *87*
Proverbs 15:8, 28:9, *87*
Proverbs 16:18, *119*, *211*
Proverbs 18:7, *119*
Proverbs 23:7, *118*
Proverbs 29:18, *101*
Proverbs 29:23, *119*
Proverbs 29:25, *120*
Proverbs 3:12, *155*
Proverbs 3:3, *183*
Proverbs 3:32, *132*
Proverbs 3:5-6, *151*
Psalm 103, *150*
Psalm 103:12, *120*
Psalm 103:1-3, *150*
Psalm 103:14, 35, *107*, *262*
Psalm 103:3-4, *46*
Psalm 103:5, *190*
Psalm 107:10-16, *46*
Psalm 107:17:20, *46*
Psalm 107:20, *158*
Psalm 107:23-30, *47*
Psalm 107:4-9, *46*
Psalm 107:8, *63*
Psalm 118:15, *53*
Psalm 119:103, *220*
Psalm 119:105, *161*, *256*
Psalm 119:114, 147, *256*

Psalm 119:130, *53*, *114*, *256*
Psalm 119:170, *256*
Psalm 119:28, *256*
Psalm 119:50, *256*
Psalm 119:89, *256*
Psalm 119:9, 11, *256*
Psalm 119:9,11,50,105,114,165, *274*
Psalm 138:3, *172*
Psalm 139:16, *262*
Psalm 139:23-24, *181*
Psalm 139:24, *161*
Psalm 139:5, *128*
Psalm 141:2, *88*
Psalm 18:30, *151*, *186*
Psalm 18:6, 34:15, *186*
Psalm 21:3, *63*
Psalm 22:3, *57*
Psalm 23, *171*
Psalm 23:4-5, *242*
Psalm 23:6, *63*
Psalm 25:14, *132*
Psalm 25:3, *45*
Psalm 27:13, *63*
Psalm 27:5)., *132*
Psalm 29:2, 100:2, *99*
Psalm 30:5b, *267*
Psalm 31:19, *63*, *128*
Psalm 31:9, *132*
Psalm 33:11, *283*
Psalm 33:18, *151*, *282*
Psalm 34:15, *87*
Psalm 34:7, *98*
Psalm 38:12, 119:110, *119*
Psalm 4:1, 4:3, 4:8, 5:2-3, 5:11-12, 7:1, 7:10, 9:10, 16:1, 17:6, 18:1-6, 18:16-19, 18:27-28, 18:30-36, 22:11, 25:1-5, 27:1-14, *50*
Psalm 40:2, *158*
Psalm 42:1, *154*
Psalm 46:1, *282*
Psalm 46:1, 9:9, 59:16, 144:2, *172*
Psalm 46:10, *216*

Psalm 51:10, *41*
Psalm 51:12, *32, 93*
Psalm 55:16-17, *45*
Psalm 65:11, *63*
Psalm 66:18, *55*
Psalm 70:2, 71:13, 83:17, *128*
Psalm 77: 14, *185*
Psalm 77:10-11, *185, 248*
Psalm 77:10-12, *62*
Psalm 77:1-3, *185*
Psalm 8:2, *57*
Psalm 8:3, *132*
Psalm 8:5, *39, 70, 273*
Psalm 85:10, 86:15, 89:14, *183*
Psalm 91, *279*
Psalm 91:1, *132*
Psalm 91:11, *69*
Psalm 94:11, 139:2, *218*
Revelation 1:8, *283*
Revelation 11:15, *33, 83*
Revelation 12:10, *250*
Revelation 12:11,17, *49*
Revelation 12:7-10, *129*
Revelation 12:9, *253*
Revelation 17:14, 19:16, *259*
Revelation 3:10, *166*
Revelation 3:16, *166*
Revelation 3:16-17, *165*
Revelation 3:8, *165*
Revelation 4, *87*
Revelation 5:10-12, *88*
Revelation 5:12, *57*
Revelation 5:13, *88*
Revelation 5:8, *88*
Revelation 5:9-10, *88*
Revelation 6-10, *69*
Revelation 8:3-4, *89*
Romans 1:18-32, *52*

Romans 1:30, *119*
Romans 12 :1-2, *178*
Romans 12:1, *147, 233*
Romans 12:1-2, *40, 66, 284*
Romans 12:2, *228*
Romans 14:11, *33, 46*
Romans 14:12, *168*
Romans 15:13, *101*
Romans 15:4-5, *107*
Romans 16:25, *132*
Romans 3:23, *114*
Romans 5:14-17, *39*
Romans 5:16, *270*
Romans 6:16, *95*
Romans 7:14-24, *141*
Romans 8, *182, 183*
Romans 8:1, *262*
Romans 8:1, 31-35, *186*
Romans 8:11, *205*
Romans 8:1-2, *127, 251*
Romans 8:15, *35, 211, 279, 285, 286*
Romans 8:17, *70*
Romans 8:22, *69*
Romans 8:26, *2, 14*
Romans 8:26,27, *92*
Romans 8:26-27, *85, 218, 267*
Romans 8:28, *151*
Romans 8:29, *228*
Romans 8:33-34, *251*
Romans 8:38-39, *251*
Romans 8:6, *141*
Romans 8:7, *141*
Romans 9:23, *128*
Ruth 1:13, *17*
Ruth 1:20,21, *17*
Ruth 2:12, *17, 172*
Ruth 4:17, *18*

www.ingramcontent.com/pod-product-compliance
Lightning Source LLC
Chambersburg PA
CBHW021422070526
44577CB00001B/14